**50% OFF!**

NCMHCE Online Test Prep Course

We consider it an honor and a privilege that you chose our NCMHCE Study Guide. As a way of showing our appreciation and to help us better serve you, we have partnered with Mometrix Test Preparation to offer you 50% off their online NCMHCE Prep Course.

Mometrix has structured their online course to perfectly complement your printed study guide. Many NCMHCE courses are needlessly expensive and don't deliver enough value. With their course, you get access to the best NCMHCE prep material, and you only pay half price.

WHAT'S IN THE NCMHCE TEST PREP COURSE?

- **NCMHCE Study Guide**: Get access to content that complements your study guide.
- **Progress Tracker**: Their customized course allows you to check off content you have studied or feel confident with.
- **750+ Practice Questions**: With 750+ practice questions and lesson reviews, you can test yourself again and again to build confidence.
- **NCMHCE Flashcards**: Their course includes a flashcard mode consisting of over 530 content cards to help you study.

TO RECEIVE THIS DISCOUNT, VISIT THE WEBSITE AT

link.mometrix.com/ncmhce

USE THE DISCOUNT CODE:
STARTSTUDYING

IF YOU HAVE ANY QUESTIONS OR CONCERNS, PLEASE CONTACT MOMETRIX AT SUPPORT@MOMETRIX.COM

FREE VIDEO

Essential Test Tips Video from Trivium Test Prep!

Thank you for purchasing from Trivium Test Prep!
We're honored to help you prepare for your exam.
To show our appreciation, we're offering a

FREE *Essential Test Tips* Video

Our video includes 35 test preparation strategies that will make you successful on your big exam. All we ask is that you email us your feedback and describe your experience with our product. Amazing, awful, or just so-so: we want to hear what you have to say!

> To receive your FREE *Essential Test Tips* Video, please email us at
> **5star@triviumtestprep.com.**

Include "Free 5 Star" in the subject line and the following information in your email:

1. The title of the product you purchased.
2. Your rating from 1 – 5 (with 5 being the best).
3. Your feedback about the product, including how our materials helped you meet your goals and ways in which we can improve our products.
4. Your full name and shipping address so we can send your
   FREE *Essential Test Tips* **Video**.

If you have any questions or concerns please feel free to contact us directly at:
5star@triviumtestprep.com.

Thank you!

– Trivium Test Prep Team

NCMHCE Exam Prep 2025-2026:

Study Guide and Practice Test for
National Clinical Mental Health Counseling
[2nd Edition]

B. Hettinger

Copyright ©2025 by Trivium Test Prep

ISBN-13: 9781637984512

ALL RIGHTS RESERVED. By purchase of this book, you have been licensed one copy for personal use only. No part of this work may be reproduced, redistributed, or used in any form or by any means without prior written permission of the publisher and copyright owner. Trivium Test Prep; Accepted, Inc.; Cirrus Test Prep; and Ascencia Test Prep are all imprints of Trivium Test Prep, LLC.

NBCC was not involved in the creation or production of this product, is not in any way affiliated with Trivium Test Prep, and does not sponsor or endorse this product.

Image(s) used under license from Shutterstock.com

Table of Contents

Counseling Attributes and Skills — 1
- Core Counseling Attributes 1
- Working with the Client 7
- Counseling Interventions 12
- Conflict and Confrontation 15
- Multicultural Counseling 18
- Answer Key 27

Group Counseling — 29
- Working with a Group 29
- Attributes in a Group Counseling Context ... 37
- Conflict in Groups 40
- Answer Key 42

Professional Practice and Ethics — 43
- Professional Practice 43
- Consultation and Self-Assessment 54
- Documentation 59
- Ethics 65
- Answer Key 73

Intake, Assessment, and Diagnosis — 75
- Intake and Interview 75
- Assessing the Client 81
- Assessment Instruments 85
- Diagnosis 99
- Answer Key 104

Treatment Planning — 107
- Developing a Treatment Plan 107
- Establishing Goals 111
- Client Education 115
- Treatment Termination 118
- Answer Key 123

Areas of Clinical Focus: Mood and Anxiety — 125
- Anxiety and Stress 125
- Mood Disorders 131
- Other Issues 135
- Answer Key 140

Areas of Clinical Focus: Family and Relationships — 141
- Relationships 141
- Childhood and Family Issues 149
- Answer Key 156

Areas of Clinical Focus: Physical Intersections — 157
- Physical Health 157
- Substance Use Disorders and Eating Disorders 162
- Gender and Sexuality 169
- Answer Key 172

Online Resources vii

Answer Key 104

Areas of Clinical Focus: Social Issues — 175

Career and Finances 175
Culture, Religion, and Spirituality 182
Answer Key 190

Human Growth and Development — 191

Elements of Developmental Psychology 191
Cognitive and Language Development 196
Lifespan Developmental Theory 200
Personality 206
Motivation and Stress 209

NCMHCE Practice Test — 215

Case Study 1 215
Case Study 2 218
Case Study 3 222
Case Study 4 226
Case Study 5 229
Case Study 6 233
Case Study 7 236
Case Study 8 239
Case Study 9 243
Case Study 10 246
Case Study 11 249
Answer Key 255

Online Resources

Trivium includes online resources with the purchase of this study guide to help you fully prepare for your NCMHCE exam.

Review Questions

Need more practice? Our review questions use a variety of formats to help you memorize key terms and concepts.

Flash Cards

Trivium's flash cards allow you to review important terms easily on your computer or smartphone.

From Stress to Success

Watch "From Stress to Success," a brief but insightful YouTube video that offers the tips, tricks, and secrets experts use to score higher on the exam.

Reviews

Leave a review, send us helpful feedback, or sign up for Trivium promotions—including free books!

Access these materials at: www.triviumtestprep.com/ncmhce-online-resources

Introduction

Congratulations on choosing to take the National Clinical Mental Health Counseling Examination (NCMHCE)! By purchasing this book, you've taken the first step toward becoming a counselor.

This guide will provide you with a detailed overview of the NCMHCE, so you will know exactly what to expect on test day. We'll take you through all of the concepts covered on the exam and give you the opportunity to test your knowledge with practice questions. Even if it's been a while since you last took a major test, don't worry; we'll make sure you're more than ready!

What Is the NCMHCE?

The National Clinical Mental Health Counseling Examination (NCMHCE) is developed by the National Board for Certified Counselors (NBCC) as part of its certification program. The NCMHCE measures the skills necessary to safely practice as an entry-level counselor.

To qualify for the exam, you must have graduated from or be an advanced graduate student in a counseling program accredited by the Council for Accreditation of Counseling and Related Educational Programs (CACREP). In some states, candidates with other related helping degrees may qualify to take the NCE and earn licensure.

What's on the NCMHCE?

There are eleven case studies on the exam. Each case study is followed by thirteen multiple-choice questions, for a total of 143 questions. Questions are multiple-choice with four answer options. All questions are aligned with the CACREP common core areas.

One of the case studies is unscored, as are its accompanying questions, or pretest questions. These questions are used by the NBCC to test their suitability for inclusion on future tests. You'll have no way of knowing which questions are unscored, so treat every question like it counts.

The NCMHCE has no guess penalty. That is, if you answer a question incorrectly, no points are deducted from your score; you simply do not get credit for that question. Therefore, you should always guess if you do not know the answer to a question.

You will have three hours and forty-five minutes to complete the test. Before the timed portion of the exam begins, you will take a ten-minute tutorial. There are no scheduled breaks during the exam.

What's on the NCMHCE?

SUBJECT	APPROXIMATE NUMBER OF QUESTIONS PER SUBJECT	PERCENTAGE
Professional Practice and Ethics	15 – 28	10% – 20%
Intake, Assessment, and Diagnosis	28 – 43	20% – 30%
Treatment Planning	15 – 28	10% – 20%
Counseling Skills and Interventions	36 – 50	25% – 35%
Core Counseling Attributes	15 – 28	10% – 20%
Total	143 multiple-choice questions (130 scored)	3 hours and 45 minutes

Questions on **Professional Practice and Ethics** address the counselor-client relationship; counselor-client roles; monitoring the therapeutic relationship; explaining counseling processes, procedures, risks, and benefits; and client rights and responsibilities. Counselors should understand how to assess their own competency to work with specific clients and their needs, seek supervision, and offer referrals as needed. Questions cover ethics and legal issues in counseling: confidentiality, its limits, and its application to electronic communication; agency policies; obtaining informed consent, including assessing client competency to grant it; providing accommodations to clients with disabilities, and advocating for client issues. Questions may also address documentation, such as client record keeping, creating and maintaining documentation, payment, fees, and insurance benefits. Finally, counselors should understand research methods and statistical concepts and know the importance of practicing self-care.

You will be tested on conducting **Intake, Assessment, and Diagnosis.** These questions cover client interviews, including initial, biopsychosocial, cultural formulation, and diagnostic. Be prepared to show your ability to assess a client's presenting problem, levels of distress and mental health functioning, and perform a mental status exam (MSE). Assessing for trauma and substance use may also be covered, as will ongoing assessments for at-risk behaviors, assessing outcomes, and using appropriate assessment instruments. Questions will address determining diagnoses and any co-occurring diagnoses, which level of care is needed, and screening clients for services. Questions may also relate to obtaining client self-reports, evaluating interactional dynamics, and assessing counseling effectiveness.

A portion of the questions deals with **Treatment Planning**. Prepare for questions about developing treatment plans, goals, and objectives. Collaboration with clients, their support systems, and other providers will also be addressed. Questions may cover establishing goals and identifying the barriers and strengths that affect attaining those goals. Other possible topics are different levels of treatment, transitions, using assessment instruments, revising the treatment plan, and educating the client on the value of the treatment plan. Finally, client follow-up and termination processes will be covered.

The bulk of the test addresses **Counseling Skills and Interventions**. Expect questions that pose scenarios with clients and ask which therapeutic intervention you would use or which skill could be demonstrated. Issues covered by these questions include establishing the therapeutic alliance, crisis intervention, transference, defense mechanisms, and group counseling.

Finally, the test covers **Core Counseling Attributes**. Questions address self-awareness; genuineness; congruence; positive regard; understanding of gender, sexuality, and multicultural issues; empathetic attunement and responding; conflict resolution; group issues; and more.

How Is the NCMHCE Scored?

Once you have completed your test, you will receive your unofficial score from the proctor and may print a hard copy of your score to take with you. You will receive your official results electronically four weeks after the end of the testing window. Remember, you may not use your NCMHCE credentials until you have received your official results, even if you pass the test.

The NCMHCE is a pass/fail test. Of the 143 questions on the test, 130 are scored. Your raw score is how many of the 130 scored questions you answered correctly. That score is then scaled based on the level of difficulty of the questions you answered correctly.

If you pass the test, the Center for Credentialing & Education (CCE) will report your official scores to your licensing organization within thirty days. If you do not pass the test, you may appeal, or you may retake the test after a three-month waiting period.

The number of correct answers needed to pass the exam will vary slightly depending on the questions included in your version of the test. (In other words, if you take a version of the test with harder questions, the passing score will be lower.) For security reasons, different versions of the test are administered during every testing window.

How Is the NCMHCE Administered?

To register for the exam, you must first apply through the Center for Credentialing and Education (CCE). You must register online at http://www.cce-global.org under the "ProCounselor" tab. After your application is accepted, you will receive an exam eligibility email with instructions on how to register for the exam. If you wish to retake the exam, you may do so, but only after a three-month waiting period.

The NCE is administered at Pearson VUE testing centers around the nation. Plan to arrive at least thirty minutes before the exam to complete biometric screening. Bring at least one form of government-issued photo ID and be prepared to be photographed and have your palms scanned. You may also be scanned with a metal detector wand before entering the test room. Your primary ID must be government issued, include a recent photograph and signature, and match the name under which you registered to take the test. If you do not have proper ID, you will not be allowed to take the test.

You will not be allowed to bring any personal items into the testing room, such as calculators or phones. You may not bring pens, pencils, or scratch paper. Other prohibited items include hats, scarves, and coats. You may, however, wear religious garments. Pearson VUE provides lockers for valuables. You can keep your ID and locker key with you.

About Trivium Test Prep

Trivium Test Prep uses industry professionals with decades' worth of knowledge in their fields—proven with degrees and honors in law, medicine, business, education, the military, and more—to produce high-quality test prep books for students.

Our study guides are specifically designed to increase any student's score. Since our books are shorter and more concise than typical study guides, you can increase your score while significantly decreasing your study time. We're pleased you've chosen Trivium to be a part of your professional journey.

1 Counseling Attributes and Skills

Core Counseling Attributes

Counseling Attributes

Many basic counseling attributes form the foundation of the therapeutic relationship with a client and distinguish the professional counseling relationship from other interpersonal relationships:

1. **Genuineness** is a counseling attribute that refers to authenticity.
   - Counselors should say what they mean and mean what they say.
   - Counselors should be authentic in sessions with clients and not put on a false front.
   - For example, if a counselor smiles when greeting a client, the smile should be authentic and not forced.
2. **Congruence** is similar to genuineness. The psychologist Carl Rogers defined congruence as the genuineness necessary for a counselor to provide unconditional positive regard and empathy. Rogers believed that when counselors show congruence in their sessions, they appear more trustworthy, which strengthens the therapeutic alliance.

Counselors should be fully attentive to both their clients and themselves while practicing transparency:
   - Counselors' insides should match their outsides.
   - Counselors should be completely honest with clients about what the counselors experience.
   - For example, if a counselor cringes in response to a client's remark, a congruent counselor will explain that reaction to the client.
3. **Nonjudgmental stance** requires counselors to remain open-minded to the client's experience and refrain from evaluating the clients, their issues, or their behaviors.
   - This attribute emphasizes the benefits of practicing self-awareness and self-reflection.

- Judgment can be communicated both verbally and nonverbally, so counselors must learn to remain neutral in words and body language during sessions with clients.
- A counselor can exhibit a nonjudgmental stance with a client by
  - keeping facial expressions pleasant and neutral;
  - staying in a relaxed body posture;
  - maintaining eye contact regardless of what the client says.

4. **Positive regard** expands on the nonjudgmental stance. A counselor practicing positive regard
   - projects an attitude of acceptance of the client as a person;
   - adopts a worldview and philosophy of seeing all people as worthy of dignity and respect regardless of their thoughts, emotions, or behaviors, which are separate from people's inherent worth.
   - A counselor exhibits positive regard by
     - verbally affirming that the client is worthy of dignity and respect no matter what;
     - treating the client with dignity and respect in sessions;
     - reinforcing the idea that clients are not defined by their thoughts, feelings, or behaviors;
     - clarifying that even if counselors disapprove of a client's behavior, they accept the client as a person.

PRACTICE QUESTION

1. A client discloses to the counselor that he uses illicit substances at night when his kids are in bed. The counselor believes this behavior is risky and could endanger the children. Which of the following statements would BEST reflect the implementation of counseling attributes?

   A) "You need to stop using immediately, as it could put yourself and your children in danger. What if there is an emergency and you're unable to respond?"

   B) "The potential of something bad happening concerns me, and I don't agree with your choices, but I am here to help you if you would like to make better ones. I know you can do it."

   C) "If this continues, I will have to report you to child welfare for putting your children at risk. You could be facing serious charges."

   D) "What kind of parent does something like that? You should reconsider your choices and think about your kids from now on."

Self-Awareness

As an objective participant guiding a therapeutic process with clients, a counselor must practice clinical detachment while conveying empathy. This requires awareness of self. **Awareness of self** is a practice of reflection and observation both in and outside of the moment.

Awareness of self in the moment is a skill whereby the counselor notices his own thoughts, beliefs, emotions, and behaviors without judgment and recognizes how these impact the client. By noticing and evaluating, the counselor can adjust based on the client's reactions. For example, a counselor may find himself reacting emotionally to a client:

- The client may react with surprise.
- The counselor can then choose how to handle the situation without judging his own emotional reaction.
- Sharing an emotional reaction with a client may increase trust.
- The counselor may react negatively to a client's disclosure.
- In practicing self-awareness, the counselor can recognize a negative reaction, evaluate it, and put it aside so the client does not feel judged.
- The counselor may choose to share the process of self-awareness and invite the client to do the same.

Another aspect of self-awareness is the practice of self-reflection on one's own or in consultation with others. Before meeting a client of a significantly different cultural background, for example, the counselor might reflect on her values and beliefs about the client's culture and how those beliefs could impact the client in the session. By practicing self-reflection beforehand, counselors can

- check whatever bias they may have;
- educate themselves about the culture;
- meet the client without bringing that bias into the session.

The counselor's verbal and nonverbal communication impact clients in both positive and negative ways. Clients can tell if something is not right with the counselor, and that may interfere with building a therapeutic relationship. Therefore, the counselor needs to remain self-aware in sessions and must read the client's cues to understand the client's reaction and make adjustments as needed.

 HELPFUL HINT

Counselors can also practice self-reflection with a supervisor or other colleague to help bring awareness to any bias or prejudice that could adversely affect the client relationship.

PRACTICE QUESTION

2. During a session with a client, a counselor makes a statement and notices the client flinch. What is one thing the counselor can do in the session to demonstrate self-awareness?

   A) continue the session as if nothing happened
   B) ask the client what he got out of the session when it is over
   C) point out the client's reaction and seek understanding from the client
   D) discuss the situation with a supervisor at the next supervision meeting

Communication and Active Listening

The basic elements of communication and active listening form the foundation of a counselor's rapport and relationship with the client. To build a strong rapport with a client, the counselor must

- be engaging;

- be an active listener;
- avoid interrupting the client.

Clients will trust that the counselor cares about their issues and advocates for their well-being. A counselor who actively listens will deliver on guarantees, establish and maintain boundaries, and build trust with the client. Building trust can take time, but doing so makes managing the client's condition easier for all involved.

The theory of basic communication is made up of several components:

- **sender**: the individual or thing sending the message
- **channel**: the method by which the sender transmits the message
- **receiver**: the individual or thing translating the message
- **destination**: the individual or thing for whom the message is targeted
- **message**: the information transferred from the sender to the recipient

People use these elements in everyday conversations without even realizing it. The sender will transfer information through the channel to the receiver, who interprets or translates the message to the destination. In recent times, oral conversation has given way to texting, emailing, and using social media; sometimes, the intended tone of the message can be lost without aural cues.

Active listening means paying attention to the speaker, not just hearing his words. The listener makes eye contact with the speaker to indicate interest in what is being said. An active listener repeats important points the speaker has made to ensure understanding, asks follow-up questions, and does not interrupt. The goal is threefold: to convey to the speaker that the listener understands the message, to show the speaker that the listener cares about what the speaker is saying, and to let the speaker know that the listener empathizes with the speaker.

TABLE 1.1. Dos and Don'ts of Client Communication

DO...	DON'T...
• make eye contact with the client	• use medical jargon
• introduce yourself and use the client's name	• threaten or intimidate the client
• speak directly to the client when possible	• lie or provide false hope
• ask open-ended questions	• interrupt the client
• speak slowly and clearly	• show frustration or anger
• show empathy for the client	• make judgmental statements
• be silent when appropriate to allow the client time to think and process emotions	• make accusations
• use person-first language	• tell the client what to do
• maintain pleasant facial expressions	• force clients to answer questions
• use relaxed body language	

In addition to active listening, a variety of techniques are used for therapeutic communication:

- **Sharing observations** may open up the conversation to how the client is feeling.
- **Using touch**, such as a gentle hand on the shoulder or arm, when appropriate or welcome, can offer comfort. However, this may not be appropriate in mixed-gender relationships, with those who have experienced trauma, or with those with other relational differences.
- **Silence** allows the client a moment to absorb or process information and sit with emotions to experience them fully.
- **Summarizing and paraphrasing** information back to a client helps ensure or confirm understanding and convey empathy.
- **Asking relevant questions** that pertain to the situation helps the counselor gather information for decision-making and can lead to insight for the client.
- **Reframing** is a technique that counselors use to offer the client another way to consider a situation. It offers an alternative perspective while demonstrating that the counselor understands the client.

Communication includes both verbal and nonverbal components:

- **Verbal communication** uses language to convey information. Characteristics of verbal communication include tone, volume, and word choice.
- **Nonverbal communication** includes behavior, gestures, posture, and other nonlanguage elements of communication that transmit information or meaning.

Finally, attending and reflecting are foundational skills for counselors:

- **Attending** is a basic skill whereby the counselor communicates to the client that she is present and listening.
  - Attending is a vital skill for establishing rapport with clients because it lets them know that the counselor's attention is solely on the client.
  - A counselor can practice attending verbally through greetings, showing interest in the client's life, and asking questions, when necessary, to clarify what the client said.
  - A counselor can convey attending to a client nonverbally through eye contact, facial expressions, and gestures that encourage a client to keep talking.
- **Reflecting** is a skill that demonstrates attention, understanding, and empathy. Just as a mirror shows a reflection, reflecting in the therapeutic setting is a way of repeating what the client says.
  - Reflecting shows that the counselor is listening.

- A counselor uses this skill to increase the connection with the client.
  - When clients feel that they are truly heard, they feel valued, which increases positive feelings toward the counselor.
- A counselor demonstrates reflecting by repeating what the client just said.
  - For example, a client tells a story about a family conflict and says, "I just wanted to hit someone, but I didn't."
  - The counselor might say, "You wanted to hit someone, but you didn't."
  - This shows the client that the counselor heard what he said and invites him to say more without asking a direct question.

PRACTICE QUESTION

3. Which of the following scenarios demonstrates attending behaviors by the counselor?
   A) maintaining eye contact with the client and smiling to encourage the client to keep talking
   B) using a laptop to type notes while the client talks
   C) fidgeting and looking at the clock many times throughout the session
   D) sitting tensely and still with a neutral facial expression

Empathy

Empathy is the ability to understand and accurately perceive the feelings and experiences of clients from their perspective. Carl Rogers viewed empathy as a state of being for counselors that facilitates being non-judgmental and accepting.

Empathy differs significantly from sympathy. Although both involve emotions, empathy does not involve the counselor's personal experience, nor does it involve judgment. Sympathy, on the other hand, is the process of pitying or feeling bad for someone without really understanding that person's perspective; this means it includes judgment.

Sympathy is a surface-level intellectual understanding based on personal experience. Empathy is a deeper understanding and sharing of emotions based on the other person's perspective. Empathy builds connection; sympathy does not.

- **Empathetic attunement** combines empathy with attending skills. When using empathetic attunement, the counselor is aware of the client's emotions as well as his own.
  - The counselor communicates verbally and nonverbally that he recognizes the client's emotions.
  - For example, if a client starts to cry in a session, the counselor can demonstrate empathetic attunement by staying silent and relaxed, being present with the client, and allowing her to experience that emotion without judgment or comment.

- **Empathetic responding** is a verbal response from the counselor that tells the client she understands what the client is feeling and why he feels that way.
    - This skill shows the client that the counselor respects and understands his emotions and the reasons for them.
    - Using the example of the client who feels like hitting someone during a family conflict, the counselor might empathetically respond by saying, "You feel intense anger because you feel that person is not listening to you."

PRACTICE QUESTION

4. A client tells the counselor that her spouse just gave notice of divorce. The client is in shock and asks questions in rapid succession, wondering what she missed, what is wrong with her, and what will she do now. She is taking short, shallow breaths and talking fast. How can the counselor demonstrate empathetic attunement in this situation?

    A) try to answer the client's questions or help her answer her own questions
    B) tell the client to calm down and speak more slowly so the situation can be discussed productively
    C) help the client identify the cognitive distortions forming in her mind that contribute to her feelings
    D) allow the client to continue to express her frustration without judging her

Working with the Client

Establishing the Counseling Relationship

Individual counseling follows a template:
- Assess client issues.
- Determine diagnosis.
- Set goals based on the diagnosis.
- Design an evidence-based plan of treatment for the diagnosis.

Everything flows together and relates back to the diagnosis. Even as new information emerges over the course of treatment, any changes to the treatment plan must still directly relate to the client's diagnosis. For clients to be correctly diagnosed, they must

- feel safe enough with the counselor to truthfully disclose information needed to form a correct diagnosis;
- feel like the counselor is not judging them; embarrassment and shame often accompany mental health issues.

The importance of the **therapeutic relationship** can therefore not be understated. The counseling relationship is the most important factor that predicts treatment outcomes. For clients to accept the proposed treatments, they must first trust the counselor enough to be honest about their experiences and issues:

- Without trust, the client may not feel comfortable sharing everything with the counselor.
- If the client does not share openly, it can lead to the wrong diagnosis and the wrong plan of treatment.

For example, a person with depression who does not trust the counselor might not disclose a serious trauma, like childhood sexual abuse. Without that information, the counselor may make the wrong recommendations for treatment. While the client may experience some relief, he will not truly benefit from the treatment plan if therapy does not address the underlying issues.

The foundation of the counseling relationship is the therapeutic alliance. The **therapeutic alliance** is an unwritten agreement between the client and the counselor based on trust, boundaries, and mutual respect. It is not a friendship but rather a formal treatment relationship.

In the therapeutic alliance, clients feel safe to explore issues and be vulnerable with the counselor. At the same time, they know that the counselor will hold them accountable and maintain professional boundaries. Clients need assurance that the counselor will not judge them.

The therapeutic alliance is also an equalization of power between the client and the counselor. Often, clients enter into counseling viewing the counselor as a person of authority, much like many people view physicians. In that type of relationship, clients may expect the counselor to tell them what to do to get better. Unlike the client-physician relationship, however, the counselor in the therapeutic alliance

- makes it clear that clients lead the way and establish their own goals;
- uses therapeutic techniques, not force or coercion, to help clients achieve their goals.

PRACTICE QUESTION

5. At her first appointment, a client asks the counselor for help with sleep difficulties that interfere with functioning. After talking about the sleep issues, the client says, "Okay, that's my problem, tell me how to fix it." Which aspect of the relationship should the counselor address to create a therapeutic alliance?

    A) explain that counseling is client-focused and not counselor-focused

    B) establish the counselor's position as an expert and tell the client what to do

    C) question the client's experience and tell her there is nothing wrong with her

    D) explain to the client that the problem is all in her head and the issue is not really about sleep

Motivation to Change

Motivation is the driving force behind people's actions. Counselors should assess clients' sources of motivation in the context of managing their mental health to better educate, encourage, and advocate for them:

- **Intrinsic motivation** is the desire to achieve a goal, seek challenges, or complete a task that is driven by enjoyment and personal satisfaction (for example, exercising because it is enjoyable). Motivation comes from within the client.
    - People who are intrinsically motivated to pursue change are more likely to follow through with counseling.
    - For example, a woman who struggles with depression and irritability and who is intrinsically motivated may come to counseling because she wants to be a happier person.
- **Extrinsic motivation** is the desire to accomplish a goal that is driven by external rewards or punishment (for example, exercising to prevent anxiety). Extrinsic motivation comes from forces outside the client.
    - People who are extrinsically motivated may follow through with counseling, but they are less likely to do so than those who are intrinsically motivated.
    - For example, an adolescent forced into therapy by his parents may only come to counseling to avoid punishment. This will impact the level at which he engages in the process.
    - Another example is a client referred to therapy by a drug court proceeding whereby her success in therapy will determine whether or not she goes to jail for a drug offense. In this case, extrinsic motivation may positively influence the client.

Counselors should also consider a client's motivation for change as it pertains to the stated problem. In other words, a client may have intrinsic motivation to feel better but may not be ready to make the behavioral changes necessary to do so.

In these cases, the counselor should help clients discover and tap in to their motivations to change. This will move them from the stages of change talk to change action. The **transtheoretical model** allows counselors to identify which stage of change clients are in and how to guide them to a stage of change where they are motivated to engage in change behavior.

- Clients with an **external locus of control** will attribute their successes or failures to outside forces. These clients tend to blame others for what they experience and feel there is little to nothing they can do to change these experiences. Some of these clients will feel helpless and hopeless that anything can change, while others recognize that even if those outside forces impact their success or failure, there are options to counter them.

- Clients with an **internal locus of control** will attribute their success or failure to themselves. Some of these clients will unrealistically take the blame and responsibility for everything that happens to them; others use their strengths to overcome adversity.

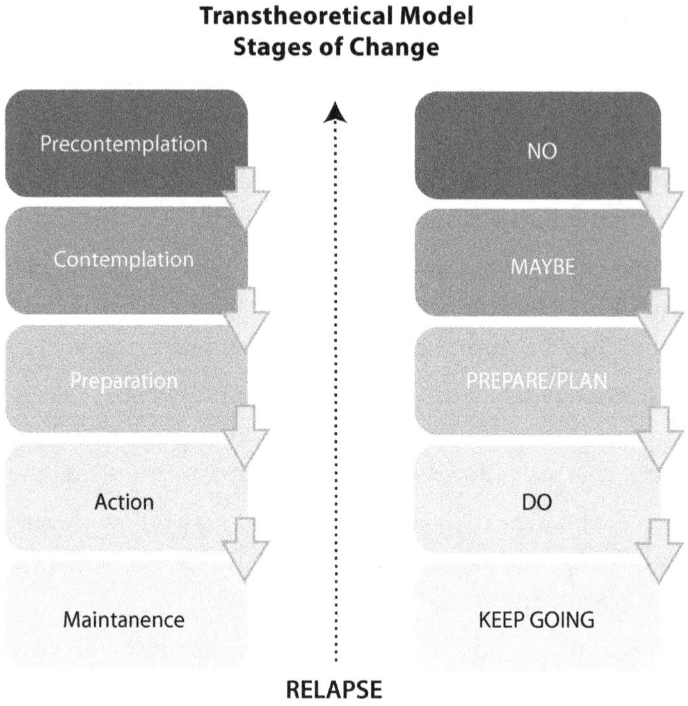

**Transtheoretical Model
Stages of Change**

Precontemplation → NO

Contemplation → MAYBE

Preparation → PREPARE/PLAN

Action → DO

Maintanence → KEEP GOING

RELAPSE

Figure 1.1. Transtheoretical Model

PRACTICE QUESTION

6. A college student comes to therapy seeking help for depression. The client says he is doing poorly in school and wants to quit. During the assessment, he says school is too hard, the professors are unfair graders, and his peers sabotage his work. What do the client's statements indicate?

   A) The client has an internal locus of control.

   B) The client is depressed.

   C) The client has an external locus of control.

   D) The client is motivated to change.

Client Education

Counselors should provide educational resources on relevant topics (for example, stress management, assertiveness training, divorce adjustment). This type of education in the context of mental health is often referred to as **psychoeducation**, or education focused on sharing evidence-based information about a mental health issue and how to cope with it.

Psychoeducation is valuable because it helps clients understand the what, how, and why of what they are experiencing. For example, a counselor who diagnoses a client with generalized anxiety disorder would teach her about the diagnostic criteria for the condition, evidence-based causes for the disorder, what options are available to her for treatment, evidence-based means of coping with the disorder, and the potential prognosis for the disorder based on research. Often this education can help clients understand that they are not alone in this experience, that their experiences are valid, and that there is hope for treatment. When seeking social support, it can also help when clients explain to other people in their lives what they are experiencing. Strategies for teaching include the following:

- **Lectures** (groups or one-on-one) are effective for conveying cognitive knowledge, particularly to auditory learners. A counselor uses this strategy to convey information on a specific subject to a client individually or to a group.
- **Group discussions** in which clients can ask questions and share information are effective for social learners and can help with affective learning (for example, changing attitudes) and practicing skills in a safe environment.
- **Role-playing** is a good way to teach affective skills (like responding to peer pressure) and to practice relational and communication skills in a safe environment.
- **Instructional materials**, like films or pamphlets, may be used as part of a larger education plan; however, they may be ineffective if clients are disengaged or the materials do not match the client's needs and learning abilities.
  - Counselors may provide instructional materials to clients within the context of treatment to support additional learning. For example, during a session, the client learns about healthy coping skills and discusses coping skills to try during the next week.
  - A counselor might give the client a pamphlet that defines healthy coping skills and provides a list of healthy coping skills to try, including ones that were discussed in the session. This serves as a reminder for the client and reinforces what happened in the session.

Some specific strategies to engage clients in the learning process include the following:

- Link new information to current behavior; new learning is better received when it focuses on what the client already knows.
- Be clear, explicit, and specific.
- Suggest alternatives or adaptations that apply directly to clients and their situations.
- Be transparent about the goals of the learning process and why these are important.
- Involve other health providers (like dieticians) to engage clients and reinforce learning.
- Invite people from the client's social support network to participate in the learning process.

Finally, technology can engage clients and connect them to providers and support communities. **Webinars** or **live events** are often available in the community and geared toward specific client populations (for example, parents). When recommending these resources, the counselor should verify the credentials of presenters as well as the validity and quality of the information presented.

PRACTICE QUESTION

7. A mother brings her teenager to therapy because of significant mood changes and increased social isolation. During the assessment, the counselor diagnoses the teenager with PTSD due to recent bullying at school. How can the counselor use psychoeducation in a session with the mother and teenager?

    A) explain the symptoms of PTSD and ways to manage the symptoms during treatment

    B) refer the client to a psychiatrist for medication

    C) bring in another counselor to work with the mother

    D) tell the mother to keep the teenager home from school until symptoms subside

Counseling Interventions

Counselors must be able to apply evidence-based counseling interventions. Ethical and competent counselors receive proper education and training before using these interventions with clients. Counselors must take care to use therapeutic techniques properly; the improper application of evidence-based interventions could harm the client.

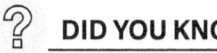

DID YOU KNOW?

In some cases, third-party payers will not reimburse counselors for interventions unless they can provide documentation of authorized training.

Cognitive Behavioral Therapy

Cognitive behavioral therapy (CBT) is based on the theory that thoughts and feelings influence behaviors. The theory further suggests that many of the thoughts that influence behaviors occur without a person's conscious knowledge.

The point of using CBT as therapy is to guide clients to become aware of those thoughts and identify the unhealthy ones. Clients can then learn to take control of their thoughts and separate the thoughts from their behaviors. Because several mental health issues are associated with negative thoughts and beliefs, the counselor can use this theory-based counseling intervention with clients who have a variety of diagnoses. The counselor's role in CBT is to

- help clients explore their thoughts and beliefs;
- analyze where thoughts and beliefs originated;
- evaluate the truth or effectiveness of thoughts and beliefs;
- revise or create new thoughts and beliefs that help clients achieve their therapeutic goals.

Dialectical Behavior Therapy

Dialectical behavior therapy (DBT) uses concepts from CBT but also considers the significant impact of strong emotions on thinking and behavior. As implied by the name, DBT suggests that opposing forces exist in a state of tension. For example, a person practicing DBT understands that he may feel very strong negative emotions, but his whole life is not ruined. Someone using DBT would understand that he might perform badly on an exam, but that does not mean he is unintelligent or that he has no future. The goal of DBT is to help clients learn to balance between extremes and choose constructive or positive behaviors despite strong emotions. The therapy itself focuses on helping clients

- learn mindfulness;
- learn to regulate their emotions and tolerate distress;
- identify dysfunctional thinking patterns;
- choose healthy coping skills.

Another characteristic of DBT is establishing and maintaining boundaries with clients to teach them how to do the same in their lives. Implementation of DBT interventions requires the counselor to engage in additional education and training.

DID YOU KNOW?

Dialectical behavior therapy was originally created to treat women with borderline personality disorder and high rates of suicidality.

Eye Movement Desensitization and Reprocessing

Eye movement desensitization and reprocessing (EMDR) is considered an evidence-based treatment intervention for clients with post-traumatic stress disorder (PTSD) and other diagnoses. This treatment is based on the theory of information processing. According to this theory, memories associated with traumatic events are not stored properly. The techniques used in EMDR employ bilateral stimulation while recalling a memory to store it properly in the brain and reduce the strong emotions attached to it.

To apply bilateral stimulation, a counselor may ask a client to hold two joysticks that vibrate alternatingly or to wear a headset that plays tones or clicks in one ear, then the other. This therapy can be very effective for clients with the following diagnoses:

- PTSD
- phobias
- bipolar disorder

HELPFUL HINT

Counselors should not use EMDR with clients until they are properly educated and trained by a qualified EMDR trainer.

Acceptance and Commitment Therapy

Acceptance and commitment therapy (ACT) is based on the theory that people can choose positive behavior even if their thoughts and feelings are negative. In other words, negative thoughts or feelings do not have to dictate a person's behavior. This therapy uses techniques such as

- mindfulness;
- changing the way a client thinks and behaves regarding strong feelings;

Counseling Skills and Attributes 13

- establishing values;
- encouraging clients to take action consistent with those values.

This therapeutic intervention can be used for clients with a variety of mental health issues. One example of its use is to help clients manage the discomfort of withdrawing from substance use or to manage the cravings involved in substance use recovery. The client may feel she needs the substance, and her thoughts tell her she needs it to curb the discomfort. The client can choose to exercise instead because she has the goal of remaining abstinent. Although there is no requirement to receive education and training to use ACT as an intervention, it is recommended.

Solution-Focused Brief Therapy

Solution-focused brief therapy (SFBT) involves bringing attention to clients' internally held strengths and developing these into skills to solve their problem behaviors. SFBT is effective in three to ten sessions and is used for clients working on

- substance use disorders;
- depression;
- eating disorders;
- anger management.

SFBT interventions include

- the miracle question (asking clients to envision an alternate reality where their problem does not exist);
- exception questions (focusing on when the client is not experiencing their problem);
- presupposing change questions (helping clients recognize change that has occurred in their lives);
- scaling questions (having clients rate their experience or feelings on a scale of worst to best);
- coping questions (reviewing times clients have used coping mechanisms and shown resiliency).

PRACTICE QUESTION

8. A client comes to therapy with social anxiety that prevents him from having a social life because he thinks people are judging him. Which type of therapy would benefit this client?

    A) acceptance and commitment therapy (ACT)
    B) dialectical behavior therapy (DBT)
    C) eye movement desensitization and reprocessing (EMDR)
    D) cognitive behavioral therapy (CBT)

Conflict and Confrontation

Conflict and Crisis

Conflict in the therapeutic relationship can generate insight and provide beneficial therapeutic moments. **Transference** describes a situation in which the client interacts with the counselor as if the counselor were someone else in the client's life. These interactions can be positive or negative, but either way, they are unhealthy:

- A positive example of transference might be treating the counselor as if she were a friend.
- A negative example might be directing anger at the counselor when the client is angry at his spouse.

In either case, the counselor's skill at bringing awareness to the interaction and processing it with the client can be a constructive therapeutic moment. For example, if the client behaves toward the counselor in anger, the counselor can direct the client's attention to the emotion of anger. The counselor could ask the client to describe what she is feeling in the moment and determine the cause and object of that anger. Also, the counselor might invite the client to engage in a dialogue in which she imagines the counselor is the object of her anger, which allows her to process the emotion through role-play.

When discussing transference, it is also appropriate to bring attention to **countertransference**, which is the counselor's transference toward the client transference. For example, a client treats the counselor as if he is a friend, perhaps telling him that he reminds her of her friend, and then discloses a painful experience. The counselor reacts to the client's transference by sharing a similar painful experience instead of simply listening to the client. That disclosure is countertransference and often happens without the counselor realizing it, which is another reason counselor self-awareness and self-reflection are important:

- Countertransference can shift the focus from the client's therapeutic needs and toward the counselor.
- It also compromises the counselor's objectivity because the professional boundary has been blurred by the disclosure of personal information.

Defense mechanisms are another source of conflict within a therapeutic relationship. These are techniques clients use to protect themselves from feelings of anxiety or hurt. There are a number of defense mechanisms that people use. Some of the more common ones appear in Table 1.2.

TABLE 1.2. Defense Mechanisms

MECHANISM	DEFINITION	EXAMPLE
Denial	ignoring reality	A parent denies that his child is misusing substances despite obvious signs.

continued on next page

TABLE 1.2. Defense Mechanisms (continued)

MECHANISM	DEFINITION	EXAMPLE
Repression	deciding to avoid thinking about something distressing	A client pushes away memories of an ex-partner who treated her badly.
Regression	engaging in childlike behavior or emotions	A woman speaks in baby talk when someone gets angry with her.
Intellectualizing	focusing on rationalizing an issue rather than the emotions	A client's loved one dies; he only talks about the person's illness, the course of treatment, and the inevitability of death without acknowledging the sad emotions.
Compartmentalizing	keeping a part of one's life separate from the others to reduce distress	A client works a very dangerous job but keeps it completely separate from her home life.

Constructive confrontation is a helpful therapeutic tool counselors use to call attention to the client's behaviors and feelings in the present moment, especially when there is incongruity. This method is useful to confront transference and defense mechanisms.

For example, if a client is talking about something distressing but is smiling or laughing, the counselor might stop the client and share his observation about her behavior. By confronting the client about the difference between the painful experience she is discussing and the outward emotional expression, the counselor can guide her to increased self-awareness and, possibly, some insight.

Risk assessments for **crisis** situations should be part of every assessment counselors conduct with clients. It is also necessary to ask clients how they define a crisis and what a crisis might look like for them. Everyone's interpretation of a crisis is different. Counselors cannot rely solely on their own judgment. Potential crisis situations can include

- suicide risk;
- self-harm;
- danger to self;
- danger to others;
- interpersonal violence;
- situational violence;
- a health emergency for self or loved ones;
- sudden changes in education, employment, or housing;
- natural disasters;
- accidents;

- sudden change in relationship status;
- psychotic episodes;
- substance use lapse;
- sudden strong mood changes, such as mania or depression.

Safety planning is a client-led process whereby the counselor and the client discuss

- what determines a crisis;
- what the client will do in a crisis;
- whom the client will reach out to in a crisis;
- under what conditions outside help will be sought.

Depending on the client's situation, a safety plan will be put in writing so that the client and counselor can each keep a copy and the client can share the plan with others who will be involved in the plan. As clients progress through treatment, their needs will change, so safety plans should be revisited and revised over the course of treatment. Safety plans include the following information:

- how to tell if the client is in crisis
- whom to call when the client is in crisis
- whom not to call when the client is in crisis
- what supporters should do
- what supporters should not do
- under what circumstances to call for outside help
- which outside help to call
- how to tell when the client is no longer in crisis

Counselors need to keep boundaries with clients and ensure that they understand when it is appropriate to contact the counselor when in crisis and when to call others. Most counties in the United States have a crisis hotline; some have hotlines specific to sexual assault and domestic violence. If a counselor works for a community mental health agency, the organization will likely have emergency and crisis policies in place for clients.

HELPFUL HINT

Risk assessment should occur at intake and periodically throughout the counseling relationship.

DID YOU KNOW?

Counselors must establish boundaries in crisis planning: some clients use crisis situations to seek attention from counselors.

PRACTICE QUESTION

9. During a session, a client has tears in her eyes while discussing her mother. She screams at the counselor, "I don't care what my mother thinks!" What therapeutic tool can the counselor use to help the client process her outburst?

    A) summary reflection
    B) positive reframing
    C) constructive confrontation
    D) empathetic attunement

Conflict Resolution Strategies

Conflict resolution is important in both the counseling relationship and the group counseling context. Some strategies to resolve conflict include conflict avoidance, giving in, standing one's ground, compromising, and collaborating.

Conflict avoidance involves not acknowledging the conflict. **Giving in** means acquiescing to the other party, thereby giving her what she wants or letting her have her way. **Standing one's ground** is a way of competing with the opposing party in the hopes that he does not win the battle. **Compromising** involves seeking out common ground as a stepping-stone to negotiating and resolving the conflict. **Collaborating** consists of actively listening to the opposing party's perspective, discussing areas of like-mindedness and common objectives, and confirming that both parties understand each other's viewpoints. This strategy is sometimes difficult, but it can be rewarding when it is effective.

PRACTICE QUESTION

10. Jolie manages a department in a mental health clinic. Mary, one of her employees, is constantly at odds with Nicole, another employee. Mary has seniority over Nicole but is not her direct supervisor. Mary wants Jolie to write Nicole up for disrespecting her. Jolie listens to both sides but takes no action and goes about her work as if no conflict has occurred. What type of conflict resolution strategy is Jolie employing?

    A) compromising

    B) conflict avoidance

    C) giving in

    D) collaboration

Multicultural Counseling

Multicultural Issues

Culture refers to the collective behaviors and beliefs characteristic of a particular group, be they ethnic, social, or religious. Culture includes the shared values, language, and religion of the people living in a location or region. It also includes how people feed, clothe, and shelter themselves. Shared traits include

- norms of behavior (greetings and interactions on a day-to-day level);
- values (the moral beliefs and codes that guide a culture's textual and subtextual behavior);
- language (cultural communication, including through formal language, slang, and colloquialisms).

Some cultures view the rest of the world through the lens of **ethnocentrism**, the belief that one's culture is superior to others, and those other cultures are judged by the former's values and assumptions. **Cultural bias** is a phenomenon whereby a person's worldview is informed by his own culture, and he therefore perceives the rest of the world through that lens.

Cultural bias impacts interpersonal relationships, including therapeutic relationships, especially when it comes to practicing nonjudgment and empathy. Competent counselors will practice self-awareness regarding their cultural biases and take steps to reduce these so they do not interfere with the therapeutic relationships they have with clients. Additionally, cultural bias can influence a counselor's diagnosis of a client because it provides a lens through which the counselor views a client's behavior, thereby preventing the counselor from seeing the client's concerns through her own unique experiences.

Multicultural issues play a significant role in mental health and can affect

- the way people think about mental health issues;
- the causes for mental health issues;
- seeking treatment;
- appropriate diagnosis and treatment;
- recovery;
- a client's preferences for and expectations of a counselor.

Culture can impact internal and external stigma related to mental health. Cultural issues also influence family relationships, friendships, and social support networks, and define what constitutes socially acceptable behavior. Counselors must educate themselves about the potential multicultural issues they may encounter with clients. A culturally competent counselor asks clients about their own cultural perspectives and understands how important cultural perspectives are to them.

HELPFUL HINT

Cultural bias is evident in research: most psychological research has been conducted using White, middle-class participants. Therefore, the results do not reflect or apply to the experiences of people of other populations.

HELPFUL HINT

In some cases, a counselor must be prepared to acknowledge that a client would be better served by working with another counselor who is more able to meet the client's cultural needs.

PRACTICE QUESTION

11. Self-reflection and seeking knowledge about multicultural issues can help counselors reduce which of the following?

A) anxiety
B) cultural bias
C) conflict
D) empathy

What Is Multicultural Counseling?

In **multicultural counseling**, issues of culture and identity are openly addressed as concerns how they impact a client's functioning. When clients present for therapy, they often focus on the symptoms they experience in an effort to fix them. However, in multicultural counseling, a counselor will redirect to further explore issues such as

- race;
- ethnicity;
- family;
- religion;
- socioeconomic status;

- environment;
- identity.

Multicultural counseling explores how those factors contribute to a client's symptoms. It also considers how those cultural factors function as risk or protective factors. Multicultural counselors might also discuss with clients how they view therapy and what their expectations are for the therapeutic process.

Culture impacts the way people experience mental health issues. It is therefore also appropriate, for example, to ask a client who says she is depressed how she experiences depression and how the cultural factors that impact her most play a role in what she experiences.

For example, a client might report that he experiences depression as sadness, fatigue, loss of appetite, and a desire to socially isolate. Perhaps he feels as though his family expects him to stop feeling depressed because he comes from a culture that does not believe depression is a mental health issue or that it requires treatment. The family's invalidation of the client's depressive symptoms may be a contributing factor to his treatment plan in addition to addressing the symptoms of depression.

Multicultural competence is demonstrated by counselors who

- regularly practice self-awareness regarding their own cultural bias;
- pursue knowledge of other cultures;
- can interact with people of different cultural backgrounds effectively and respectfully.

Counselors must continually pursue multicultural competence. For example, a non-Native counselor might live in a state with a significant Native American client population. That counselor should network with counselors in the Native American community to learn about available resources and how to integrate appropriate Native American concepts or ideas in treatment.

Multicultural competence also requires a degree of cultural humility, especially when the counselor is not immersed in the client's culture. Using the Native American population as an example, a White counselor might ask a Native American client about his tribal affiliations and how important that connection is to him. The counselor might also ask the client how he feels about discussing his personal issues with a non-Native counselor. A multicultural counselor will be able to have that conversation respectfully and honestly while inviting the client to discuss cultural issues of importance to him.

The **emic perspective** is a way of learning about and perceiving culture by becoming a part of that culture. Taking this perspective can lead to a more in-depth understanding of the values and beliefs inherent to a culture in a way that an outsider cannot perceive.

The **etic perspective** is a way of learning about and perceiving culture from the outside of that culture. This perspective enables a person to acquire knowledge and to answer questions about a culture but often does not go deeper than a superficial understanding.

The **transcultural perspective** is an approach to counseling that references five dimensions:

1. culture knowledge
2. understanding power, privilege, and oppression
3. positionality and self-reflexivity
4. partnership
5. cultural competence

- A counselor understands that a client may already experience hardship due to cultural issues and seeks to understand the client's cultural perspectives on issues related to counseling.
- A counselor using a transcultural perspective will explore the client's culture on his terms and discuss what it means for the counseling process. Counselors understand that the client is the expert on his own life, experiences, and struggles.

The **Association for Multicultural Counseling and Development (AMCD)** is a professional counseling organization dedicated to providing professional development for counselors to improve cultural competence. The AMCD also advocates for human rights and policies to enhance cultural diversity within the counseling profession.

PRACTICE QUESTION

12. What is the BEST way for counselors to demonstrate cultural competence with clients?
    A) avoid talking about their own culture
    B) match the client with a counselor who has the same cultural background
    C) discuss cultural issues with clients of other cultural backgrounds respectfully
    D) read a book about multicultural counseling

Considerations in Multicultural Counseling

A multicultural counselor practices the basic skills and core attributes of counseling (genuineness, congruence, nonjudgmental stance, positive regard) and keeps sessions focused on clients and their needs. Additionally, counselors pursue knowledge of cultural issues by learning about the populations within their community that they may encounter in a therapeutic setting. This means that they learn about the general values, beliefs, and behavioral norms of each group. Acquisition of knowledge leads to awareness of

- the counselor's own cultural biases;
- the counselor's attitudes toward people of different cultural groups;
- the attitudes of various cultural groups toward each other.

Acquiring knowledge enables the counselor to put knowledge and awareness into practice with clients by

- asking about cultural issues during the assessment process;
- creating a safe environment for the client to discuss cultural issues.

The counselor can further demonstrate knowledge about cultural differences by drawing attention to the differences between the counselor and the client and seeking understanding about how culture influences a client's mental health.

Psychologist Gilbert Wrenn drew attention to the culturally encapsulated counselor. **Culturally encapsulated counselors** are counselors who

- look at the world and other people only through their own cultural lens;
- do not venture outside that lens;
- ignore anything contrary to that lens;
- treat clients as if they can all be treated the same way;
- views themselves as free of bias and are therefore not open to learning.

To avoid becoming culturally encapsulated, the counselor must practice and demonstrate respect for and acceptance of diversity. The first way to do this is to recognize the various aspects of diversity that affect people.

The **RESPECTFUL counseling** acronym provides a useful framework for counselors to approach multicultural issues. Each of the letters represents areas of diversity within people. This model can serve as a template for discussing issues during assessment or throughout the counseling process:

- **R**eligious/spiritual issues
  - Does the client hold religious or spiritual beliefs? Why or why not?
  - How do those beliefs or lack thereof influence the client? Are they important to the client?
- **E**conomic class issues
  - What is the client's experience with socioeconomic class?
  - How has the client's socioeconomic experience affected his life, worldview, and choices?
- **S**exual identity issues
  - How does the client identify sexually? Is this important to her?
  - How has the client's sexual identity affected her life, relationships, and family?
- **P**sychological developmental issues
  - Did the client have any developmental or psychological issues during his childhood that impacted him either positively or negatively?
  - Did he get treatment for any of these issues?
  - How did the experience impact the client?
- **E**thnic/racial identity issues
  - How does the client identify ethnically/racially?

- How has her identification shaped her values and beliefs?
- Has she encountered discrimination? How has that impacted her life?
- **C**hronological issues
    - How old is the client? What is the client's developmental stage?
    - How were previous developmental stages resolved?
    - How does the client's age impact him now?
- **T**rauma/threats to well-being
    - Does the client have a history of trauma?
    - What does the client experience in terms of the effects of trauma?
    - How does that trauma influence her perception of herself and others?
    - How does it impact her relationships?
- **F**amily issues
    - How does the client define family?
    - How does the client describe his family of origin?
    - How are those relationships now?
    - How does family influence the client's choices and identity?
- **U**nique physical issues
    - Does the client have different or limited physical abilities?
    - Are those differences something the client was born with or acquired?
    - How do the client's unique physical issues impact her life, functioning, and relationships?
- **L**anguage/location of residence issues
    - Is the client a native of the location in which he lives, or did he immigrate there from another city, state, or country?
    - Does the client have a non-Native immigration status?
    - Does the client speak a second language?
    - Is English the client's first or second language?
    - How do these issues and experiences impact the client?

PRACTICE QUESTION

13. A counselor who refuses to acknowledge cultural differences and claims she has no cultural bias could be characterized as what?

    A) culturally encapsulated

    B) stuck in her ways

    C) conservative

    D) liberal

Specific Cultural Groups

Every client who presents for therapy is a unique individual, and each session with that client will be unique. Counselors should check their assumptions about clients—whether based on cultural bias or any other preconceived ideas—at the counseling office door. By maintaining a client-focused approach to therapy and adopting the core attributes of a counselor, one can approach each session with each client with an open, nonjudgmental mind.

Counselor self-examination is a practice of consistent self-reflection whereby counselors examine their own cultural diversity, attitudes, beliefs, and values, and how those influence how they interact with clients. Several concepts aid in self-examination and working with clients from different cultural backgrounds:

- **White privilege** refers to the unearned social status and advantages held by White people.
    - For example, White characters and figures generally have more widespread positive representation in the media than do people of other races. Perhaps a White child sees more characters or toys that look like him than would a Black, Latino, or Asian child.
    - This disparity can be harmful to individuals who are not White, as they will not grow up and live with similar experiences.
- **Racial microaggressions** are small behaviors and messages that occur in everyday situations and are characterized by a bias toward a marginalized group.
    - They include questions, comments, and actions.
    - They can be both intentional and unintentional.
    - One example would be to presume that an individual is dangerous because of her race, ethnicity, or gender; for instance, a pedestrian crosses the street to avoid a person of a different race.
- The term *model minority* describes myths that are commonly associated with Americans of Asian descent.
    - This can include the idea that children of Asian descent are smarter than other children, more musically inclined than others, and pushed harder by their parents than are other children.
    - These seemingly positive stereotypes might be downplayed or considered less offensive or harmful than negative stereotypes about education or ability.
    - Stereotypes associated with positive attributes can be just as harmful to the individual as negative stereotypes.
- **Unconscious bias** refers to the attitudes and stereotypes people do not consciously realize they have about others.
    - Unconscious bias results in behaviors that can be interpreted as offensive.
    - Education and self-reflection can help bring unconscious bias into the conscious mind so the counselor can reduce it.

Counselors should also be aware of **historical hostility and minority racial identity development (MRID)**. According to MRID, trauma is passed from one generation to the next. The following are all vehicles for historical trauma:
- how a group of people feels about themselves
- how a group views others
- how the group perceives systems
- how the group interacts with other people and systems

These attitudes, values, beliefs, and behaviors can be passed through generations. Groups of people who have been subjected to hostility, oppression, and discrimination throughout history carry the trauma of those experiences throughout the subsequent generations within their families.

The MRID model is a framework that explains the various stages minority groups go through to develop their cultural identities. It includes four stages that range from devaluing their minority identities to developing confident identities as minorities within the majority population.

Cultural groups often contain more **within-group differences** than **between-group** differences. For example, there are distinct differences between collectivist and individualist cultures; however, within the collectivist culture, there will be even more differences.

Within-group differences are even visible within families. Therefore, even if a counselor knows someone from a particular cultural group, that does not mean the next person she meets from that group will hold the same values, beliefs, and behaviors.

PRACTICE QUESTION

14. A family who has immigrated to the US from Haiti comes to therapy for help with adjustment issues. The parents are devout Christians and value traditional family and gender roles. The three teenagers are rejecting the family's religious preferences and are strongly influenced by US popular culture. What is this an example of?

    A) unconscious bias
    B) within-group differences
    C) between-group differences
    D) model minority

Gender Issues

Culturally competent counselors also recognize diversity regarding gender. They must demonstrate knowledge of and sensitivity to gender orientation and issues pertaining to gender. Congruence, unconditional positive regard, and empathy are important during sessions with lesbian, gay, bisexual, transgender, queer, intersex, and agender (LGBTQIA+) clients:

- **Gender** refers to a person's subjective experience of gender, which may or may not be congruent with the gender assigned to that person at birth.

- Gender characteristics may fall within a range of masculinity and femininity. A person's identified gender will impact that person's gender roles and gender identity.
- **Gender issues** can refer to a variety of experiences, including
  - gender orientation;
  - gender identity;
  - gender dysphoria;
  - how to talk to family about gender;
  - discrimination at school or work;
  - navigating intimate/romantic relationships.

Gender socialization is the process individuals undergo when learning and conditioning themselves to the societal expectations and attitudes of their gender. Gender socialization is a lifelong process that can impact a person's beliefs, thoughts, feelings, and behaviors. Early socialization is most often shaped by parents, caregivers, and others within the family of origin. As a child grows up, socialization is further shaped by friends, school, the media, and the community.

Gender role conflict occurs when people are in a rigid or restrictive environment that leads them to devalue themselves or restrict how they express themselves. These individuals are unable to live as their true selves in their environment, which is harmful and distressing. Gender role conflict can be assessed by using the **gender role conflict scale**, a thirty-seven-item assessment that can be self-administered and explores four domains:

1. success, power, and competition
2. restrictive emotionality
3. restrictive affectionate behavior between men
4. conflicts between work and family relations

PRACTICE QUESTION

15. A person who grows up being told that a woman should aspire to be a wife and mother has experienced which of the following regarding the idea of femaleness?

    A) therapy

    B) gender socialization

    C) gender orientation

    D) diversity

Answer Key

1. **B)** The counselor demonstrates genuineness and congruence by stating that she does not agree with the client's choices, shows nonjudgment by keeping the behavior separate from the person, and expresses positive regard by encouraging the client to work toward better choices.

2. **C)** A self-aware counselor will read the client's nonverbal feedback immediately, recognize something is wrong, and address it in the session as soon as possible to maintain a good therapeutic relationship with the client.

3. **A)** Attending behaviors, like eye contact and other nonverbal signals, communicate that the counselor is present and paying attention to the client.

4. **D)** The client is in shock, not thinking straight, and needs to express these emotions. The counselor can demonstrate empathetic attunement by giving her time and space to feel what she needs to feel without judgment.

5. **A)** This client expects the counselor to be the expert professional and give direction, but the therapeutic alliance relies on equal power and trust between client and counselor.

6. **C)** The client's statements suggest that he blames his failure on the school, professors, and peers—not himself; this demonstrates external locus of control.

7. **A)** Psychoeducation can help the teenager and the mother understand what the teenager is experiencing.

8. **D)** Cognitive behavioral therapy would focus on identifying and addressing the client's thoughts and beliefs related to how others view him.

9. **C)** The counselor can use constructive confrontation to draw the client's attention to the discrepancy between the words she is speaking and the visible emotion she is displaying.

10. **B)** Jolie is practicing conflict avoidance by pretending that no conflict has happened.

11. **B)** Self-reflection and knowledge can reduce a counselor's reliance on his own worldview and thereby reduce cultural bias.

12. **C)** A significant aspect of multicultural counseling is applying the knowledge and skills learned within relationships with people of different cultures, which can be facilitated through respectful discussions about cultural issues.

13. **A)** Culturally encapsulated counselors look at the world and other people only through their own cultural lens, do not venture outside that viewpoint, ignore anything contrary to that lens, and treat clients as if everyone can be treated the same way. They also view themselves as free of bias and are not open to learning.

14. **B)** The group is the Haitian family. Within the family, there are differences among individuals even though they are all part of one family unit, which is an example of within-group differences.

15. **B)** Gender socialization is the process individuals undergo when learning and conditioning themselves to the societal expectations and attitudes of their own genders.

2 Group Counseling

Working with a Group

Group counseling is significantly different from individual counseling because the client is the entire group, not just one person. Therefore, the focus of intervention is on the interactions among group members. This shift requires a purposeful approach from the group counselor when determining the type, size, and duration of the group.

Group type, size, and duration depend on the goal of the group. Some groups focus on a specific purpose and benefit from interaction among members; others offer support for members with minimal interaction among them. The following section discusses the different types of groups and their characteristics.

Types of Groups

Open groups, or open-ended groups, have no set beginning or ending; members can come and go as they please. Open-ended groups might teach members a set of coping skills for substance use or follow a psychoeducational curriculum that starts again once one cycle of the program ends:

- Some open-ended groups follow a **manualized program**, which provides a curriculum for the group counselor and includes instruction techniques and exercises to use for practice.
- Manualized programs can run in cycles, allowing members to start at any time and finish when the cycle is complete.
- Examples of manualized programs include anger management and court-ordered driver education and counseling (for DUI clients).
- Other open-ended groups function as support groups, like mutual aid groups, where members receive support from each other.
- Examples of support groups include open groups for people dealing with depression or grief.
- The level of interaction among group members is superficial.

> **? DID YOU KNOW?**
> Some states regulate the ratio of group leaders to members (for example, ten to fifteen members for each facilitator). This way, the group size will depend on the number of facilitators available.

- The size of the group depends on factors such as
  - the number of group counselors;
  - room size;
  - program capabilities;
  - state rules regarding group sizes.

Open-ended groups can last as long as necessary. Some run continually; others have a start and end date. **Closed groups** are the opposite of open groups:

- New members are not allowed to join once the group begins.
- Closed groups tend to have a specific purpose as well as a start and end date.

Closed groups are effective for especially delicate matters. For example, closed groups for people who have experienced sexual assault are appropriate due to the level of trust required among group members and the weight of the topics addressed. The success of the group often depends on the trust established and the interaction among members:

- Closed groups may feature a curriculum or schedule of topics.
- Closed groups typically set criteria for membership, such as age, gender, or experience with the topic.

Psychoeducational groups, or **curriculum groups**, focus on a specific topic and typically have start and end dates. Psychoeducational groups are usually open, with the stated purpose of teaching a skill or providing information. Topics include

- anger management;
- parenting skills;
- life skills.

These groups follow an evidence-based program whereby the facilitator presents information to the group. Group interaction focuses on the topic.

Process groups focus on the interaction among group members. In process groups, counselors help members process their thoughts, feelings, and behaviors on a deep level. The purpose is to address challenges that members face in the present. Process groups treat issues such as

- depression;
- anxiety;
- PTSD;
- substance use;
- relationship issues;
- other mental illnesses.

Interactions among group members allow them to increase self-awareness and gain insight from other members by sharing experiences and perspectives. Additionally, process groups allow members to practice various skills, such as:

- assertiveness;

- creating boundaries;
- working through conflict.

These groups require a deeper level of trust among their members; therefore, process groups are often closed or semi-closed.

A **homogenous group** facilitates bonding among members based on what they have in common, which provides a focus for the group's purpose. Members of a homogenous group are chosen because they have characteristics or traits in common, such as

- gender;
- age (for example, members who are under eighteen);
- mental health issues (for example, members with a certain diagnosis).

Members of **heterogeneous groups** are chosen for the diversity of their characteristics or traits. Many open groups are heterogeneous: anyone of any age with any issue may participate. This diversity of experiences, backgrounds, traits, and issues that each person brings to the group can help other members.

PRACTICE QUESTION

1. A counselor wants to create a group for parents of children with disabilities to help them learn more about coping and to create a network of people who can support each other through tough times. Which of the following groups would be appropriate?

   A) an open twelve-step group

   B) an open and homogenous group

   C) a closed and heterogenous group

   D) a closed process group

Group Activities and Psychoeducation

Structured activities provide overall structure and routine to an open group. A counselor can use structured activities during a session in a variety of ways.

For example, in an open group, members might use the structured activity format to each say their name and provide a brief update on their progress. Then, there might be a presentation of a relevant topic followed by group reactions and commentary on the topic for a set amount of time. Finally, the group might close with a structured activity, such as each member summing up the session.

This structured method gives group members a sense of stability and trust in the group process, helps them feel comfortable with the routine, and keeps sessions predictable. Structured activities may also be used for

- building trust among group members by helping them get to know each other;
- lessons to keep the progress of the group moving toward its end goal;
- sample situations that members may encounter, which allow them to role-play in group;

- moving a group out of stagnation or resolving a conflict;
- teaching skills;
- engaging new group members.

There are many ways to use psychoeducation as part of the group process. In some groups, the focus is on the presentation of educational materials. Psychoeducation can also be used to normalize and validate a group member's experience. For example, if a member of a substance use group talks about having cravings that feel out of control, the counselor can use psychoeducation to explain the effects that drugs have on the brain and what the brain goes through during the healing process and recovery.

PRACTICE QUESTION

2. A counselor is creating a drop-in group for people who have experienced grief or tragic loss. There is no sign-up process for the group, nor does the counselor have any information about the people who will participate or what they are dealing with. What is the BEST reason to have structured activities in this particular group?

    A) to help group members feel comfortable and welcome by providing a predictable routine

    B) to weed out participants who do not belong in the group

    C) to allow group members to interact with each other in the present and gain insight

    D) to let potential participants know the group is a closed group

Interactions in Groups

There are many ways counselors can manage **leader-member dynamics**. The title of "group leader" can be misleading because group counselors act more as facilitators than leaders. The purpose of a group is to facilitate interactions among group members, and while a counselor may present material or topics for the group to address, the real work takes place when members inspire insight in each other.

Many interactions between leaders and members are positive, but an effective group leader will remember the group's function and resist trying to control all aspects of the group. The following are some ways to keep leader-member dynamics from becoming disruptive to the group:

- Have the members establish group rules and reiterate them at each meeting. When the group creates the rules, the leader is no longer in an authoritative position.
- Defer to the group. For example, if a member challenges the leader's qualifications or reasons for being there, the leader can reflect that question back to the group and ask if anyone else feels that way, why they feel that way, and what impact that has on the group.

This takes the focus of discussion off of the leader and back to the members.

- Remind members that the group is not about the leader. This is another skill whereby the group leader reflects the interaction between a member and the leader back to the group.
- Invite the group to decide. If a member's behavior toward the leader becomes too disruptive, it may be appropriate to ask the group to determine if the member's behavior violates group rules and, if so, to act. Deferral to the group puts the power of the member's fate in the hands of the members and not the leader, thus giving group members authority over each other.

Managing leader-member dynamics is similar to the relationship between basketball players and the referee. The action of the game is the ball between the players, but sometimes the ball bounces to the referee. The referee's job is not to take the ball and join the game but to direct the ball back to the players to continue the game. Most groups require a **leader** or **facilitator**:

- For some groups, the counselor acts as the group leader or facilitator.
  - State regulations may require a counselor to be present at a therapy group.
- Some group types require the presence of the counselor, but the counselor may defer group leadership to a member.
- Other groups may not need a counselor as a leader, especially if they are support groups and not therapy groups.
  - Examples include mutual aid groups like Alcoholics Anonymous (AA) or peer support groups.
  - In such groups, it is wise to have someone act as a leader if only to get the group started and ended on time.
  - Chairpersons, coordinators, or facilitators manage logistics and ensure adherence to the group format and rules.

By having a coordinator or facilitator, the groups can remain open to all potential participants, and members and potential participants will know what to expect when they attend. Effective group leaders understand the group's purpose and function, which then determines the level of facilitation the group will require:

- In psychoeducational groups, the leader might be responsible for presenting the material and coordinating discussion afterward.
- In process groups, the leader might be responsible for noticing interaction among members, calling attention to something happening in the group for deeper processing, or addressing issues related to members who are too quiet or too overpowering.
- An effective group leader can facilitate resolutions for therapeutic purposes when conflict arises.

TABLE 2.1. Characteristics and Skills of Effective Leaders

CHARACTERISTIC/SKILL	DEFINITION
Detachment	the ability to keep the focus of the group on the members and not on the leader
Observation	the ability to notice therapeutic events when they happen in a group and point them out
Empathy and encouragement	the ability to draw out group members who are not participating and include them
Reflection and summarization	the ability to rephrase what group members are saying to make a connection with what other members are experiencing
Confrontation and mediation	the ability to recognize conflict or the potential for conflict and guide group members through fixing it themselves
Teaching and clarifying	the ability to add educational information to the group discussion that applies to what is going on in the group and find ways members can use what they learn outside of the group
Management	the ability to keep members on task or focused and help them enforce group rules when necessary

Co-leaders can be very effective in groups since one person cannot notice or address everything that happens. A co-leader can be

- another licensed counselor;
- a counseling intern;
- a peer.

Co-leaders can take on various roles: training new counselors as group counselors, presenting specialized material, or acting as additional observers. Peers, or people further along their recovery journey than other members, can also be very helpful to engage group members.

Before the group session begins, the co-leaders should discuss each of their roles. For example, one co-leader may take the role of lead facilitator while the other observes and interjects, or each co-leader may divide up responsibilities equally.

Although **leader-member interactions** are not usually the focus of group counseling, it is helpful when group members trust the leader. The counselor can promote and encourage interactions between the leader and members through

- introductions;
- self-disclosure;
- asking clarifying questions;
- other counseling skills (for example, reflection, summarization, and attending).

The counselor's role in facilitating the group is to promote and encourage interactions among members. There are several ways to do this:

- Using **direct questioning**, the counselor might ask one group member how he reacted to what another member said.
- To **establish commonality** among members, when one member shares something about a family member who died, for example, the counselor might ask if anyone else has experienced the loss of a family member.
- **Linking** is a technique group counselors use to connect what one member says or experiences to another member to establish a connection, empathy, or understanding.
- **Feedback** in group therapy can be used by the counselor or members to share reactions to another group member—what that person said, did, or shared.
  - In addition to sharing reactions, feedback can include providing encouragement or recommendations.
  - An effective group counselor will facilitate feedback among members but may also use feedback as an instructive tool for the rest of the group.
- **Self-disclosure** is the process of sharing one's perspectives or experiences and generally refers to the counselor's sharing of personal experiences for a therapeutic purpose.
  - Self-disclosure can be useful for establishing a trusting relationship with the group members or for instructive purposes, but it should be used with care.
- Finally, the counselor can bring up **previous information** shared by a member in group to apply to a current situation.
  - For example, if a member shared a coping skill in a previous session that could help someone in the current session, the counselor might ask the first member about what he did and ask if he could explain it again.

Confidentiality in group therapy is held by the counselor, not necessarily the group. This means that the counselor has a legal and ethical obligation to keep what happens or who is a member in the group confidential. The agency hosting the group may have rules regarding group confidentiality that all members will be expected to uphold.

Group members are not legally or ethically obligated to uphold the same standards as the counselor; however, confidentiality is essential for groups to be successful, which is why members need to establish rules of confidentiality. This is one of the first items of business in a new group:

- Counselors should facilitate the creation of confidentiality rules to include how group members recognize each other outside of group and on social media.

 HELPFUL HINT

A word of caution when bringing up previously shared information: the counselor cannot bring up information the client shared with the counselor outside the group, which would be a breach of confidentiality.

- The group should determine the consequences of breaking confidentiality and how such a situation will be handled if it happens.

Another key role of the group counselor is to identify therapeutic moments that occur and point them out to members. The counselor can do this purposefully by asking questions of members and inviting feedback.

For example, if someone shares an experience, the counselor might ask the group if anyone else has experienced something similar or if they have any feedback for that member. The counselor can also do this indirectly by allowing the group to interact and then interjecting on occasion to share an observation of a theme or pattern. The counselor can also use summarization at the end of group sessions to identify patterns and themes that emerged in that session.

PRACTICE QUESTION

3. A member of a process group for people in recovery from substance use says she does not like the group counselor because he is young and never had any substance use issues, so she questions how he can do his job. What is the BEST response the counselor can make?

    A) "If you don't like it, you are free to leave the group."
    B) "All right, I'll find you someone else."
    C) "That's a good point. What do others think about this?"
    D) "There's nothing you can do but accept it."

Group Stages

There are several defined **stages in the group process**:

- forming
- storming
- norming
- performing
- mourning

The **forming** stage of the group process is the start of the group when members join, introduce themselves, and determine their positions in the group. This part of the group process involves establishing the group rules, getting used to the format, and gaining an understanding of what the group will accomplish.

The **storming** stage involves conflict among group members. This can include testing boundaries, ascertaining whether other members really belong in the group, challenging the authority of the counselor, or resisting the way the group has decided to operate. Not every group goes through this stage, but the group's success depends on a healthy resolution; otherwise, members will be stuck in this stage and not get to the group's actual work.

The **norming** stage involves healing and repairing following the storming stage. If there is no conflict within the group, it occurs immediately after the forming stage. This is the stage when group members become comfortable with each other, understand what is expected of them, and settle into the routine of the work.

The **performing** stage describes the phase of real group work being done. The leader's function is reduced because members take on the roles of encouraging interaction with each other. It is in this stage that much of the therapeutic work is accomplished.

The **mourning** stage occurs at the end of the group and begins the process of group termination. During group therapy, members can become close and the end of group can be a sad event. Therefore, to ensure a successful termination of the group, the leader might facilitate an event or ritual to commemorate the successes of the members and to celebrate their accomplishments. Honoring this stage of the group process helps members transition out of the group.

Counselors need to be aware of which stage the group is in to make sure members are ready for a particular intervention. If a proposed intervention is not appropriate for the stage, then it will not be effective. For example, a role-play intervention to teach assertiveness might not be effective during the storming stage because of the level of group conflict; however, adjusting that intervention to teach healthy conflict resolution skills would be appropriate. A counselor should therefore always think about whether members are ready for a particular intervention and if it will help them move toward the stated goals.

PRACTICE QUESTION

4. At the end of a group counseling session, the counselor highlights the way three members achieved deep insight into their issues, and thanked the other four members for helping with validation, feedback, and encouragement of those three members. Which developmental stage is this group likely in?

    A) forming
    B) norming
    C) storming
    D) performing

Attributes in a Group Counseling Context

Group Therapeutic Factors

A counselor demonstrates all of the core counseling attributes in a group context. Important core counseling attributes include

- self-awareness;
- genuineness;
- congruence;
- nonjudgment;
- positive regard;

- active listening;
- attending;
- reflecting;
- empathy.

See Chapter 1, "Core Counseling Attributes," for more details. In addition, the following attributes are important for group counseling:

- facilitation of group topics and group membership
- management of time, rules, and tasks
- observation of group members
- redirection of topics back to the group
- modeling appropriate behavior and healthy relationship skills
- identification of therapeutic moments
- enforcement of group rules
- fairness of treatment of and among group members
- conflict resolution skills
- calling out inappropriate behavior
- facilitating behavioral corrections
- teaching skills and therapy concepts

There are multiple therapeutic events and factors that occur in group therapy that a counselor watches for and facilitates. Group counselors foster the emergence of **group therapeutic factors** by knowing what they are and how to recognize them in a group context. Once a counselor recognizes when these factors occur, it may be appropriate to call attention to them in the group.

Self-disclosure is the sharing of personal information and experiences; it usually refers to the counselor. The purpose of self-disclosure is to further the therapeutic process. Often this is done with the intent to establish trust with the client, to move the client out of stagnation, or to inspire insight.

Self-disclosure can also include the counselor sharing feelings in the present to bring something into awareness. For example, a counselor may disclose feelings of tension within the group to initiate a conversation about conflicts among members.

Self-disclosure among group members is a key component of group therapy and requires that members share their thoughts, feelings, and experiences. The counselor may need to navigate self-disclosures by inviting reticent members to share and limiting the sharing of those who tend to dominate discussions.

Interaction in group therapy refers to the interpersonal engagement among group members. The interaction should not be between members and the counselor but among the members themselves, so that they can learn from each other rather than from the counselor. A counselor who notices how members interact may draw attention to a more quiet member to encourage their participation.

In group therapy, **acceptance and group cohesiveness** refers to members feeling like they belong in the group, that other members accept them for who they are, and that the member relationships are important to them. Group members feel safe and not judged, which results in a healthy environment for therapeutic progress.

When group members come to an understanding of their issues, or if they gain a new perspective or awareness of what they experience, this is referred to as **insight**. The new understanding or perspective helps members see their experience a little differently and even provides what they need to move beyond their issues.

Catharsis refers to an internal experience of change or a sudden realization that leads to a strong emotional reaction. The sudden realization may be associated with something that happened in a person's past or the identification of a triggering event.

Guidance occurs when either the group counselor or other group members provide educational information or advice.

Altruism is an aspect of group therapy whereby group members help each other, thus shifting the focus from themselves to other people. Helping other members provides a sense of value and gratitude among all members, which can improve how members think about themselves. A counselor may point out situations in which one group member helped another in order to draw attention to it and thus magnify the therapeutic effect.

Vicarious learning is learning from the experiences of other people. The self-disclosure of group members allows the other members to hear the good and the bad in the hopes that the listener makes different choices based on the experiences of someone else.

Hope is a strong motivator, and it can fuel a person's desire for change. Without hope, people feel helpless to change their situation. Within a group situation, the **instillation of hope** can come from members who share a common experience and who can show other members that healing is possible. Hearing the stories of someone who has been in the same situation can provide members with inspiration and a model of how healing is possible.

Existential factors involve recognizing what gives life meaning and the shared experience of being human. This may include discussions about big questions surrounding life and death, universal truths, and spirituality. Existential discussion in group therapy can help members come to terms with what they are dealing with by giving it some meaning or purpose outside of themselves.

PRACTICE QUESTION

5. In a highly emotional group session, one member is crying. After a moment of letting him experience his emotions, another member goes over to him and puts a hand on his shoulder. The crying member looks at the second member, and the two make eye contact and smile. The counselor says, "Thank you for reaching out and offering comfort and validation." Which therapeutic factor is the counselor calling attention to?

    A) instillation of hope

    B) existential factors

    C) self-disclosure

    D) altruism

Conflict in Groups

The counselor can use many strategies to facilitate the resolution of **interpersonal conflict in the group setting**. First, the counselor needs to approach all conflicts as if they are a therapeutic opportunity from which group members can learn. Conflict has a way of bringing issues to the surface and inspiring insight; therefore, the counselor should approach conflict with an attitude of curiosity and exploration.

It is essential to focus on the present when doing this in the group. Often, conflict among two or more group members is representative of something else, but that something else cannot be discovered without exploring what is happening in the moment. Counselors should follow certain steps to make the most of conflict:

1. The counselor should first call attention to the conflict and bring it into the present.

2. The counselor should then bring each party's awareness to their individual experiences of the conflict.

3. Group members should be asked to offer their observations and feedback about the conflict.

4. The counselor should guide the parties while they work through the conflict, after which the group processes how it went and what they learned from it.

Group counselors should not let conflict go to waste. Each conflict presents a learning opportunity for group members to not only gain insight into their behaviors but also to learn how to work through conflict in a healthy way.

Counselors must recognize and address harmful group behaviors and intervene if members do not. Often, that intervention includes pointing out the person's behavior and exploring it. This intervention shows everyone that the counselor values the cohesiveness of the group by enforcing group rules and protecting members. If the behaviors violate group rules, then the group must decide whether to enforce the rules and determine the consequences. One method of intervention is blocking. In **blocking**, the group counselor immediately stops a member's behavior if it is

- inappropriate;
- counterproductive;
- harmful to others.

After stopping the behavior, the counselor references the group rules and the reason for blocking the member's behavior. If the member violated the group's rules, the counselor may defer to the group to determine what to do about the member.

For example, if the group decides that name calling is not allowed and a member calls another member an inappropriate name, the counselor should immediately stop the group and block the offending member from continuing.

Unfortunately, a counselor has no power to regulate the behaviors and interactions of members outside of the group; however, part of establishing group rules would include every member agreeing to confidentiality and the way in which people interact outside of the group. If a member violates the agreed-upon rules, then it would be appropriate to address that in the group and let the group decide whether that person is allowed to continue as a member. Additionally, the counselor may speak to members one-on-one, but the most effective interventions occur within the group.

PRACTICE QUESTION

6. What should a group counselor do when there is conflict in group therapy?
    A) call attention to the conflict immediately and help the members work through it
    B) ignore the conflict and address it in a future session when tensions are not so high
    C) speak with the individual group members outside of the group and remind them to work together
    D) bring in a supervisor to deal with the conflict so the counselor does not signal favoritism

CONTINUE

Answer Key

1. **B)** An open group would be most appropriate because parents can enter or leave as they please. A homogenous group is suitable because members share the common characteristic of parents of children who have disabilities.

2. **A)** Structured activities in an open group—that allow people to participate whenever they want—offer members a familiar routine that does not rely on individual members to keep the group progressing.

3. **C)** The counselor acknowledges that the client has a valid point, thus demonstrating empathy, but then turns the question back to the group to facilitate conversation among members.

4. **D)** Performing is the stage of group therapy when real work gets accomplished. This session included positive group interactions that contributed to positive outcomes for multiple group members, so the group is likely in the performing stage.

5. **D)** Altruism is the act of one group member helping another. This counselor pointed out that one member reached out to another to offer comfort.

6. **A)** Conflict in group therapy can be beneficial as a therapeutic learning opportunity. The group should work through conflict in the present.

3. Professional Practice and Ethics

Professional Practice

Counselor-Client Relationship

The counselor in a treatment setting should demonstrate empathy while maintaining a level of clinical detachment. This is the basis for a therapeutic relationship.

The **therapeutic relationship** exists to benefit the client, not the counselor. Within a therapeutic relationship, the counselor

- limits self-disclosure;
- establishes boundaries with clients;
- focuses sessions on the client's treatment goals.

Building trust with a client in the therapeutic relationship involves

- honesty;
- empathy;
- boundaries;
- communication;
- client-led care.

In **client-led care**, clients set the agenda guided by the counselor. The counselor does not engage in coercive behaviors, such as forcing a client to participate in a particular type of therapy. Instead, the counselor explains the recommended therapies for a particular issue and allows clients to choose what will work best for them.

When clients present for treatment, they enter the therapeutic relationship with less power than the counselor. The counselor must be aware of this and equalize the power dynamic by consistently **monitoring the therapeutic relationship** and building trust as needed.

The counselor can use these techniques to monitor the therapeutic relationship:

- Determine how the client feels about the relationship and the therapy process by asking what is working and what else is needed.

Based on the answers, it may be necessary to reestablish a rapport with the client.

- Observe and assess the client's behaviors and nonverbal communication in session.

A client who starts to close up and become quiet may be losing trust in the counselor, and the counselor must call attention to the change and switch gears to reestablish trust. This might mean stopping the work of therapy and establishing common ground again.

- Provide standardized assessments to the client before a session at various intervals whereby the client can rate his interaction with the counselor.

Client rights and responsibilities are often listed in the mental health regulations of the state in which the counselor practices. These rights and responsibilities generally fall into the categories of high-quality care, client-centered practice, informed consent, confidentiality, and right to records.

High-quality care ensures that the client can expect prompt service from adequately trained professionals in an environment of physical and psychological safety.

- If the client feels she is not receiving high-quality care, she has the right to complain and request a referral to another provider.
- The client will not be subject to unnecessary or unending treatment.

In **client-centered practice**, the counselor must inform the client of all treatment options and allow him to choose his goals and treatment methods.

- The client has the right to ask questions about treatment, including methods and finances.

Clients must provide **informed consent** for treatment. To obtain informed consent, counselors must

- disclose to the client their training and expertise;
- explain how the counseling process works and what the client can expect;
- describe the boundaries of the therapeutic relationship.

Counselors may not conduct treatment interventions they are not trained for.

Clients have the right to a level of **confidentiality**. The counselor will keep the client's personal information confidential according to state and federal laws and explain to the client under what circumstances confidentiality may be broken.

Confidentiality is discussed in depth later in this chapter.

Clients have the **right to records**. The counselor should explain

- how sessions are documented;
- why sessions are documented;
- how clients can access their records.

Since many clients may not understand their records, counselors can go over the records with them.

Although this is usually covered in the first session, the counselor should make a practice of reminding clients of their rights periodically throughout therapy. The first session is usually stressful, so it is irresponsible to expect the client to remember everything that was said.

PRACTICE QUESTION

1. Which of the following BEST describes client-centered practice?
   - **A)** A counselor tells a client how many sessions she will have.
   - **B)** A client wants to focus on anxiety, so the counselor recommends therapeutic interventions.
   - **C)** A client with depression asks the counselor to disregard his history of self-harm.
   - **D)** A client asks to have ninety-minute sessions instead of the usual sixty-minute sessions.

Group Practice

In **group practice**, the therapeutic relationship between counselor and client changes. The "client" is the group as a whole, rather than each individual member.

Different types of group therapy have their own best practices; however, the general rule is that the primary mode of therapy is the interaction among group members and the counselor as the facilitator. Ultimately, group work focuses on the members working together.

The counselor clarifies how groups work at the first session as well as when new members join (if the group is an open one). The counselor explains her role as facilitator and helps establish group rules with the full participation of members.

The **counselor-client role in group therapy** is a little different than it is in individual therapy. The counselor establishes group work **expectations** like attendance requirements and other administrative policies set forth by the organization and state laws.

In group work, the counselor is required to maintain the confidentiality of the group members, but individual members are not bound by confidentiality rules. Therefore, it is up to the members to create a confidentiality agreement among themselves when establishing group rules.

Group rules (in group counseling) are most effective when the members both set and agree to them. While there may be organizational policies and state laws that apply to group work, members should set a majority of the working rules. These may address

- confidentiality;
- how group members should treat each other;
- the extent to which the members want the facilitator involved;
- whether someone can be removed from the group for disrespectful behavior.

The group should also discuss and agree on the process for member removal. Once the rules are established, they are usually posted in the room and revisited each time someone joins the group.

Termination criteria depend largely on the type of group:

- In **open-ended groups**, members come and go as they please; termination is not necessary.
- Curriculum-based or **closed groups** have a start and an end point, so termination occurs when the group curriculum is finished.

Another criterion for termination is the violation of group rules. If a member violates rules after agreeing to comply with them, she will be asked to leave. These situations should be documented.

 HELPFUL HINT

Some groups are open-ended but require clients to attend a certain number of sessions. In these situations, termination occurs once the requirements are met.

PRACTICE QUESTION

2. It is the first session of a closed group therapy meeting. There will be fifteen sessions focusing on dealing with childhood trauma. The facilitator should do which of the following FIRST?

    A) explain to group members that any confidentiality breaches will lead to removal from the group and could result in legal actions

    B) ask group members to share their childhood trauma stories

    C) explain the differences between group and individual therapy and guide the group in creating rules

    D) invite the organization's administrator to the first group to explain the rules members must abide by

Policies and Procedures

The counselor is obliged to explain agency policies at the first session and any time these issues arise during the therapeutic relationship. This is typically done during the informed consent discussion.

Policies generally address

- attendance and appointments;
- payment;

- how the organization documents the counseling process;
- how a client's records will be used, how requests for records will be handled;
- how the organization approaches confidentiality;
- threats to self and others.

Additionally, the organization may have policies regarding working with children and adolescents, including sharing information with parents.

During the first session, the counselor should also explain counseling processes, procedures, risks, and benefits.

Counseling **processes** define the parameters of the relationship and include

- how many sessions the client can expect to attend;
- what methods the counselor will likely use;
- assessment, diagnosis, and treatment planning methods.

Counseling **procedures** address specific issues such as

- what the client should do if he cannot make an appointment;
- what happens if the client does not show up for an appointment;
- under what circumstances the counselor will terminate the relationship;
- under what circumstances the counselor will refer the client;
- what to do in case of a mental health emergency.

Counseling comes with risks and benefits. These should be explained to the client as part of informed consent.

TABLE 3.1. Risks and Benefits of Counseling

RISKS OF COUNSELING	BENEFITS OF COUNSELING
• The client's symptoms may get worse before they improve.	• The client can cope with mental health symptoms.
• Current relationships with family or friends may change or end.	• The frequency and severity of the client's symptoms decrease.
• Therapeutic intervention may not be effective for the client.	• The client's quality of life and daily functioning improve.
• The counselor may not be appropriate for the client.	• The client's relationships improve.

CONTINUE

PRACTICE QUESTION

3. A counselor is meeting with a client for the first time. The client appears distraught, saying he feels quite awful. He denies he is in crisis but feels he needs mental health treatment. Which of the following is an appropriate counselor response?

    A) welcome the client and immediately address his problems and concerns to make him feel better faster

    B) call a supervisor to assist with crisis management based on the observed behavior

    C) obtain informed consent, including reviewing policies and procedures, before beginning counseling

    D) explain the counselor's credentials and plan for helping the client

Statistical Concepts and Methods Used in Research

Counselors must stay current on research trends in mental health counseling and understand the statistical concepts and methods used in research. Research involves a combination of qualitative and quantitative research. Some studies use mixed methods.

Qualitative research addresses how and why things happen. This research relies on interviews, focus groups, and other open-ended evaluation techniques. Qualitative research generally uses fewer participants in an effort to explore a topic more deeply. While this research can lead to statistical results, it is important to review the methods used to achieve these results before applying them in practice. Often, the results of qualitative research can lead to more questions.

Quantitative research relies more on numbers and data points that can be measured and quantified. This form of research relies more on standardized assessments and methods of measuring behavior. It may involve experimental conditions. Quantitative research presents results using numerical data.

It is best practice to ask several questions when reviewing research to inform the practice:

- How old is the research?

It is important to consider when the study was conducted as well as when it was published. There is often a significant period between the actual study and the publication of the results, which may influence the applicability of the results. For example, a study published in 2020 that was conducted from 2013 to 2015 may not be relevant due to social and cultural changes that may have taken place since the study was done.

- How many participants were involved, and what were their characteristics?

Studies with few participants tend to be less generalizable than those with large groups of participants. Furthermore, characteristics such as age, race, gender, geographic location, and socioeconomic status of participants can impact results. A counselor looking for research about depression treatment in adolescents from a particular cultural group would not find relevant information in a study about the elderly in a different cultural group. When deciding whether the research applies to their clients, counselors should consider if the participants are representative of their client population.

- What methods were used in the research?

If a study reports significant positive results but does not compare the methods to a control group, the results may not be as positive as they seem. Or, if a study purports to be about children with ADHD, it is important to understand how the researchers determined that the participants have ADHD. Examination of the methods of the study will help counselors determine if the study presents results that make sense.

- What are the limitations of the study?

Limitations presented at the end of the study will reveal flaws in the research and researchers' comments about how their study could have been improved.

This may call attention to issues that might have limited the research in some way, such as a small number of participants or a focus on only one cultural group.

Research can be stated in terms of statistically significant results and clinically significant results. Statistically significant results do not always mean that the results are clinically significant or clinically appropriate.

- Over how many months or years did the study take place?

The period over which a study is conducted can impact the validity of the results. For example, a study on addiction treatment may only evaluate the results for the duration of the treatment and for a short time following the treatment. Addiction, however, can be a lifelong challenge, so a counselor should question whether positive results after a short period could be sustained after a longer period.

- What other studies support the research?

Strong research is that which has been replicated under either the same or different conditions. When deciding between two evidence-based practices, the one with fifteen different studies will likely be more valid and reliable than the practice with only two studies.

PRACTICE QUESTION

4. A counselor is considering several group therapy treatment options while planning an intervention group for women with addictions in prison. Using knowledge of statistical concepts in research, which of the following would present the strongest research picture?

   A) one research study of a group intervention that evaluated women with addiction in an urban setting over ten years

   B) multiple studies evaluating the intervention of women with addictions that took place seven years prior with no further research conducted

   C) a study of a group that used a similar intervention in one women's prison located in a foreign country

   D) several research studies of an addiction group intervention evaluated in several women's prisons over the past five years that included follow-up studies after the women were released

Evidence-Based Practice

Evidence-based practice describes methods and interventions used by counselors that are supported by research and professional best practices.

Evidence-based practice creates a standard of client care, beginning with a comprehensive assessment of the client's presenting problems. That assessment informs a diagnosis, which must be backed up with evidence that the client meets the criteria, including formal assessments and clinical interviews. The diagnosis then informs the treatment plan, which consists of a list of goals and objectives for addressing the symptoms associated with the diagnosis.

$$\text{assessment} \longrightarrow \frac{\text{diagnosis}}{\text{formal assessments + clinical interviews}} \longrightarrow \text{treatment plan}$$

Figure 3.1. Evidence-Based Practice

To meet the goals and objectives, the counselor uses evidence-based therapeutic interventions supported by research as valid approaches for that specific diagnosis.

Counselors are expected to abide by evidence-based practices while also ensuring they receive the proper training to implement the evidence-based interventions.

There are many evidence-based manualized treatments that target specific diagnoses and specific clients, which present treatment interventions with step-by-step modules that counselors can use with clients to ensure program fidelity or adherence to proper use of the intervention.

Evidence-based practice holds counselors to a professional standard of care. It also builds public trust between the counseling profession and potential clients. Counselors should therefore not use treatment intervention methods that are not supported by research for a particular diagnosis.

PRACTICE QUESTION

5. Evidence-based practice includes standards of care informed by research that begins with which of the following?
    - A) a comprehensive assessment of a client that yields a diagnosis
    - B) determining which treatment a client needs
    - C) consultation with the client's previous providers
    - D) researching available treatments for the client's diagnosis

Accommodations

Clients with **disabilities** should be accommodated. Most health care organizations have policies and procedures in place to accommodate clients with disabilities. For instance, clients who are deaf, hard of hearing, blind, or who have low vision should be offered interpretation services or other assistance as appropriate. Whenever possible, the counselor should ask the client what his preferred method of communication is.

Cognitive impairments can often result from trauma or injury, like a stroke. In these cases, clients may not be able to speak due to motor impairments. Or they may have neurological conditions that prevent them from processing communication. The counselor should ask the client or the client's representative which method of communication works best and remain aware of changes in the client's cognitive status.

The **Americans with Disabilities Act (ADA)** prohibits discrimination against individuals determined to be disabled. The ADA defines disabilities to establish which individuals need to be protected under the law. These individuals must have a mental or physical impairment that substantially limits one or more major life activities. The person may have a record or history of such impairments or may be perceived by others, such as an employer, as having such limiting impairments.

Most compliance with the ADA is initiated at the organizational level. Still, counselors must adhere to the ADA in their physical practice by providing

- sufficient space for wheelchairs or other assistive devices;
- ADA-compliant furniture (can accommodate people of various weights and body types);
- materials in alternative formats if requested (large-print forms, for example);
- frequent breaks to support cognitive challenges.

Part of the assessment process will include asking the client if she requires any accommodations.

Persons with disabilities may require **accommodations** adjustments in their job duties or environment. Employers must provide these accommodations as long as they are reasonable and do not cause "undue hardship" to the employer, such as high expense or difficult installation.

Counselors may be called on to provide documentation of a client's disability.

First, the counselor must get the client's written permission to share the information. The counselor must then limit documentation to issues covered within the counseling relationship.

If the client has cognitive challenges and the counselor has assessed the client for that, then the counselor can provide supportive documentation for that issue. However, if the client is requesting accommodation for a physical disability, the counselor cannot provide supporting documentation for the client's physical condition. The counselor could, however, provide information about how the physical disability impacts the client's mental health.

Language barriers can occur when a counselor does not speak the client's primary language or speaks it as a second language. Counselors who do not speak the client's language have options:

- The client brings someone he trusts to act as an interpreter. The interpreter will have to sign confidentiality forms.
- The counselor can use professional interpreting services. Many health care organizations have relationships with professional interpreting services. Being under contract, interpreting services agree to abide by HIPAA and confidentiality rules.

HELPFUL HINT

It is a good idea to review with the client what information will be disclosed.

HELPFUL HINT

The counselor must always communicate with the client, not with the interpreter.

HELPFUL HINT

In the spirit of client-centered practice, the client should choose the translation option.

It is important for the client to feel comfortable with the interpreter. The counselor is responsible for checking in about this and ensuring that the client understands that he can ask for someone else.

Conducting counseling sessions with an interpreter present can be challenging for both the client and the counselor, so counselors may wish to undergo additional training on providing these services with compassion and empathy.

Distance counseling and **telemental health** are becoming an important part of counseling services. Two of the most significant issues in providing services this way are confidentiality and security.

Organizations that permit this type of interaction with clients often create organizational policies for how counselors may provide services and what methods are allowed. Part of the reason for these policies is that insurance companies will not pay for services conducted via certain media. For example, an insurance company may pay for counseling services delivered via a licensed and secure video therapy service but will not cover services provided via a counselor's personal phone or online messaging.

Technology-based services that facilitate distance counseling and telemental health include

- telephone;
- video chat;
- online messaging;
- texting.

The technology used for therapy must be secure, and clients must be informed that even though the counselor, the organization, and the technology provider are legally obligated to provide secure services, there is always the chance that security will be breached.

Another concern with distance counseling and telemental health is the risk associated with a client in crisis. In an office environment, clients in crisis can receive immediate care and therapeutic intervention, whereas if a client tells a counselor over the phone that she is considering harming herself or someone else, the counselor's intervention options are limited. Therefore, organizations need to have policies in place for how to deal with these situations.

Benefits of distance counseling and telemental health include the following:

- Clients can obtain therapy services at their convenience without having to travel to an office, thereby increasing accessibility.
- There will be fewer cancellations and no-shows.
- Clients can participate in therapy more frequently.

Risks of distance counseling and telemental health include

- data security breach;
- difficulty observing nonverbal communication;
- confidentiality of the client if there are other people in the client's location;
- challenges establishing a therapeutic relationship.

Although there are many benefits to providing distance counseling and telemental health, technology creates an additional barrier between the counselor and the client. Potential problems include

- difficulty establishing a therapeutic relationship;
- interference with accurate assessment;
- difficulty interpreting nonverbal communication.

Counselors who want to offer distance counseling and telemental health should pursue continuing education and training that will help reduce these potential problems.

PRACTICE QUESTION

6. A client gave a counselor permission to disclose confidential information when filling out a disability accommodation request form for his employer. The human resources director left the counselor a message requesting more information. What should the counselor do?

    A) obtain written consent from the client to speak to the human resources director and agree on what information the client will allow the counselor to share

    B) return the call to human resources to provide the needed information as quickly as possible

    C) call the client and let him know the counselor will be returning the call to human resources to answer these questions

    D) ignore the voicemail message and do not mention the call to the client

Advocacy

Counselors are in a unique position to advocate for professional and client issues. Because counselors are privy to the needs, causes, and consequences of mental health issues, that knowledge can be useful for public policy, health care policy, and prevention programs.

Professional advocacy may occur in several forms:

- lobbying for laws that protect the liability of counselors in client safety situations
- advocating for changes in licensure requirements
- asking for credentialing requirements for joining insurance panels

Counselors should join professional organizations to stay informed about issues pertaining to the profession.

Counselors advocate on behalf of clients to help them secure services. Advocating for a client's needs may include connecting them to a vocational rehab organization to help them find a job.

Counselors also advocate for clients on a broader social level. For example, counselors can be instrumental in advocating for public policy that increases client access to mental health services.

While advocacy is an honorable endeavor, a counselor advocating on behalf of clients must consider whether that advocacy is appropriate and ethical. If advocacy might result in a breach of confidentiality or create a dual relationship, then it may not be appropriate.

PRACTICE QUESTION

7. Which ethical issue must a counselor consider before advocating for a client?
    - A) amount of time required
    - B) whether the client issue is important
    - C) breach of confidentiality
    - D) the counselor's qualifications

Consultation and Self-Assessment

Self-Assessment

Counselors must continually **assess their competency to work with a specific client** through a process of self-awareness and objective evaluation. Choosing to work with a client when not qualified to do so violates professional ethics and could potentially harm the client.

- Counselors must be honest about the education and training they have received.

- Counselors should pursue continuing education and additional training to keep up with best practices.
- When meeting a client for the first time, counselors must objectively evaluate whether they are qualified to work with the client based on the client's presenting problem.

Being forthcoming about training and education usually applies to certain interventions with clients. For example, if a counselor has not received training and certification to perform EMDR, she must disclose this to a client requesting EMDR and offer another method of therapy or refer the client to someone who is trained.

Self-evaluation about competency to work with clients is more complicated. For example, if a client presents with severe addiction and the counselor is not trained in working with addiction, he must disclose that to the client and refer the client to someone who is qualified. Finally, consultation with a supervisor can help the counselor evaluate her effectiveness and competencies, including creating plans for professional development.

A prominent adage among counselors is, "When in doubt, consult." Counselors who work in community mental health clinics or organizations have access to an on-site supervisor, clinic director, or someone who acts as the senior counseling professional. **Supervision and consultation** are not just for inexperienced counselors; they provide support to all levels.

A counselor should seek supervision or consultation in specific situations:

- difficulties with client assessment, diagnosis, and treatment planning
- when a client's progress appears to stagnate
- when a client is in crisis
- when presented with an ethical situation
- when faced with a court order or other legal issue

A significant benefit of seeking supervision and consulting with a colleague when dealing with a client issue or an ethical issue is documented evidence that additional help was requested with an incident. In legal situations, this can act as a level of protection and ensure that proper procedures are followed.

When consulting with a supervisor or colleague within the organization that employs a counselor, client confidentiality should be honored, but those consultations tend to fall under the confidentiality exception that clients agree to in informed consent. Counselors in private practice who establish a consultation relationship with another colleague should also disclose to clients the potential for consultation and explain how the counselor will keep the client's information confidential.

Consultation and supervision should be limited to issues pertaining to the counseling process, not gossip or disclosure of client information that is not relevant to treatment.

PRACTICE QUESTION

8. Why is it inappropriate for a counselor to provide treatment using methods she has not been fully trained for?
    A) The client will not know to ask about the therapy.
    B) An untrained counselor could harm a client.
    C) The client will not receive any benefit from it.
    D) The counselor could make money from referring the client elsewhere.

Referrals

Not every client is appropriate for every counselor, and vice versa. A counselor should **provide a referral** in certain situations:

- The counselor does not have adequate training to work with the client's issues.
- The counselor and client cannot establish a productive therapeutic relationship.
- An ethical issue such as dual relationships precludes a counselor from working with a client.
- The counselor experiences an issue that would disrupt the client's treatment.
- The counselor is quitting, retiring, or otherwise leaving the organization or the profession.

When providing referrals, there are several **best practices** recommended for counselors:

- Give the client plenty of notice, if possible.
- Provide the client with several choices for other providers and offer to facilitate the transfer.
- Ask the client if he wants a joint session or a phone introduction with the new provider.
- Ask the client if she wants the counselor to give the provider information about her; if so, discuss what information to share.

A counselor should **provide information to third parties** as required by law. These generally include

- insurance companies;
- health care professionals;
- legal guardians.

Information provided to insurance companies and other health care professionals is regulated under state law and HIPAA, with those policies outlined in the informed consent.

A counselor should share the minimum amount of information necessary to honor the confidentiality of the client. For example, to get reimbursement for services rendered, the counselor may need to disclose the diagnosis and treatment plan objectives to an insurance company. However, the counselor should not include process notes that include intimate details of the client's session. Those are not required to secure payment and should therefore remain confidential.

Within the comprehensive care model, organizations often encourage counselors to consult with a client's physician or case manager. This should be discussed with the client and included in the informed consent discussion. When the counselor shares information with other members of the care team, she should let the client know when and what information was disclosed. For example, for court-mandated clients, the court usually requests reports of the client's progress in treatment. This may include attendance records and progress toward goals, but it should be limited to required information only.

When the counselor provides services to a client with a legal guardian, he may be required to disclose some information to the guardian. Again, that information should be limited. The counselor should discuss disclosure of other information with the client and receive permission to disclose it; then the information can be shared in the client's presence.

For example, an adolescent client may not want the full extent of her substance use shared with her parents. The counselor is not required by law to tell them, but he feels it would be therapeutic for the client and the family. The counselor may rehearse the disclosure with the client and then facilitate a family session where the adolescent discloses the substance use to the parents. However, it is not the counselor's responsibility to tell the parents unless required to do so by law. Doing so without the client's consent could damage the therapeutic relationship and harm the client.

PRACTICE QUESTION

9. A counselor has been working with a client weekly for six months. The counselor is diagnosed with an illness that will require him to leave work for at least three months. Which action should the counselor take?
    - **A)** assure the client that he can keep up with weekly sessions
    - **B)** coordinate with the client and refer her to another counselor
    - **C)** tell the client that the counselor will be out for three months and will contact the client when he returns
    - **D)** have the receptionist cancel the client's appointments and schedule with another counselor

Self-Care

Being a counselor can be a challenging, stressful job. Counselors often work with clients who are dealing with illness, death, or financial hardship. The emotional toll of managing these clients can be immense.

At the same time, counselors may also have to navigate complex systems like hospitals, insurance companies, and government agencies. The impact of these stressful situations cannot be underestimated.

Because of these strains, counselors should not overlook their own **self-care**. The first step in practicing self-care is practicing **self-awareness**. Understanding one's limits and the signs of strain can let the counselor know when it's appropriate to engage in self-care.

Counselors who work with clients who have experienced traumatic events are subject to **secondary trauma**, a condition that mimics the symptoms of PSTD. Although less severe than PTSD, secondary trauma interferes with the counselor's ability to function. Furthermore, when stress is left unattended for too long, counselors can suffer from burnout. **Burnout** is one of the primary reasons counselors leave the profession.

Signs of exhaustion, stress, and burnout can include the following:

- increased anxiety
- worrying about clients after hours
- taking work home
- difficulty concentrating
- sleep disturbances
- emotional lability
- social isolation
- increased irritability

 **DID YOU KNOW?**

Counselors cannot serve clients well if they are not taking good care of themselves. In fact, counselors who do not practice self-care become more at risk of harming their clients either through ignorance or negligence.

Counselors should develop proactive practices for self-care and self-awareness. This may include regularly scheduled activities to promote health and happiness. There are many ways a counselor can fulfill the goal of being healthy and happy:

- routine exercise
- eating a well-balanced diet
- getting adequate sleep
- enjoying hobbies
- relaxing
- spending time with friends and family
- refraining from overuse of alcohol or other substances

The counselor should also set physical and emotional boundaries with clients and be willing to ask for assistance when confronted with unmanageable tasks. A crucial boundary for counselors is the one between work and personal life. While counselors should check in with themselves, it is also recommended that counselors in an agency setting check in with each other. Counselors should also talk with spouses, partners, or family members about signs of stress and let them know how to point out those signs when they notice them. Sometimes others will notice the signs of stress before the counselor does.

PRACTICE QUESTION

10. A positive, proactive method for managing stress and burnout in counseling might include which of the following?

    A) scheduling lunch away from the office and leaving work right at closing time

    B) taking on as many clients as possible to keep busy

    C) talking to colleagues about stressful clients

    D) refusing to work with difficult or complex clients

Documentation

In counseling, if something is not documented, it did not happen. Therefore, counselors must create and maintain documentation appropriate for each aspect of the counseling process in compliance with state law, for insurance reimbursement, and to document client progress.

Creating and Maintaining Documentation

The counselor is responsible for maintaining accurate, objective documentation of the client's care. Accurate documentation has obvious benefits for the client's care, but it is also important for the counselor. Counselors can use accurate, timely documentation to prove they have complied with standards of care and practice, which is important for professional advancement and a possible legal defense. Counselors should

- only document facts; opinions do not belong in the official documentation;
- record details of the client visit as soon as possible after the visit;
- always record if the client agrees or refuses case management, interventions, or other types of care;
- record all communication with people or organizations involved in the client's care, including the client's family, medical providers, employer, and insurance companies;
- document the care plan, including assessments, interventions, evaluations, and the outcomes of each;
- document all instances of consultation about the client with supervisors and colleagues, including what was discussed and with whom, and recommendations;
- document modifications of the care plan, the rationale for the changes, and whether the client agreed;
- include all legal documents, including advance directives and informed consent forms;
- document discharge plans and client education.

Many organizations require documentation and regular review by the clinic director to ensure compliance with state law.

There are two types of notes taken by the counselor that are added to the client's documentation.

Progress notes are the official record of a session and tend to follow a **SOAP note** format:

- <u>S</u>ubjective information about the client and what she is experiencing
- <u>O</u>bjective findings from assessments or observation
- <u>A</u>ssessments that include findings of the client's diagnosis or evaluations of how the client is progressing in the treatment plan
- <u>P</u>lans that include next steps, both therapeutic and otherwise

Progress notes may be shared with others.

- Insurance companies receive progress notes when determining reimbursement.
- Progress notes may be included in client records requests from other providers.
- Progress notes are subject to inspection by agency quality control personnel and government regulators.

When clients request a copy of their records, these are the notes that are included. When the courts request records, these are the notes that are subject to a subpoena.

The second type of notes, **process notes**, are considered a counselor's private notes. Process notes are not required to be part of the client's official record. Process notes generally include

- hypotheses;
- theories;
- the counselor's thoughts regarding client treatment;
- questions to address during supervision.

Process notes are considered privileged and are not generally accessible to the client or other parties except in certain circumstances:

- If a client is involved in a legal action, it is possible that the counselor's records, notes, and documentation will be shared with the court.
- When a counselor leaves an agency, the documentation stays with the agency; the counselor's notes will influence how future providers interact with that client.

Not all counselors use process notes. Still, counselors should consider the impact of every piece of documentation on the client.

There are certain times when the counselor should **review client records**:

- When starting with a new client, reviewing his records can provide relevant historical information about his issues. These can be

HELPFUL HINT

When writing progress notes, keep them clinical and focused on the client's treatment plan.

requested as part of the intake process or by asking the client to bring the records to the first session.

- When taking a referral from another counselor, the client's records can be helpful for understanding which therapeutic interventions worked and which did not. These can be requested as part of the referral process.

- During a quarterly review process, often required by state law or for funding purposes, client records are subject to review. For example, many agencies that provide substance abuse treatment services must conduct client reviews every thirty or sixty days to determine the client's progress in treatment. It is also considered best practice to review client records quarterly to determine if the present course of treatment is appropriate, to evaluate client engagement, and to ensure that documentation is compliant with state law.

- Before discharging a client, the records must be reviewed to create a discharge summary.

PRACTICE QUESTION

11. A client with severe anxiety frequently talks about other people in session, especially his family members, because he believes his anxiety is all their fault. Which of the following would be included in a well-written progress note?

   A) the counselor's observations of the client's anxiety symptoms

   B) specific unpleasant remarks made by the client's mother to him

   C) actions the client's brother takes to bully him

   D) what the client said about his last counselor

Payment, Fees, and Insurance Benefits

Counselors should be aware of payment, fee, and insurance benefit issues. Agencies and clinics generally have staff or departments to address these issues. It is best practice to allow the administrative staff to handle billing and insurance so that any challenges do not infringe on the therapeutic relationship.

However, a counselor must be aware of the policies governing care to be able to answer questions and navigate the treatment process. For instance:

- Insurance providers decide how many sessions of therapy are appropriate for a particular diagnosis.
  - If therapy is going to take longer than originally planned, the counselor must request authorization for more sessions.
  - The counselor must submit documentation in support of that request.
- Payments, fees, and insurance benefits also determine session length, frequency, and mode of delivery.

> **DID YOU KNOW?**
>
> If counselors provide therapy they are not trained to do, the insurance company can refuse to provide reimbursement.

- Some insurance companies cover forty-five-minute sessions; others allow sixty-minute sessions.
- Counselors should be aware that an insurance provider will only pay for the determined amount of time. This may affect how many clients they can see in a day as well as how long a session might be.
- A counselor usually cannot bill an insurance company for services provided outside of established parameters.
- Insurance companies do not reimburse counselors for the time it takes to complete documentation.
- Some insurance companies will not provide reimbursement for therapies that are not evidence-based; some even list which therapeutic interventions are acceptable.
  - During the credentialing process, counselors must disclose to the insurance company which methods of therapeutic intervention they have received training for.
- The insurance company may also dictate the mode of service delivery that is acceptable for reimbursement.
  - Some insurance companies will not reimburse counselors for unscheduled telephone sessions or home visits.
  - Counselors must know what they are allowed to do based on the client's insurance benefits.

PRACTICE QUESTION

12. What is a clinically relevant reason a counselor must pay attention to the client's insurance provider?
    A) to explain the client's health care benefits to them
    B) to determine whether the counselor wants to work with the client
    C) to understand how many sessions the company will pay for
    D) to act as intermediary between the insurance company and agency administration

Health Care Laws and Legislation

NCCs should be familiar with the important elements of several pieces of health care legislation.

The **Affordable Care Act (ACA)**, popularly known as "Obamacare," changed behavioral health care coverage. Key elements of the ACA include the following:

- Insurance companies cannot deny coverage due to a preexisting condition or charge more because of the condition or based on gender.
- Adults who cannot obtain health insurance through a job may remain on their parents' policies until the age of twenty-six.

- Essential health benefits must be covered. These include
  - mental health;
  - substance use disorders.

Congress passed the **Health Insurance Portability and Accountability Act (HIPAA)** in 1996. HIPAA allows workers to continue or transfer health coverage when they change or lose a job. HIPAA also focuses on how health care information is handled.

The HIPAA Privacy Rule and the Security Rule, developed by the Department of Health and Human Services, protects the privacy and security of certain health care information. This **protected health information (PHI)** includes

- demographic information, such as name, address, phone numbers, SSN;
- information included in the medical record;
- payment history.

The NCC must follow HIPAA privacy and security policies. PHI must be safeguarded, released, and disposed of in the manner described by HIPAA. Only personnel who require clients' PHI should have access to that information for treatment or administrative purposes, such as billing and scheduling.

When medical records are no longer needed (a period usually specified by state regulations), they must be destroyed so the information cannot be retrieved.

PHI can only be released under specific circumstances:

- A **Privacy Rule Authorization form** must be signed by the client.
  - This form allows the provider to release information to the parties included in the form.
- Clients may also authorize the provider to release their PHI to others, usually family members.
- PHI can be shared within the health care team only when it is considered relevant to treatment.
  - PHI should not be shared with anyone not directly involved in the client's care.

Counselors may also need to share PHI with outside government agencies.

- State law specifies that the practitioner must warn authorities if harm (exploitation or abuse, for example) to the client is suspected.
- If counselors are aware of HIPAA violations and do not report them, they and the organization at fault can be held liable.

Annual HIPAA training is a component of most mental health providers. This ensures that faxing, internet communications, and phone delivery of clients' health care records, including personal notes and billing, are properly handled.

HELPFUL HINT

HIPAA's Security Rule establishes rules pertaining to the transfer of electronic records. The Privacy Rule sets national standards for the protection of health care information.

The **Mental Health Parity and Addiction Equity Act (MHPAEA)** was enacted in 2008 to fill in the gaps in the Mental Health Parity Act of 1996 (MHPA). According to the MHPAEA:

- Insurance plans that offer mental health care benefits must manage them as they manage medical/surgical benefits.
  - The insurance company cannot place limits on mental health benefits that it does not place on medical/surgical benefits.
  - These rules also apply to substance use disorders.
- The MHPAEA specifies limitations on how insurance companies can cover mental health and substance use disorder benefits.

Agencies or counselors who provide services to clients with substance abuse issues must also abide by **42 CFR Part 2**, a federal law that offers strict confidentiality rules for clients with substance use disorders. It was originally written for agencies that receive federal funding to provide substance abuse treatment only, and those organizations and providers are not allowed to acknowledge that a person is a client at the organization.

In agencies and organizations that provide both mental health and substance abuse treatment, it is best practice to include the privacy provisions of 42 CFR Part 2 as part of the confidentiality policies.

DID YOU KNOW?

Not every health insurance plan was required to offer mental health benefits under the MHPAEA. However, the ACA has greatly extended insurance plan coverage and lists mental health care as an essential health benefit.

PRACTICE QUESTION

13. Which of the following is MOST likely a violation of HIPAA?
    A) using a password to log onto a shared computer
    B) shredding records when they are expired
    C) accessing the mental health record of a client's parents
    D) faxing the results of an assessment to a client's primary care provider

Electronic Health Records

The **Health Information Technology for Economic and Clinical Health (HITECH) Act** was written to encourage the use of electronic health records (EHRs) and related technology. The Centers for Medicare and Medicaid Services (CMS) have several objectives for using EHRs:

- Electronic exchanges of summary of care: An **exchange of summary of care** (also referred to as a discharge summary) refers to the movement of a client from one setting to another. For example, the exchange of summary of care is used when a client is discharged from an inpatient to an outpatient facility.
- There is greater ease of sharing records with supervisors and other members of a client's care team.
- Documentation compliance is improved.
- Clients can access an online portal to check on appointments and reminders.

PRACTICE QUESTION

14. A provider wishes to use electronic health records. Which objective BEST helps to eliminate gaps in care?

- **A)** reporting specific cases
- **B)** structured electronic transmission of laboratory test results
- **C)** use of electronic prescriptions
- **D)** electronic exchanges of summary of care

Ethics

Ethics and the NCC

Ethics are moral principles, values, and duties. Whereas laws are enforceable regulations set forth by the government, ethics are moral guidelines established and formally or informally enforced by peers, the community, and professional organizations. Ethics include norms and duties.

Norm is short for *normal*, a term used for a behavior or conduct that is valued and usually expected. Norms are also often described as aspirational ethical principles because they are not enforceable by law, but counselors aspire to the highest ethical standards to maintain trust between the public and their profession.

Duties are commitments or obligations to act in an ethical and moral manner. These fall under the minimum ethical standards and are usually part of the state regulations. Counselors can be held legally accountable for violating ethical standards.

Core ethical principles include autonomy, beneficence, nonmaleficence, justice, veracity, and fidelity.

- **Autonomy** is acknowledging that a client is a unique individual with the right to her own opinions, values, beliefs, and perspectives.
- **Beneficence** describes acting with the intent of doing the right thing or the most good. The counselor has an obligation to act in the best interest of the client, regardless of other competing interests.
- **Nonmaleficence** describes the intent to do no harm. This principle addresses the counselor's responsibility to keep the client from harm in the care setting.
- **Justice** can be considered fairness. The counselor should be fair to clients in counseling matters and regarding administrative issues.
- **Veracity** is the practice of complete truthfulness with clients and families.
- **Fidelity** concerns honoring promises or commitments made to a client.

The National Board for Certified Counselors (NBCC) has a Code of Ethics. A **code of ethics** is a statement of the expected behaviors of its members. This code may also set standards and disciplinary actions for violations, including suspension, censure, fines, or expulsion.

Some key elements of the NBCC Code of Ethics follow:

- NCCs must take appropriate action to prevent harm.
- NCCs may only provide services they are qualified for.
- NCCs should promote the welfare of clients, students, and those individuals they supervise or provide services to.
- NCCs must communicate truthfully.
- NCCs should recognize that their behavior reflects on the counseling profession, and avoid damaging actions accordingly.
- NCCs should encourage the participation of clients, students, or supervisees, and recognize the importance of supervision.
- NCCs are accountable for their actions and should adhere to professional standards and practices.

If a counselor has an ethical concern, she is encouraged to contact the NBCC for advice.[1]

When addressing ethical concerns with a client case, the counselor should consult with a supervisor or colleague and document the ethical decision-making process in the client's record.

> **DID YOU KNOW?**
>
> NCCs are expected to hold each other accountable for professional ethics and are obligated to report violations.

PRACTICE QUESTION

15. A client tells the counselor that he wants to try EMDR to work on anxiety. The counselor is not trained in EMDR. What should the counselor do?

   A) refer the client to a qualified practitioner
   B) suggest avoiding EMDR and instead focus on techniques the counselor is trained in
   C) explain that EMDR will be discussed later in treatment
   D) ask her supervisor for guidance

Nonmaleficence

Nonmaleficence is the principle of not doing harm. It requires counselors to consider the impact of their actions (and inaction).

The potential for nonmaleficence in counseling includes referrals. A counselor should refer a client to another provider if

- the client's treatment progress seems stagnant;
- the counselor does not have the expertise to treat the client's particular condition.

A counselor might have good intentions in wanting to continue working with the client, but by not referring the client, he is harming her: another

[1] NBCC Code of Ethics, https://www.nbcc.org/Assets/Ethics/NBCCCodeofEthics.pdf

counselor might be able to help the client progress through her issues more quickly.

Another example of nonmaleficence application in clinical practice is hospitalization, especially **mandatory psychiatric treatment**. Some states have a provision that stipulates a person can be committed to a psychiatric facility against his will for a minimum period, often seventy-two hours, if he presents a danger to himself or others. While this may sound like a positive action to save someone's life, it must be considered whether that forced commitment will harm the client.

If a client shows signs of suicidality, proactive measures such as developing a crisis plan can be instrumental in providing the client with the help she needs without resorting to a potentially traumatic experience.

In any type of ethical dilemma, a counselor needs to balance state laws and agency policies with the principles of beneficence and nonmaleficence. Consultation and documentation are vital in these situations for reasons noted previously.

PRACTICE QUESTION

16. A client presents for therapy with a medium risk for suicide. Although a crisis situation is not imminent, the client may experience a crisis at some point. A counselor practicing nonmaleficence would do which of the following?

A) work with the client to develop a crisis plan that includes family and friends for social support

B) explain to the client that any crisis situation will land him in the psychiatric hospital

C) avoid discussing the problem until the client actually experiences a crisis

D) continue with therapy interventions and do not discuss suicide any further

Dual Relationships

The clinical therapeutic relationship requires the counselor to refrain from any type of **dual relationship** with clients. A dual relationship is when the counselor has both a counseling relationship with the client and a relationship outside the clinical setting.

Avoiding dual relationships reduces the chance of a counselor exploiting a client or conveying the perception of power and authority. For example, if a counselor has any type of personal relationship with a client outside of the treatment setting, it is unethical for her to provide services to that client. In general, counselors should avoid

- any sexual or romantic relationship with former or current clients;
- a counseling relationship with someone with whom the counselor had a previous sexual or romantic relationship.

Any counselor who becomes aware of another counselor engaged in dual relationships or of sexual harassment or exploitation is obligated to follow procedures for reporting the legal and ethical violation.

 HELPFUL HINT

The NBCC Code of Ethics states that a counselor cannot engage in a dual relationship with a client for two years following the termination of a counseling relationship. However, state laws and regulations may have longer timelines. It is the counselor's responsibility to know and follow those laws.

A dual relationship can also apply to business relationships. In some states, business relationships are permissible with clients; however, these relationships are still unethical. For example, if a client is a carpenter and the counselor needs work done on her home, it is unethical to hire that client as a carpenter. Business relationships such as these have the potential for exploitation and the expectation of favors.

PRACTICE QUESTION

17. A client comes to therapy but explains that he does not have the money to pay for therapy. He has a house-cleaning business and offers to trade services by cleaning the counselor's house and office in exchange for therapy. How should an ethical counselor respond?

   A) accept the offer of trading services

   B) accept the offer but limit the trade to cleaning the office

   C) decline the offer

   D) explain the law to the client and refer them to a clinic that offers free mental health services

Privacy

In the age of social media, privacy is of particular concern for counselors and clients. Clients may share personal information in a public forum, but it is unethical for a counselor to use social media, technology, or other resources to find information about clients without their written permission.

Social media privacy is also appropriate to address in group therapy. Group members may have access to information about other members. Group rules should stress not only the importance of confidentiality but also of privacy.

Counselors consulting with supervisors or other care team members about the client should consider the client's privacy and only provide information relevant to his treatment plan.

Counselors should also avoid accepting gifts from clients except in cases of cultural significance or therapeutic significance. Gift exchanges can create confusion about the nature of the therapeutic relationship, and the counselor needs to consider that as well as the impact that nonacceptance could have on the client's well-being.

 HELPFUL HINT

If the counselor decides it is appropriate to accept a gift, the reasoning should be documented.

PRACTICE QUESTION

18. When is it acceptable for a counselor to look up a client's social media presence?

   A) when a client is mandated to treatment by the judicial system

   B) not acceptable; constitutes an invasion of privacy

   C) before the first session so the counselor can get to know the client

   D) if a client makes comments in session that make the counselor uncomfortable

Consent

Client **consent** is required for treatment. A client must provide **informed consent** for a counselor to perform a treatment or procedure, or if she is going to take part in a research study.

For informed consent to be valid, the counselor must cover key elements:
- description of procedures
- risks
- benefits
- alternatives

The counselor must also assess **client competency** to provide informed consent. A competent client understands
- the procedure or practice;
- the risk and benefits involved;
- possible consequences.

Finally, the client must acknowledge having provided consent. Most states have regulations for practices that include having a signed informed consent form for each client.

State regulations vary regarding the age of consent. The age of consent to sign informed consent forms ranges from fourteen to sixteen. Regardless of the legal age of consent, a good way to establish trust with adolescent clients or with clients unable to provide legal consent for themselves is to gain the client's assent for treatment. Obtaining **assent** means
- going through the entire informed consent process with the client;
- explaining the role of the counselor;
- making sure the client understands the therapeutic process
- ensuring that the client agrees to participate freely.

Obtaining assent helps establish trust with clients and engages them in the therapeutic process. This can be especially powerful for those who may feel they are being coerced into treatment.

DID YOU KNOW?

Informed consent forms may need to be updated once per year to remain valid.

HELPFUL HINT

To obtain assent, many counselors use a form similar to the informed consent form.

PRACTICE QUESTION

19. While obtaining informed consent is required by law, obtaining assent is not. Why is it a good idea to obtain assent anyway?

A) Clinic administrators want documentation that everyone involved in therapy has signed the proper forms.

B) Parents will probably not tell their children what the process of therapy will include.

C) Even if clients are not of legal age to consent, it is important to the therapeutic relationship that they understand the process and agree to participate.

D) It protects the counselor from future legal action.

Confidentiality

Confidentiality means that the counselor will keep the client's personal information confidential according to state and federal law. The counselor must also explain to the client when and under what circumstances confidentiality may be broken. In general, confidentiality requires that counselors must not disclose client information to anyone not authorized by the client.

Confidentiality is a vital aspect of the counseling relationship and is protected not only by professional ethics but also by law.

There are several **limits to confidentiality** that are usually explained in writing in the informed consent process:

- Client information will be shared with clinic personnel for record-keeping and billing purposes.
- Client information may be shared with a clinical supervisor or colleague for the purposes of consultation for the benefit of the client.
- Client records may need to be included in state or federal auditing procedures.
- Client information may be shared if the client expresses a desire to hurt themselves or someone else.
- Client records may be shared in the case of a medical emergency.
- Records may be shared if the client discloses that she has experienced abuse or that she perpetrated abuse that falls under the requirements of mandated reporting.
- If the client brings someone else to the session and grants the counselor permission to waive confidentiality, client information may be shared.
- A court order may require a counselor to break confidentiality.

Counselors should abide by the principle of sharing the least amount of information needed to get the job done. Furthermore, it is best practice that any breaches of confidentiality be shared with the client either before or immediately after the breach, including what information was shared. Also, the counselor should document the incident, along with the personal information disclosed, in the client's records.

Social media and electronic communication should be considered risks for confidentiality breaches. Information posted on social media is not private, as the platform owners can access a person's data at any time. Therefore, counselors should be careful what they post about themselves on social media.

Some counselors use social media as a professional referral opportunity that includes a business page with how to contact them. However, connecting with clients as friends on social media is unethical. Also, communication with clients via social media is not recommended due to the confidentiality risks.

It is not ethical for counselors to look up clients on social media to learn more about them. Electronic communication may be used for setting appointments, but it is recommended to only use electronic communications for therapeutic purposes if that is part of an agency's protocols for conducting telehealth or distance counseling.

Communicating with clients on social media outside of the counseling relationship would ethically be considered a dual relationship unless it is conducted outside of the legal time allotted. States set the rules about this period; in some cases, a counselor may have to wait two to five years before engaging in a dual relationship with a client, and that includes social media friendships.

PRACTICE QUESTION

20. A client collapses during a therapy session, and the counselor needs to call an ambulance. Since this is an emergency, what can the counselor reveal to the emergency medical personnel?

    A) the client's history of childhood sexual abuse and how it causes significant distress

    B) the reasons why the client is in therapy

    C) no information because he does not have permission from the client

    D) the client's name, how the client collapsed in session, and any physical conditions that may have contributed to the collapse

Legal Aspects of Counseling

NCCs are vulnerable to legal action. There are multiple situations that may result in legal system involvement, including

- disability evaluations;
- workers' compensation evaluations;
- workplace accommodations;
- school accommodations for children;
- custody disputes;
- divorce disputes;
- abuse and neglect cases of children, adults, people with disabilities, or older adults;
- use of therapeutic interventions that are not evidence-based or are unlawful;
- criminal cases involving mental illness or substance abuse;
- duty to warn cases;
- complaints against a counselor to the licensing board.

Counselors must be aware of and understand

- state laws;
- regulations;
- standards of care;
- agency policies;

- the differences between subpoenas and court orders in their state;
- the procedure for responding to subpoenas and court orders.

Consistent supervision and consultation on client cases and thorough documentation of this help protect the counselor by showing that she followed policy and regulations. Counselors should seek advice from a supervisor or legal representative in these cases. Agencies usually have policies for handling these situations, but legal requirements will determine how a counselor must respond to requests for information by attorneys.

Not every state requires a counselor to provide records to a subpoena. Furthermore, when presented with a request for client records by someone within the legal system, it is important to discuss this with the client and document what and how the information was shared.

Therefore, two rules of best practice apply to protect counselors in legal situations:

1. If it is not documented, it never happened.
2. Consult, consult, consult.

Many clients are referred for treatment by courts or systems affiliated with the courts. For example, child protective services may require that families or individuals engage in services. Also, mental health courts and drug court programs are becoming more widespread as incarceration diversion efforts. In these cases, there are special considerations for documentation requirements and sharing information with the courts and the rest of the client's care team.

Counselors should take extra care during the informed consent process to not only meet the needs of the referring system but also protect the privacy and confidentiality of the client to preserve the therapeutic relationship.

DID YOU KNOW?

Complaints against a counselor can be made against both the agency and the individual counselor, including HIPAA violations. Therefore, counselors should carry professional liability insurance to protect their interests. They should not rely on their employer to do so.

PRACTICE QUESTION

21. A counselor has been working with an adult client for several months. Without warning, the counselor receives a letter from an attorney working on behalf of the client's spouse, requesting the client's mental health records. What should the counselor do?

    A) send the attorney a letter clarifying which records are being requested

    B) consult with a supervisor or legal representative to determine the next steps

    C) ask the client what the attorney's purpose is in requesting the records

    D) fax a copy of the client's records to the attorney

Answer Key

1. **B)** In client-led care, counselors provide guidance, but clients determine the agenda.

2. **C)** The counselor's role is group facilitator—the group is the client. Therefore, the counselor needs to guide the group in establishing rules of conduct not otherwise covered.

3. **C)** Although the client demands immediate help, he is not in crisis. The counselor can offer the client empathy and understanding about his needs, but before offering help, the counselor is obligated to obtain informed consent. Part of that informed consent is explaining policies and procedures so the client can make an informed decision about whether he wants to proceed.

4. **D)** This option includes several best practices in research, including studies on the same population the counselor works with, the same setting, multiple studies with a large number of participants, and an evaluation of how well the treatment serves the clients after they leave prison. Not only is this collection of studies valid for the application the counselor is considering; it also shows positive results over a long period, thus increasing the likelihood that the counselor's clients will benefit from the intervention.

5. **A)** The first step in the process of evidence-based practice is conducting a thorough assessment of the client. Formal assessments and clinical interviews should be used to demonstrate that the client meets the criteria for a specific diagnosis. Once a diagnosis is made, then a treatment plan can be created.

6. **A)** The counselor may only speak or disclose information to other parties after receiving written permission from the client; otherwise, it is a breach of both confidentiality and the Health Insurance Portability and Accountability Act (HIPAA). If the client only provided written permission for the counselor to fill out a form, the counselor must receive written permission to talk to the human resources director, as it is a separate instance of sharing the client's personal information. Some states and organizations also require counselors to discuss with their clients what information will be disclosed and why. Even when it is not required, this is considered best practice to maintain trust between the client and the counselor.

7. **C)** Advocating on behalf of a client might risk breaching the client's confidentiality.

8. **B)** Without proper training in a given technique, there is a significant risk that the counselor will inadvertently harm a client.

9. **B)** When a counselor will be unavailable for any length of time, it is best practice to refer the client to another provider to continue the same level of care.

10. **A)** Proactive boundaries and time away from clients can help counselors balance work stress and life.

11. **A)** Progress notes include objective observations of the client's symptoms and progress through treatment. While the other items may influence the client's symptoms, the details are not relevant to the treatment progress. Instead, a counselor might note "client's anxiety increases due to mom's verbal taunts."

12. **C)** Insurance companies often dictate the number of sessions they will cover.

13. **C)** Under the Health Insurance Portability and Accountability Act (HIPAA), counselors are not allowed to access the medical records of people they are not providing care for.

14. **D)** Electronic exchanges of summary of care improve coordination of care.

15. **A)** The counselor is not trained in the technique the client wants to try, so she should offer to refer him to a qualified practitioner. Practicing EMDR with the client would violate the NCC's Code of Ethics, which says that NCCs may only provide services they are qualified for. It also violates the principles of veracity, nonmaleficence, and justice. Postponing the conversation (Option C) could also cause harm by preventing the client from accessing the treatment sooner. The counselor should not need to ask her supervisor for advice; she should understand these ethical principles.

16. **A)** Counselors understand the risk associated with suicidality and the potential for a traumatic experience in mandatory psychiatric treatment. So, a counselor practicing nonmaleficence will work with the client to create a crisis plan that will help mitigate a crisis without requiring mandatory hospitalization.

17. **D)** While the counselor should decline the offer, an ethical counselor would explain the conflict related to dual relationships and refer the client to a clinic that offers free services.

18. **B)** It is unethical for a counselor to use social media, technology, or other resources to find information about a client without his written permission.

19. **C)** Obtaining assent from underage clients makes them feel part of the process, helps them understand the counselor's role and how therapy will work, and establishes trust with the counselor.

20. **D)** In a medical emergency, the counselor may reveal confidential information about the client, but only enough to help the emergency medical personnel do their job. Therefore, the client's name, a description of how she collapsed, and any known physical conditions that could impact her medical treatment are appropriate to disclose. Following the incident, the counselor should document the incident, including what was disclosed in the client's record, and share this information when the client is stabilized.

21. **B)** The client's confidentiality and privacy are paramount. Depending on state law and agency policy, the counselor may not be required to turn over any records. Counselors should always consult with a supervisor or legal representative and document the consultation before taking action.

4 Intake, Assessment, and Diagnosis

Intake and Interview

Intake Forms

When meeting with a client for the first time, counselors conduct an intake assessment to get to know the client. Clients are often asked to complete intake forms before their appointment and bring them to discuss with the counselor.

Intake forms are kept in the client's chart. These forms enable clients to explain in their own words why they are seeking counseling.

Several versions of intake forms can be used. Standard intake forms are specific to the location where treatment is being offered.

The general categories of information on these forms can include

- personal contact information;
- emergency contact information;
- relevant insurance information;
- list of current symptoms;
- medical concerns and medications;
- current substance use;
- history of mental illness including trauma, suicidal ideation, suicide attempts, and homicidal ideation;
- privacy consents, including consents for prescribing doctors, if relevant.

Some treatment centers provide intake documentation for the counselor to complete that serves as a guide for the initial interview. In other cases, the counselor begins by reviewing the categories listed on the client's intake form and expanding on any items that need clarification. Common issues are

- mental health history;
- history of trauma and abuse;

- current substance use;
- suicidal ideation;
- homicidal ideation.

**WELLNESS CENTER
COUNSELING INTAKE FORM**

Today's date: _____ Student ID #: _____ Gender: _____

Name: _____ Date of birth: _____

Ethnicity: _____ Education Level: _____ Major: _____

Campus address: _____ City: _____ State: _____ Zip: _____

Home address: _____ City: _____ State: _____ Zip: _____

Phone (h): _____ (email): _____ (cell): _____

Emergency Contact Person: _____ Phone: _____

Relationship to you: _____ Referred by: _____

Do you work: _____ Where: _____ Position: _____

Counseling History

Have you had previous counseling: _____ Dates: _____

Name of counselor: _____

Explain why: _____

Reason for this appointment request today: _____

List any concerns you have: _____

Are you currently taking any medications: What: _____ Why: _____

Have you ever thought about, or attempted suicide: _____

Has anyone in your family, or friends committed, or attempted suicide: _____

If yes who: _____

What are your positives: _____

Figure 4.1. Sample Intake Form

If the client is seeking specialized treatment, the counselor will spend more time exploring the presenting concern rather than areas that do not seem as relevant to the issue. For example, if a client is seeking treatment for depression, the counselor should focus on depression symptoms and corresponding life events rather than other issues.

PRACTICE QUESTION

1. Who completes intake forms?
   A) the counselor
   B) the client
   C) the facility
   D) the administration

Readiness to Change

Most people come to counseling because they want to change something in their lives. The **transtheoretical model (TTM)**, developed by researchers James Prochaska and Carlo DiClemente, offers a useful perspective on the birth and growth of behavioral change. It defines a five-step process that is determined by an individual's readiness or willingness to change:

1. precontemplation stage (not ready to change)
2. contemplation stage (getting ready to change)
3. preparation stage (ready to change)
4. action stage (performing the action that will bring about change)
5. maintenance stage (integrating the action into one's lifestyle and making it habit)

A counselor must determine readiness and willingness to change in all clients. A client's willingness shows how successful she will be in self-managing her condition(s).

PRACTICE QUESTION

2. Gene is a forty-eight-year-old male who wants to stop smoking. He has given some thought to it, but he still enjoys his two-pack-a-day habit and will not listen when his daughter lectures him about quitting. What stage of the transtheoretical model is Gene in?
   A) contemplation
   B) precontemplation
   C) maintenance
   D) action

Initial Interview and Interviewing Techniques

The purpose of a client interview is for the counselor to collect relevant health information to determine if the client is appropriate for a particular level of care and to begin developing the treatment plan.

For the **initial interview**, the counselor will meet with the client individually. Before beginning, the counselor should discuss confidentiality and situations during which confidentiality might be broken. The underlying goal of any interview is to assess the client's concerns and work toward developing an appropriate treatment plan.

 HELPFUL HINT

Counselors should be mindful of their body language while a client is sharing. If a client feels uncomfortable or as though she is being judged, she is more likely to stop sharing openly.

A key reason to conduct the **initial interview** is for the counselor to establish a rapport with the client. Establishing a **rapport** means building trust and understanding. A strong counselor-client rapport means the client will feel more comfortable with the counselor and offer more information.

Asking **open-ended questions** allows the client to lead the conversation in a way that is specific to him and his experiences. Open-ended questions teach the counselor more about the client than "yes" and "no" questions. For example, asking a client, "Tell me about your family" will reveal more information than "Do you have any children?" Thoughtful open-ended questions start a conversation.

Motivational interviewing (MI) strategies can be used with clients who are resistant and unsure about engaging in treatment. MI skills include

- open-ended questions;
- reflective listening;
- rolling with resistance;
- summarizing statements.

 DID YOU KNOW?

Rolling with resistance means understanding direct confrontation is not always effective. Rolling with resistance includes avoiding arguments, using reflective listening, and helping the person develop solutions.

Using these strategies can help create an environment where clients feel more comfortable talking about their concerns.

At the end of the interview, the counselor should summarize the gathered information and highlight important points for the client to ensure that nothing was missed. The client should be informed of the next steps, given an opportunity to ask questions, and given the counselor's contact information.

In behavioral health interviewing, the client may have a mental disability that prevents productive interviewing. A family member or guardian may assist in obtaining all pertinent information to establish a care plan. This can also include children who need mental health treatment. The care plan will be the foundation to develop a treatment strategy with achievable goals for the client.

PRACTICE QUESTION

3. In which situation should a counselor use motivational interviewing strategies?

    A) The client is lacking external motivation for treatment.

    B) The client has been hesitant but is answering questions truthfully.

    C) The client is unsure if he needs to make a change in his life.

    D) The client sought treatment because she is concerned about her mental health.

Structured Clinical Interview

A structured clinical interview is part of a client's initial intake exam. It is primarily conducted through **client self-report**, when the client describes his symptoms to the counselor based on questions the counselor asks.

There are some standardized structured clinical interviews, like the **Structured Clinical Interview for DSM-5 (SCID-5)**. The SCID-5 is most commonly used in research settings to screen participants for certain diagnoses that would disqualify them from participating in the study.

There are four main reasons to use the SCID-5:

1. to evaluate for all the major DSM-5 diagnoses
2. to select the population for a study
3. to identify current and past mental health concerns within a study's population
4. to help students and new mental health professionals improve their clinical interviewing skills

Currently, the SCID-5 is only approved for use with adults over eighteen. Some clinics use the SCID-5 as part of their clinical intake. Others use their own version of structured questions, or even use an unstructured format. In either case, the goal is to provide a set list of questions (some open-ended) that can be used to screen for and rule out diagnoses and presenting issues in clients.

There are ten core diagnoses covered in the SCID-5. The included diagnoses are:

1. mood episodes, cyclothymic disorder, persistent depressive disorder, and premenstrual dysphoric disorder
2. psychotic and associated symptoms
3. differential diagnosis of psychotic disorders
4. differential diagnosis of mood disorders
5. substance use disorders
6. anxiety disorder
7. obsessive-compulsive and related disorders
8. feeding and eating disorders
9. externalizing disorders
10. trauma- and stressor-related disorders

The SCID-5 is a comprehensive assessment that can take anywhere from fifteen minutes to several hours. Because it primarily relies on self-report, it may not be an appropriate assessment tool for individuals with significant intellectual issues or an inability to self-report for other reasons (such as poor language ability or highly disorganized thought).

During a structured clinical interview, the counselor relies on both formal and informal observations. A **formal observation** includes items like the content of the responses the client gives to questions.

Informal observations include the client's body language, affect, and the emotive quality of the client's behavior. Interactional dynamics are an important part of informal observations. **Interactional dynamics** can include not only how a client is interacting with family members during a session but also how she

 HELPFUL HINT

In general, it is not considered best practice to diagnose from only one meeting or assessment. Diagnosis can be ongoing, especially with more complex cases. A diagnosis can change if new information emerges.

speaks about friends, colleagues, and family members, and even how she interacts with the counselor.

The goal of a structured clinical interview is not to determine a firm diagnosis but rather to have a working diagnostic theory, a good understanding of the client's presenting problem and any environmental factors contributing to the problem, and the foundations for building a treatment plan with the client.

Cultural competence is a key concern in structured clinical interviews. A client who has visions or hears voices that are related to religion or culture should not be diagnosed with hallucinations, especially when these are corroborated by the client's community. Knowing diagnostic standards for cultural differences and having a strong understanding of the client's background are essential for effective structured clinical interviewing.

PRACTICE QUESTION

4. Which of the following is key to a structured clinical interview?
   A) collateral reports from family
   B) client self-report
   C) transtheoretical model
   D) client goals

Other Types of Interviews

There are several specific types of interviews counselors can conduct, including

- biopsychosocial interview;
- diagnostic interview;
- cultural formulation interview.

Templates for guiding the interview and creating documentation exist for all these types of interviews.

A **biopsychosocial interview** studies the relationship between the client's biological, psychological, and social health.

- Biological effects can include
  - medical health concerns;
  - disabilities;
  - effects of substance use.
- Psychological health refers to the client's mental health concerns and coping skills.
- Social health includes clients' relationships with others and their families.

A biopsychosocial interview shows the counselor how these three areas intertwine and impact the client's distress.

 HELPFUL HINT

During an initial interview, counselors can use any interview type.

A **diagnostic interview** assesses specifically for potential mental health diagnoses. These interviews tend to be more structured to ensure that the necessary information is covered to make an accurate diagnosis.

The **cultural formulation interview (CFI)** is a sixteen-question assessment used to recognize the cultural impacts on a client while assessing for an appropriate diagnosis. The CFI uses open-ended questions to give the client space to talk about his concerns regarding the cultural norms he experiences.

An **unstructured interview** has no standardized questions. This allows the counselor to guide the interview in ways that the counselor believes will lead to the most relevant information. An unstructured interview often allows for a more open discussion about the client's concerns, goals, and motivations.

The main topics covered in an unstructured clinical interview include:
- age and sex
- the reason for seeking counseling
- work and education history
- current social activities
- physical and mental health concerns; past and present
- current medications and any drug and/or alcohol use
- family history of mental health and physical health concerns
- the counselor's observations of client behavior during the session (e.g., anxious, detached, euthymic)

PRACTICE QUESTION

5. Which of the following is the BEST interview type to use with a new client in an outpatient mental health clinic?
    A) cultural formulation interview
    B) biopsychosocial interview
    C) diagnostic interview
    D) structured clinical interview

Assessing the Client

General Types of Assessments

A **psychological assessment** is used to assess and treat psychological, psychiatric, and personality disorders as well as developmental delays. Psychological testing can be further categorized into four main types: clinical interview, assessment of intellectual functioning (IQ), personality assessment, and neuropsychological assessment.

The **clinical interview** is a basic but integral component of any psychological testing. Also known as an "intake" or "admission interview," it is generally a comprehensive assessment to collect information about an individual's background and family relationships. Only a licensed clinician may perform a clinical interview.

The **intellectual functioning (IQ test)** is used to measure typical intelligence and is divided into subsections that evaluate verbal comprehension, perceptual reasoning, working memory, and processing speed.

The **personality assessment** was developed to help health care professionals gain better insight into an individual's personality. Two different types of objective tests used to evaluate this are the Minnesota Multiphasic Personality Inventory-2 (MMPI-2) and the Sixteen Personality Factors Questionnaire (16PF).

A **neuropsychological assessment** is used to measure capacity regarding memory, reasoning, concentration, motor skills, and other cognitive elements.

PRACTICE QUESTION

6. Which of the following assessments is the FIRST one a counselor should conduct with a new client?

    A) IQ test
    B) personality assessment
    C) clinical interview
    D) neuropsychological assessment

HELPFUL HINT

The concept of reliability can be thought of in the same way as a person who is reliable. A reliable person behaves as expected every time. A reliable assessment instrument does too.

Reliability and Validity

It is important to understand if the data are reliable and valid. **Reliability** refers to the consistency of the measurement. Take, for example, a performance-scoring system. To be reliable, the system must measure employees in the same manner. Though their scores may be different, *how* they are measured is consistent.

Validity refers to what is being measured and whether it is relevant. In the example of a performance review, if an employee's performance on a non-work-related issue is being measured, that item is not valid. It may be a reliable measurement, but it is not accurate or relevant to the actual review.

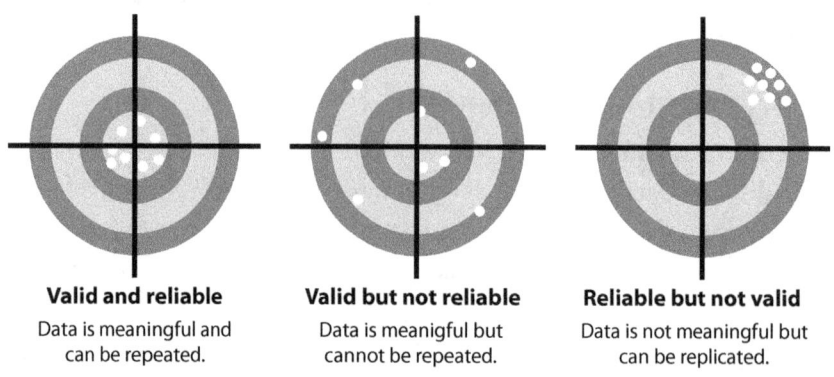

Valid and reliable
Data is meaningful and can be repeated.

Valid but not reliable
Data is meaningful but cannot be repeated.

Reliable but not valid
Data is not meaningful but can be replicated.

Figure 4.2. Reliability and Validity

PRACTICE QUESTION

7. Which of the following is an example of high validity?
   A) a math exam to determine how well the students know the material
   B) an oven that can consistently change temperatures but does not display the correct temperature
   C) using GPA to determine athletic ability
   D) a scale that is five pounds off but always reads the same weight

Mental Status Exam

A **mental status exam (MSE)** is an informal assessment typically conducted during the initial clinical interview. It does not involve formal questions for the client or even a formal scoring method; instead, it is based on the counselor's observations and impressions of the client's behavior and how he presents himself.

Although the MSE is based on the clinician's personal observations, the counselor's goal is not to state her opinion of the client but rather to record her observations objectively and in a fact-based manner. She should not write, for example, "the client has a bad attitude." A more appropriate and objective observation would be, "the client sat in a slouched position during the appointment and gave one- or two-word responses to questions."

The information obtained in a mental status exam is an essential part of the counselor's initial assessment and working diagnosis. She is gathering information about the client's level of interest in treatment, insight into how he perceives his issues and the world, and potential clues that can lead to a formal diagnosis.

Appearance is a common assessment in an MSE. The counselor should observe the following:

- How is the client dressed?
- How does she hold herself? (For example, does she slouch and cross her arms or have a calm and relaxed posture?)
- Is she unkempt and unwashed or meticulously groomed?

Another domain includes **motor behavior**, which relates to a client's physical movements. Excessive fidgeting can be a sign of attention deficit hyperactivity disorder (ADHD) or anxiety disorders, while very slow movement can be a sign of major depressive disorder. Involuntary limb movements or impaired gait may signify physical disorders like Huntington's disease or schizophrenia. Documenting physical movements that seem abnormal will be essential for diagnosing more complex disorders.

Mood is based primarily on the client's self-report. It is the clinician's job to translate the client's self-report into clinically appropriate language:

- **euthymic:** normal or mildly positive mood
- **depressed/sad/dysphoric:** sad, "low" mood
- **anxious**
- **irritable**
- **euphoric/expansive/elevated:** abnormally positive mood

 DID YOU KNOW?

Poor hygiene can be a symptom of several clinical diagnoses, including mood disorders and psychotic disorders.

Clinical students often confuse mood with **affect**. While mood is how the client appears to be feeling, **affect** is how the client is presenting. Affect is observed based on the client's facial expressions, posture, reactivity, and vocal quality. (Is it expressive and variable based on speech, more of a monotone, or something in between?)

- **normal/congruent with mood:** affect matches described mood
- **labile:** affect swings wildly or is highly variable
- **constricted:** limited range of emotional display
- **blunted:** extremely limited range of emotional display
- **flat:** little or no emotional range displayed

Orientation refers to the client's state of mind. Is he aware of where he is, the date, why he is in the counselor's office? Clients with poor orientation may be suffering from brain injury, hallucinations, or dementia. Orientation typically assesses the following:

- **orientation to time:** Does she know the day and year?
- **orientation to place:** Does she know where she is, or is she confused?
- **orientation to situation:** Does she know and understand why she is in the counselor's office?

Thought process and form refers to *how* the client thinks and is based on the clinician's observations of the quality of the client's thoughts. Is the client logical with coherent, linear thought? Or does he display disorganized or tangential thoughts?

- **linear:** coherent, goal-directed, clear
- **tangential:** racing thoughts, jumps from topic to topic, difficult to follow

Categories under thought process and form include

- poverty of thought (having few thoughts);
- blocking (being unable to form thoughts);
- racing thoughts, flight of ideas (having rapid thoughts);
- loose associations (when a person's thoughts are disconnected);
- circumstantiality (when a person is able to get to the point but adds additional details along the way);
- tangentiality (when a person doesn't answer a question even though their thoughts are related to the question asked).

Thought content, on the other hand, refers to *what* the client thinks. Does the client exhibit any signs of hallucinations or delusions? Is she fixating on anything?

- **suicidal/homicidal ideation:** suicidal or homicidal thoughts, plans, means, and intention to follow through
- **hallucinations:** auditory, visual, olfactory, gustatory, tactile, hypnagogic (having hallucinations upon waking or falling asleep)

- **delusions:** grandeur, jealousy, persecutory, somatic, love, religious
- **obsessions/compulsions:** religious, contamination, fear of losing control of one's actions, sex
- **phobias:** more intense than a fear, consistent and long-term, negatively impact the client's quality of life due to avoidance of everyday activities to prevent having to deal with the fear

Speech refers to the quality of the client's language production. Is it very fast or slow? Is it loud? Speech quality can provide important information about symptoms that relate to schizophrenia, autism spectrum disorder, personality disorders, and more.

- **quality/fluency:** Does the client speak easily or stumble over his words?
- **rate:** Does the client speak very quickly or noticeably slowly? Does the client speak in a monotone, with a clipped voice, or have other unusual vocal inflections?
- **volume:** Is the client's speech noticeably louder or softer than normal?
- **quantity:** Does the client use appropriate and concise words? Does she only offer minimal or monosyllabic words, or does she provide extensive, elaborate detail?

Insight refers to how well the client can describe her own condition and circumstances. For example, a client who experiences hallucinations but is able to express to her counselor that she knows no one else can see them and doesn't believe them to be real would be described as having good insight.

HELPFUL HINT

This list of elements for a mental status exam is not exhaustive. Each clinic will have its own forms or expected observations for MSEs. This list covers the topics that are typically found in the MSE; however, questions and terminology may vary.

PRACTICE QUESTION

8. Which of the following is an element of a mental status exam?
   A) client's level of insight
   B) case notes from prior counselors
   C) an IQ assessment
   D) client's past drug use

Assessment Instruments

An important part of being an effective counselor is understanding how to choose a good assessment. Considering whether the assessment has been tested and approved for a client's age, ethnicity, language, or presenting problem can help a counselor determine what is the best choice to make when assessing a client.

Statistical analysis of large groups of clients and how accurately the assessment measures their symptoms can help the counselor determine the assessment's efficacy. The following are several important statistical factors.

Assessing Trauma

Trauma is an emotional response or reaction to distressing events. Some common exposure events include natural disasters, war, witnessing or surviving violence, witnessing or surviving abuse, witnessing or surviving rape or sexual assault, or being in an accident that leads to hospitalization.

There are four main domains of trauma symptoms.

1. **Intrusion** includes intrusive memories, nightmares, flashbacks, or reactions to triggers.
2. **Avoidance** involves changing one's behavior to avoid certain thoughts, memories, or external reminders.
3. **Negative changes in mood and affect** include memory issues, low self-worth, thoughts that the event was their fault, consistent negative emotions, a sense of detachment, or difficulty feeling positive emotions.
4. **Increased reactivity** includes symptoms like irritability, hypervigilance, elevated startle response, attention issues, sleep issues, and self-destructive behavior.

For a client to be diagnosed with **post-traumatic stress disorder (PTSD)**, he must have been exposed to a traumatic experience, exhibited symptoms across all four domains, and experiencing the symptoms for at least one month.

The **Clinician-Administered PTSD Scale for DSM-5 (CAPS-5)** is one of the most commonly used assessments for PTSD. It is a structured diagnostic interview with thirty questions. It has high validity and reliability, making it a strong assessment for PTSD. The assessment takes about forty-five to sixty minutes to complete.

The **PTSD Symptom Scale Interview for DSM-5 (PSSI-5)** is a twenty-four-question semi-structured interview used to assess for PTSD in adults. It is administered by a clinician and used to diagnose PTSD in adults.

The **PTSD Checklist for DSM-5 (PCL-5)** is a twenty-item self-administered checklist for PTSD symptoms. It can be used to make a provisional diagnosis of PTSD (contingent on further follow-up and assessment by a clinician). It can also be used as a way to monitor symptom severity over time.

The **Clinician-Administered PTSD Scale for DSM-5–Child/Adolescent Version (CAPS-CA-5)** is based on the **CAPS-5** assessment, with language and questions geared toward children. It is approved for use with children ages seven and up. Like the CAPS-5, it is a structured clinical interview that lists the symptoms that are key to a PTSD diagnosis; it has thirty questions.

The **UCLA Child/Adolescent PTSD Reaction Index for DSM-5 (UCLA-RI)** is a semi-structured interview for children and adolescents. It covers a client's history of trauma experiences and screens for trauma symptoms based on the four domains found in the *DSM-5*.

PRACTICE QUESTION

9. Suzie was recently bitten by a dog and had to go to the hospital for treatment. Her mother is worried that she may have experienced trauma from the experience. Which of the following is a symptom of avoidance?

   A) Suzie reports frequent nightmares about dogs.

   B) Suzie's mom says that she has been yelling at her brother more often.

   C) Suzie's teacher reports that Suzie has not been paying attention in class.

   D) Suzie refuses to visit a neighbor who has a dog.

Assessing Substance Use

Substance use is the nonmedically warranted consumption of medications or substances such as tobacco, alcohol, or illicit drugs. **Substance dependence** is a deep physical and/or psychological need to use a controlled substance to achieve a feeling of euphoria and/or calmness. **Substance abuse** is the continued use of a medication without medical reason, or excessive and intentional use of a controlled substance (alcohol or narcotics, for example). Finally, **addiction** is dependence on a substance or practice that is physically or psychologically habit-forming to the extent that critical pain and damage result.

The **Tobacco, Alcohol, Prescription medication, and other Substance use (TAPS) Tool** is a four-question screening tool for adults that determines if the client is using tobacco, alcohol, prescription medications, or other substances, and at what frequency in the previous twelve months. It can be self-administered or administered by the clinician.

The **Drug Abuse Screening Test (DAST-10)** is a ten-question assessment to determine drug abuse. It has been approved for adults and older young adults (ages sixteen and up). It can be administered by the counselor or the client.

The **National Institute on Drug Abuse (NIDA)-modified Alcohol, Smoking, and Substance Involvement Screening Test (NM-ASSIST)** is a clinician-administered online assessment that asks the client about lifetime prescription and illegal drug, alcohol, or tobacco use. If the client indicates any usage, the questions progress to frequency and the degree to which use has negatively impacted the client's life.

The **CAGE questionnaire** consists of four questions that can be worked into an intake assessment or an individual session. CAGE is an acronym for "cut down, annoyed, guilt, and eye-opener."

The **Alcohol Use Disorders Identification Test (AUDIT)** is a ten-item tool that helps counselors recognize when a client's drinking behaviors have become dangerous for their health.

The **Michigan Alcohol Screening Test (MAST)** is a twenty-five-item assessment that helps counselors better understand the lifetime severity of a client's alcohol use. The MAST is often used to help guide treatment plans.

The **Clinical Opiate Withdrawal Scale (COWS)** is an eleven-item screening tool administered by clinicians. It measures objective symptoms of opiate withdrawal such as heart rate, joint pain, stomach issues, goosebumps, sweating, and more. The assessment is used to help clinicians understand the level of opiate dependence and how severe a client's withdrawal symptoms are.

The **Car, Relax, Alone, Forget, Friends, Trouble (CRAFFT)** is a screening tool approved for youth ages twelve to twenty-one to determine substance use. It can be administered by a counselor or through self-assessment. It begins with three questions to determine any level of drug or alcohol use in the previous twelve months. If the client affirms any usage, screening moves on to query about six situations. The final portion is a brief intervention.

The **Drug Abuse Screening Test for Adolescents (DAST-A)** is a modified version of the DAST. It is a twenty-eight-question screening tool to determine adolescent abuse of prescription or illegal drugs, tobacco, or alcohol. It can be administered by the counselor or self-administered.

The **Screening, Brief Intervention, and Referral to Treatment (SBIRT)** is used by clinicians to determine alcohol use. It can be used with adolescents and adults. The client's reported alcohol consumption is placed into different danger levels depending on his weekly consumption, which is then discussed with him, and possible motivation for change is assessed. If the client is amenable, the final part of the SBIRT involves referral to treatment.

PRACTICE QUESTION

10. The counselor is seeing a fourteen-year-old client for the first time. She was referred for missing school and poor family relationships. Her mother suspects she has been using marijuana with friends. Which of the following would be the BEST tool to screen for drug usage?

    A) TAPS
    B) CRAFFT
    C) COWS
    D) SBIRT

Assessing Other At-Risk Behaviors

Counselors have an ethical duty to conduct ongoing assessments for **suicidal** and **homicidal** behavior, **self-injury**, and **relationship violence**. Counselors are legally required to report any serious threats of suicide or homicide to the police for intervention. Self-injury with no suicidal intent and relationship violence are not reportable events, but responsible counseling involves ongoing monitoring and assessment of these aspects of a client's life to ensure safety.

As part of ongoing assessment, counselors have a responsibility to screen for **suicidal** or **homicidal ideation (SI/HI)**—thoughts of harming oneself or others:

- Frequency and duration: How often does the client think about harming herself or others, and for how long?
- Intensity: Are the thoughts fleeting and easy to ignore, or are they pressing and disturbing?

HELPFUL HINT

Some people are afraid that asking about suicidal ideation can make a person suicidal. Research shows that this is not true and that assessing for SI can be lifesaving.

- Plan: Does the client have a plan for how he would kill himself or others, or is it more of a vague wish to be dead?
- Means: If the client has a plan, does she have the means to carry it out? For example, if the client has contemplated shooting herself, does she have access to a gun?
- Intent: How seriously is the client considering enacting his plan? Does he have a specific time and date that he is planning on; does he deny any intent; is it something in between?

Nonsuicidal self-injury (NSSI) is any form of self-injury without intent to kill oneself. The most common forms of NSSI include cutting, burning, and head banging or hitting. Other forms include scratching, hitting oneself or other objects, ingesting harmful substances, and more.

It is important to refrain from judgment or reacting emotionally when assessing for NSSI. Although cutting is the most common form of NSSI, it is important to screen for other types of NSSI behaviors, as they can be easily missed by counselors.

The **SOARS model** is a brief assessment used in clinics to screen for NSSI.

- **S**uicidal ideation: Is the NSSI motivated by or paired with suicidal ideation?
- **O**nset, frequency, methods: When did the NSSI begin; when was the most recent time; how often does it happen; what methods were used?
- **A**ftercare: How are the wounds cared for; has medical attention for the wounds ever been required?
- **R**easons: What prompts or motivates the client to harm herself (emotional release, anger, self-hatred, and so forth)?
- **S**tages of change: Does the client think about stopping; does he want to stop?

Relationship violence, also known as "domestic violence" or "intimate partner violence," occurs when one or both partners are enacting physical, emotional, financial, or psychological abuse on the other partner. Intimate partner violence is dangerous and can be life-threatening. Despite that, it is not reportable except in cases where children witness the abuse or if the abuse is aimed at an older adult.

Important areas of assessment for survivors of domestic violence include

- frequency and duration of attacks (can be helpful to use a calendar);
- type of attack (whether a weapon was used, level of injury);
- partner stability (employment, drug/alcohol use, mental health concerns, suicide threats);
- controlling behavior (money, stalking, controlling who the partner sees);
- attacks on others (children, pets, family members).

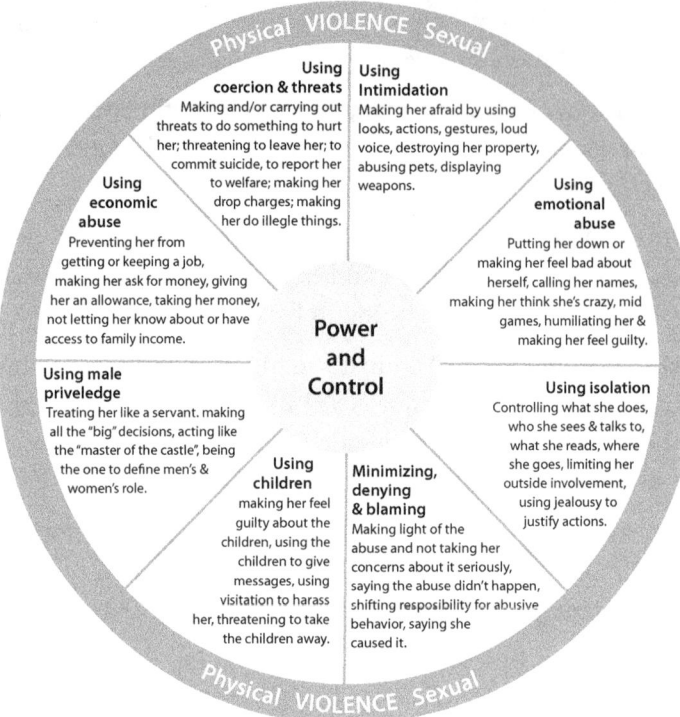

Figure 4.3. The Power and Control Wheel

Safety planning is of paramount importance for clients who experience relationship violence. It often takes a long time for them to leave their abusers. Planning where to go, saving enough money, and childcare are all crucial elements of treatment planning for clients who experience relationship violence.

PRACTICE QUESTION

11. Which of the following is the FIRST thing to determine in assessing for suicidality?
    A) if the client has access to weapons
    B) if the client has any suicidal thoughts
    C) if the client has a specific plan for killing himself
    D) if the client has planned a time and place where she would kill herself

Assessing Depression and Anxiety

Several assessment tools are available to diagnose depression and anxiety, screen for these issues, or measure the severity of symptoms in clients.

The **Suicide Assessment Five-Step Evaluation and Triage (SAFE-T)** helps identify suicide risk in clients. The counselor follows five steps:

1. Identify risk factors that can be changed to reduce the client's risk.
2. Identify protective factors that can be increased to reduce the client's risk.
3. Conduct a suicide assessment to understand the client's thoughts, plans, behaviors, and suicidal intent.

4. Determine the client's risk level and the appropriate response to ensure their safety; intervene as necessary.

5. Document the assessment of the client's risk level with the supporting evidence discussed, the interventions used, and follow-up steps.

The SAFE-T is available as a pocket card or app.

Many assessments exist to screen for depression or evaluate the level of depression in clients.

The psychiatrist David Burns developed the **Burns Depression Test** to screen for depression. The test is meant to be completed by the client. It asks about thoughts and feelings, personal relationships, physical symptoms, and suicidality.

The **Hamilton Rating Scale for Depression (HAM-D)** is commonly used for individuals who already have a depressive disorder diagnosis.

- It measures suicide risk, physical, and emotional symptoms.
- It can be used with both children and adults.
- There are two versions of the HAM-D: one includes seventeen items (HAM-D-17); the other has twenty-one (HAM-D-21).

The **Montgomery-Asberg Depression Rating Scale (MADRS)** is a ten-item tool. It helps the counselor get a better understanding of depressive symptoms in clients who have a mood disorder. Like the Hamilton Depression Scale, it is not used to diagnose; instead, it helps the counselor determine the severity of symptoms. The MADRS should be used with adult clients.

Like the MADRS, the **Zung Self-Rating Depression Scale** measures severity of depression. It is a twenty-item assessment that rates four common symptoms of depression:

1. pervasive effect
2. psychological equivalents
3. psychomotor activities
4. other disturbances

Several assessments are available for diagnosing and screening for anxiety. Some of the more common follow.

The **State-Trait Anxiety Inventory (STAI)** is useful for diagnosing anxiety in adults. Twenty assessment items cover trait anxiety: another twenty questions cover state anxiety. Differentiating between the two types of anxiety helps reveal a client's levels of anxiety on a day-to day basis (trait anxiety) as opposed to levels of anxiety in response to perceived stressors (state anxiety). The STAI can also help the counselor differentiate between depression and anxiety symptoms in a client.

The **Beck Anxiety Inventory (BAI)** is a relatively quick anxiety screening tool for adults. It can be done verbally during a session or self-reported before a session. In the BAI, the client rates the severity of several physical and emotional anxiety symptoms. This assessment is a good predictor of anxiety disorders, making it a helpful tool when trying to formulate a diagnosis. The BAI produces valid results.

HELPFUL HINT

Counselors should discuss their recommendations with clients and develop a plan collaboratively before documenting the assessment.

DID YOU KNOW?

The Hamilton Rating Scale for Depression can also be referred to as the Hamilton Depression Scale or the Hamilton Depression Rating Scale.

The BAI can also be used to help gauge the client's progress in therapy. Results before and after beginning therapy and/or medications can be compared.

Another anxiety screening tool is the **Generalized Anxiety Disorder 7-item (GAD-7)**, a quick seven-question assessment asking about the severity of anxiety. It is generally self-administered by the client and useful to track treatment progress.

The **Hamilton Anxiety Rating Scale (HARS or HAM-A)** was one of the original anxiety screening assessments. It is administered by a clinician and addresses fourteen categories of physical and psychological symptoms.

Research has found that reliability and validity of the HAM-A is improved when guidance for a structured interview is provided. As a result, the **Hamilton Anxiety Rating Scale Interview Guide (HARS-IG)** was developed. The HARS-IG is considered more reliable and valid.

PRACTICE QUESTION

12. Susan is a client who has been struggling with depressive symptoms since her husband unexpectedly passed away. Since the loss, Susan has been sleeping more than normal, has a depressed mood, and has lost a significant amount of weight. Because of Susan's symptoms, the counselor uses the SAFE-T assessment. What is the correct order of events for this assessment?

    A) document, identify risk factors, conduct suicide inquiry, identify protective factors, and determine risk level/intervention

    B) identify risk factors, identify protective factors, conduct suicide inquiry, determine risk level/intervention, and document

    C) conduct suicide inquiry, identify protective factors, identify risk factors, determine risk level/intervention, and document

    D) conduct suicide inquiry, identify risk factors, identify protective factors, determine risk level/intervention, and document

Assessing Personality

Personality assessments are used to tell a counselor about a client's behavior patterns and interpersonal interactions. These can be used to help a counselor determine how to build rapport with a client and choose treatment plans and interventions. They have also been used to assess for career paths. These assessments are a somewhat controversial tool in the world of psychology and counseling because many of them have low reliability and validity, and because one's personality changes frequently throughout a lifetime. The results are usually not shared with the client and are instead used to inform treatment.

Projective tests are assessments in which the client must interpret some type of ambiguous stimuli.

- The most well-known of these is the **Rorschach inkblot test**, which asks clients to describe what they see in an inkblot.
- Similarly, the **Holtzman inkblot technique** uses a client's interpretation of an inkblot to detect personality.

- The **Thematic Apperception Test (TAT)** is a projective test in which the client describes what is happening on different cards featuring people in ambiguous situations.

Overall, projective tests are seen as unreliable because they rely heavily on the counselor's interpretations and have low validity and reliability.

Figure 4.4. Rorschach Tests

Self-report inventories are questionnaires in which people provide information about themselves in response to various prompts. The most common is the Minnesota Multiphasic Personality Inventory-2 (MMPI-2). The **Minnesota Multiphasic Personality Inventory-2 (MMPI-2)** assesses personality traits including:

- paranoia
- social introversion
- psychopathology

The MMPI-2 is not generally used to evaluate people with healthy personalities. Rather, it measures dysfunction within an individual's personality.

The **Sixteen Personality Factors Questionnaire (16PF)** focuses on sixteen fundamental personality characteristics and functions to assist in comprehending where someone's personality may register among those characteristics. The behavioral assessment serves to provide greater understanding of an individual's behavior and causative factors or thought processes behind those behaviors.

The 16PF underwent a factor analysis that distilled the personality traits into five main traits and eventually developed into the **Big Five personality traits**, which measure the client's level of openness, conscientiousness, extraversion, agreeableness, and neuroticism.

The **Woodworth Personal Data Sheet** is regarded as the first personality test. It was developed to screen war veterans for shell shock (now known as PTSD). It is not typically used by clinicians today.

The **Myers-Briggs Type Indicator (MBTI)** is a self-administered questionnaire used to determine four personality factors with opposing domains. The domains include:

- introversion versus extraversion
- sensing versus intuition
- thinking versus feeling
- judging versus perceiving

Intake, Assessment, and Diagnosis

Though widely popular and easy to test online, the MBTI is not generally used by clinicians due to its low validity and reliability.

The **Edwards Personal Preference Schedule (EPPS)** is a series of forced-choice objective questions administered by a clinician. The assessment is designed to illuminate personality through motives and needs and to determine how one would react in certain situations. The assessment has limited validity and reliability and is not a standard personality assessment.

The **HEXACO Personality Inventory (HEXACO-PI)** addresses six characteristics:

1. humility
2. emotionality
3. extraversion
4. agreeableness
5. conscientiousness
6. openness to experience

Scoring for this assessment uses a scale, so the counselor can gauge the significance of the characteristics. However, some critics of the HEXACO Personality Inventory feel that it does not adequately reflect cultural influences.

PRACTICE QUESTION

13. Which of the following personality assessments would be the BEST choice to determine if a client has psychopathic tendencies?

   A) the Edwards Personal Preference Schedule
   B) the Big Five personality traits
   C) the Minnesota Multiphasic Personality Inventory-2
   D) the Rorschach test

Career Assessment

Career assessments are standardized inventories that allow people to explore their areas of interest and skills and what type of work environment they would thrive in. Counselors frequently use career assessments with high school and college students who are unsure of the career path they want to take, or for adults who want to revisit their current career choices. The following are some of the most common career assessment tools.

The **Strong Interest Inventory (SII)** is used for high school and college students as well as adults who are seeking guidance for a career path. It involves 291 questions across six domains in areas such as occupations and activities interests. It does not measure personality or aptitude. It is a reliable and valid assessment that counselors can use for clients who are unsure of what career path they are most interested in.

Psychologist John Holland developed a theory of career development known as **RIASEC** (realistic, investigative, artistic, social, enterprising, conventional). He theorizes that people fall into one of these six categories, which determines which work environment they are best suited for. Clients who would like to understand more about their personality and what type of environment they have the potential to thrive in would benefit from this assessment. Please see Chapter 9 for more details.

The **Self-Directed Search (SDS)** is a formalized assessment based on Holland's career development theory. It is a self-directed assessment, making it ideal for independent clients who prefer to explore career possibilities on their own.

The **Kuder Occupational Interest Survey (KOIS)** is a normed survey that compares client scores of areas of interest compared to the scores of people currently in those fields. Known as "the Kuder," it is self-administered and can be interpreted at home. For clients who are concerned about personality and interest fit within certain fields, the Kuder can help illuminate how similarly a client may feel compared to others in that field.

The **Career Beliefs Inventory (CBI)** is a counselor-administered assessment that is designed to help counselors explore areas of mental blockage, assumptions, generalizations, and beliefs about themselves and others that may be preventing them from exploring their full potential. It is ideal to use as an initial assessment for a client experiencing career difficulties, as it can provide important information for the counselor to explore with the client.

Finally, the **DiSC Assessment** groups people into four main personality profiles:

1. dominance (results-oriented, confident)
2. influence (relationship-focused, persuasive)
3. steadiness (cooperative, sincere, dependable)
4. conscientiousness (competence, clarity, accuracy)

The DiSC assessment can be used in the workplace, especially to analyze candidates and leadership qualities.

PRACTICE QUESTION

14. A client comes in concerned that he would not fit in well in his preferred career choice. Which assessment would BEST help the counselor determine the validity of that concern?
    A) Career Beliefs Inventory
    B) Kuder Occupational Interest Survey
    C) Strong Interest Inventory
    D) Self-Directed Search

Cognitive Functioning Assessments

Certain instruments and assessments are designed to measure psychological functioning. The **Rancho Los Amigos Level of Cognitive Functioning Scale (LCFS)** determines the level of brain function in post-comatose clients and clients with a closed head injury (including traumatic brain injury).

The LCFS focuses on eight areas of cognition (awareness), with each level representing a progression of improvement from brain trauma or damage:

1. No response (level 1)
2. Generalized response (level 2)—reacts inconsistently with no purpose
3. Localized response (level 3)—reacts specifically to various stimuli, with a different response each time
4. Confused-agitated response (level 4)—active but does not comprehend what has happened
5. Confused, inappropriate, nonagitated response (level 5)—less agitated, consistent reactions to basic commands
6. Confused-appropriate response (level 6)—motivated, highly dependent on others, more aware of self and loved ones
7. Automatic-appropriate response (level 7)—acts appropriately in the health care setting and at home; self-aware, oriented to place and time
8. Purposeful-appropriate response (level 8)—independently functions well within the world, has memory of how the past fits with the present and future

 DID YOU KNOW?

The Mini-Cog instrument is widely used to assess memory recall for people with Alzheimer's disease.

The **Mini-Cog assessment tool** is administered in three minutes to screen for cognitive deficiency in older adults. The Mini-Cog is used within the principal health care environment and mainly concentrates on recall abilities. An individual is asked to remember three simple words, then is intentionally distracted by the examiner, and is later asked to repeat the three words.

The **Mini-Mental State Examination (MMSE)** is brief and used to screen for dementia and cognitive functioning in older adults. There are five sections on the MMSE:

1. orientation
2. immediate memory
3. attention and concentration
4. delayed recall
5. language

The MMSE is not to be confused with the mental status exam (MSE) used in clinical intake interviews.

The **Child Development Inventory (CDI)** is a 300-item screening tool that parents complete at home and provide to the counselor. It looks at the child's development in eight areas:

1. social
2. self-help
3. gross motor
4. fine motor
5. expressive language
6. language comprehension

7. letters
8. numbers

The CDI also includes the General Development Scale which investigates health, growth, vision, and hearing, as well as a child's developmental behavior.

Cognitive functioning can also be measured by **intelligence tests**. Two main intelligence tests are

- the Stanford-Binet test;
- the Wechsler test.

French psychologist Alfred Binet wanted to develop a test measuring academic ability in order to determine which students were not learning well in the classroom and who might need special instruction. He assumed that intelligence increases with age and devised a "mental age" measurement. For example, if Bobby, an eleven-year-old, has a mental age of eleven, he is on par with his peers. If his mental age were nine, he would be behind. If his mental age were thirteen, he would be ahead.

Lewis Terman, a professor at Stanford University, used Binet's mental age system to create an **intelligence quotient (IQ)** that links intelligence to a number. To determine someone's IQ, the mental age is divided by the actual age and then multiplied by 100. So, if Bobby's mental age is twelve, his IQ would be 118.

To apply this method to adults, Terman set an arbitrary age of twenty for calculating all adult IQs. Terman developed the **Stanford-Binet IQ test** to determine IQ. Test takers are asked a variety of questions, the answers of which determine a single score.

The other major intelligence test was created by David Wechsler. It is also called an IQ test, although the resulting number is not actually a quotient. Instead, the test is standardized so that the mean (the average of the numbers) is 100, and the **standard deviation** (how spread out the numbers are) is 15 with a **normal distribution** (or bell-shaped curve).

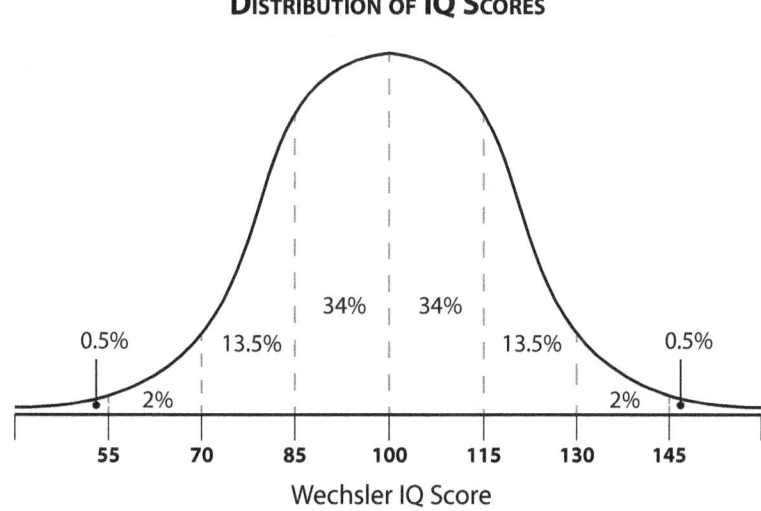

Figure 4.5. Wechsler IQ Score Distribution

A test taker's percentile (relative to the population of test takers) is determined, and the score is based on the number of standard deviations the percentile is from the mean. For example, if Shauna is in the sixteenth percentile, that places her at 34 percent below the mean (fiftieth percentile), which is one standard deviation to the left of the mean. Her IQ score would therefore be 85.

The Wechsler test comes in three different forms:
- Wechsler Adult Intelligence Scale (WAIS)
- Wechsler Intelligence Scale for Children ages 6 – 16 (WISC)
- Wechsler Preschool and Primary Scale of Intelligence (WPPSI)

Each test is composed of different types of questions (verbal and performance on the WAIS, for example). These yield subscores, which, taken together, yield a total IQ score.

PRACTICE QUESTION

15. The first IQ test was developed to determine which of the following?
    A) entry into Mensa
    B) second grade readiness
    C) graduate school readiness
    D) possible intellectual disability

Criticisms of IQ Tests

There are several criticisms of the efficacy of intelligence testing of any kind. First, the tests focus heavily on verbal skills. While the Wechsler tests require more manipulation of objects and other such performance skills, the verbal components can skew the scores of those whose verbal skills may not match their intelligence.

Additionally, intelligence tests are often accused of being biased. The questions are constructed on certain cultural norms and are not universal. If the question references information not regularly available to a certain individual, it can unfairly skew the results of the test. Defenders of the test argue that the test has the same validity—and predictive power on, for example, college grades—for all cultural groups. Others claim that the bias runs much deeper, setting up certain groups for success on both intelligence tests and college success, while unfairly impeding others.

PRACTICE QUESTION

16. Why are IQ tests frequently criticized as being biased and not universal?
    A) The tests have high validity with GPA.
    B) They ignore domains like emotional intelligence.
    C) The questions assume certain cultural norms.
    D) The questions have low reliability.

Assessing Outcomes

Assessing outcomes is an important part of rigorous therapeutic methods. Outcomes are assessed using **pretest** and **post-test measures**. For example, a client who presents with symptoms of PTSD is given the PCL-5 in the first session to determine the rate of her symptoms. After three months of weekly sessions, she reports having fewer nightmares and is better able to cope with triggers in the community. A new administration of the PCL-5 reveals that she no longer meets the clinical criteria for PTSD. This is considered a positive outcome as a result of treatment sessions with the counselor.

Pre- and post-test measures can also evaluate counseling effectiveness. Some counselors or clinics ask their clients to fill out a weekly, monthly, or termination evaluation that rates their perceptions of the counselor's efficacy. Common questions ask whether the client

- feels understood by the counselor;
- perceives improvement in symptoms;
- feels like the sessions are a good use of time.

PRACTICE QUESTION

17. Assessing a client's symptoms when she starts treatment and when she terminates with her counselor is known as which of the following?

    A) random sampling

    B) pre-test and post-test measures

    C) stratified sampling

    D) case study

Diagnosis

A **diagnosis** is an identified health condition that is based on an assessment by a trained professional. To make a diagnosis, counselors look at the client's symptoms and compare them to the symptoms listed in the *Diagnostic and Statistical Manual of Mental Disorders (DSM-5)*.

Determining and Using Diagnosis

Because diagnosis is a key component of a client's medical records, clients have the right to know if they meet clinical criteria for a diagnosis. After learning their diagnosis, clients can make informed decisions about their treatment.

Counselors should use language the client can understand when discussing a diagnosis. For example, the way a diagnosis is explained to an adult will be different from the way it would be explained to a child.

Diagnoses are used to help guide treatment. Research has found that specific presenting concerns require different therapeutic approaches. For example, cognitive therapy will not be as effective as using Dialectical Behavior Therapy (DBT) for someone living with borderline personality disorder.

Once a diagnosis is made, the counselor can determine whether additional treatment services would benefit the client. Medication management, as an example, can be an effective intervention for several clinical diagnoses.

Having a clinical diagnosis can significantly change the objectives and goals of a treatment plan. Treatment plans should be in place after the initial interview and continually be adjusted to reflect the client's progress.

Treatment plans allow for further specification and can include goals specific to a diagnosis. For example, clients struggling with obsessive-compulsive disorder may learn new and effective coping skills for their obsessions in the early phases of treatment. Once those skills have developed, the treatment plan can progress to other approaches to respond to the compulsive behaviors that are present. The next chapter discusses treatment planning in depth.

After meeting with a client for an initial interview, the counselor should take time to consider possible diagnoses. The *Diagnostic and Statistical Manual of Mental Disorders (DSM-5)* contains twenty-one sections of similar diagnoses. A counselor should get a general idea of which section the client's diagnosis may be in. Then she can begin looking at the specific symptoms for those diagnoses. Every diagnosis has different requirements, all of which are explained in the "Diagnostic Criteria" section for the diagnosis.

Many diagnoses within the *DSM-5* are rated on a mild, moderate, or severe scale, which is determined by the number of symptoms present. This is explained in the "Coding and Recording Procedures" section for each diagnosis in the *DSM-5*. Diagnoses may also have additional specifiers that would be listed in the same section.

The term *co-occurring* refers to the presence of a mental health diagnosis in addition to a substance-related disorder. Some people use alcohol and drugs to cope with symptoms resulting from a mental health condition. As a result, individuals who have co-occurring disorders need to receive treatment for both concerns for the best treatment outcomes.

Dual diagnosis refers to an individual who meets the criteria for two separate diagnoses. Symptoms for both diagnoses must be present at the same time. The term is usually used to describe the presence of a mental health diagnosis and a substance abuse disorder, but it can refer to other disorders. Dual diagnoses can be two mental health conditions, two medical health conditions, or one of each.

Comorbidity is similar to dual diagnosis, but it refers to the presence of more than one health condition. These can be medical or mental health conditions. Each diagnosis section in the *DSM-5* ends with a paragraph explaining the common comorbidities found with that particular illness.

HELPFUL HINT

Counselors may come across dual diagnoses referred to as "co-occurring disorders."

PRACTICE QUESTION

18. A counselor is reviewing initial assessment paperwork before meeting with a new client. The client has been diagnosed with PTSD with dissociative symptoms and major depressive disorder, severe. She received the PTSD diagnosis first. Three years later, she developed depressive symptoms that led to her second diagnosis. Which of the following would BEST characterize her diagnosis?

    A) co-occurring diagnoses
    B) dual diagnosis
    C) comorbid diagnoses
    D) clinical diagnosis

Levels of Care

One of the functions of an initial interview is to determine which level of care is appropriate for clients and their presenting concerns. There are a variety of options, each with its own benefits.

Residential inpatient care programs typically occur within a hospital setting. The goal is to stabilize clients so they can begin receiving treatment for their mental health concerns at a different location.

- Clients receive treatment that can include
    - psychoeducation;
    - individual therapy;
    - crisis intervention;
    - medication management.
- Inpatient programs are appropriate for individuals who have safety risks like
    - recent suicide gestures or attempts;
    - homicidal attempts.
- Inpatient programs are also suitable for clients who need a high level of care, including
    - medication management;
    - drug/alcohol detox and treatment.

In **partial hospitalization programs (PHP)**, the client attends a structured day program at a treatment facility.

- The program's structure resembles an inpatient program, but the client goes home at night.
- PHPs typically run five days a week for six to eight hours per day.
- PHPs provide clients with safety and structure for most of their day.
- PHPs are appropriate for clients who can safely live at home but still need a thorough treatment program.

- A typical client might have severe mental illness, be compliant with medication, and learning how to manage symptoms behaviorally.

In **intensive outpatient programs (IOP)**, the client attends structured programming for a few hours per day.

- IOPs usually treat addiction, eating disorders, and depressive disorders.
- IOPs typically have a psychoeducational component in addition to group treatment.
- IOPs are appropriate for
  - clients with mild disorders;
  - clients with mild and severe use disorders who have already completed residential treatment programs.

Outpatient treatment (outpatient therapy) is usually recommended to build on what clients learned in other, more intensive programs.

- The duration of an outpatient program varies depending on the presenting concern.
- Outpatient treatment typically follows successful completion of an IOP or PHP.
- Outpatient treatment is typically fewer hours per day than an IOP or PHP.
- Outpatient activities include
  - group therapy;
  - individual therapy;
  - medication management;
  - specialized treatment;
  - psychoeducation;
  - family therapy.
- Outpatient treatment programs address various mental health concerns, including
  - addiction;
  - childhood behavioral and emotional concerns;
  - mood disorders.

Psychotherapy is individual counseling between a client and a counselor that

- is appropriate for individuals with a mild mental health concern;
- allows complex clients to maintain a connection to a supportive professional after more intensive treatment;
- includes high-functioning clients;
- usually consists of weekly or biweekly individual sessions.

Self-help programs generally refer to support groups run by peers rather than mental health professionals.

- Many self-help programs address addiction, but some address other mental health concerns. These include
  - twelve-step programs (Alcoholics Anonymous, Narcotics Anonymous, for example);
  - support for families of addicts (Al-Anon, Nar-Anon);
  - eating and weight management groups (Overeaters Anonymous, Weight Watchers);
  - some grief support groups.
- Activity and attendance rate depend on the client.
- Self-help groups can be used at every level of care.

Treatment programs offer guidelines that can help the counselor decide which level of care to recommend to the client.

PRACTICE QUESTION

19. A client just completed a detox program and an inpatient addiction program to address opioid use disorder. The client has a history of trauma, anxiety, and depression. He has a safe home environment and believes that his mental health concerns triggered his substance abuse. The inpatient program recommended that he attend treatment for a few hours a day, three to four days per week while living at home. Which level of care is the client now entering?

    A) partial hospitalization program (PHP)

    B) intensive outpatient program (IOP)

    C) psychotherapy

    D) outpatient treatment

Answer Key

1. **B)** Intake forms should be completed by the client. These forms enable clients to explain in their own words why they are seeking counseling.

2. **B)** The precontemplation stage is when the individual is not thinking about behavioral change and is not ready to take steps to change.

3. **C)** Motivational interviewing (MI) is ideal for a client who is unsure about a life change (Option C). This client is in the contemplation stage of the transtheoretical model (TTM). Motivational interviewing could help the client find benefits to making changes in his life and encourage thoughtful communication about his hesitations. Option A might be an appropriate answer, but this client may have significant internal motivation. Someone with internal motivation and not external motivation will still be more open to making changes than the client in Option C. Option B describes a client who is actively participating in the interview, and Option D describes a client who seems to have internal motivation for treatment, which would encourage active participation during the interview as well.

4. **B)** Client self-report is the backbone of a structured clinical interview.

5. **B)** A biopsychosocial interview would be the best interview format to use when meeting a first-time client because it assesses physical health, mental health, and social life. This allows the counselor to determine areas of focus for the treatment plan as well as whether any specialized assessments or interview formats could also be used.

6. **C)** A clinical interview, also known as an intake interview, is an informal assessment that makes up the first part of any clinical relationship.

7. **A)** Generally, performance on math tests shows fairly accurately how well students understand the material, which makes it a valid measure of student knowledge.

8. **A)** A client's level of insight, or how aware she is of the content of her thoughts, appearance, behavior, and condition, is a key part of a thorough mental status exam.

9. **D)** Refusing to interact with anything that may remind the client of the traumatizing event is a sign of avoidance.

10. **B)** The Car, Relax, Alone, Forget, Friends, Trouble (CRAFFT) is the only assessment that is endorsed for use with adolescents and screens for drug usage.

11. **B)** The first step in assessing for suicidality is to determine if the client has any suicidal thoughts.

12. **B)** When using the SAFE-T, the counselor begins by identifying risk factors that can be changed to reduce the client's risk. Next, the counselor determines what protective factors can be increased to reduce risk. This is followed by a suicide assessment that looks at the client's thoughts, plans, behaviors, and suicidal intent. Once the counselor has all the information needed, the client's risk level can be determined and an appropriate response to ensure the client's safety can be formulated. After discussing recommendations with the client and developing a plan, the counselor should document the assessment of the client's risk level with supporting evidence discussed, the interventions used, and the recommended follow-up steps.

13. **C)** The Minnesota Multiphasic Personality Inventory-2 (MMPI-2) scores and assesses for negative personality traits associated with psychological disorders, including areas such as paranoia, antisocial behaviors, depression, and more.

14. **B)** The Kuder Occupational Interest Survey (KOIS, or "the Kuder") is normed against scores of people across ten respective fields, which is ideal for helping a client who wants to know if he has similar thoughts and feelings as other people in his chosen field.

15. **D)** Alfred Binet first developed his IQ test at the request of the French government to determine which students might have an intellectual disability as a basis to require separate classroom instruction.

16. **C)** The main criticism of IQ tests not being universal is that the questions are culturally biased toward the test makers.

17. **B)** Using pre-test and post-test techniques determines if an intervention has caused a change in symptoms or behavior.

18. **C)** The client has comorbid diagnoses because more than one disorder is present. Option A can be ruled out because neither disorder is a substance use disorder. Option B is incorrect because the client received the diagnoses at separate points in her life. If she had developed symptoms of both disorders at the same time, then Option B would be correct. "Clinical diagnosis" (Option D) simply refers to an identified health condition as determined by professional assessment.

19. **B)** The client is entering an intensive outpatient program (IOP). A partial hospitalization program (PHP) can be ruled out because the treatment recommendation is only a few days a week. Psychotherapy is generally one or two short sessions per week and would not meet the recommended level of care from the referrer. Finally, the situation describes more intensive scheduling than a typical outpatient program. After completing the IOP, the individual would likely be encouraged to continue with outpatient treatment.

5 Treatment Planning

Developing a Treatment Plan

Planning Treatment Strategies

Planning a treatment strategy is vital for achieving the client's goals. The counselor will use the list of needs discovered from the client assessment to create a care plan. A good **care plan** will include

- the problem noted;
- the goal to be achieved;
- objectives for achieving the goal;
- interventions the counselor will use;
- timeline for achieving objectives and goals;
- evaluation of the intervention.

The **main components** of a treatment plan include

- brief client background;
- diagnosis;
- problem list;
- treatment goals;
- objectives;
- interventions;
- timeline;
- method of evaluation;
- tracking progress.

The following **strategies** draw on the main components of a treatment plan and drive treatment planning:

1. The **diagnosis** acts as the anchor for the treatment plan. Every step in the treatment plan must address the diagnosis.

107

2. The **problem list** details the problems described by the client related to the diagnosis. There will likely be more than one, and there may even be multiple problems for each diagnosis. The problem list must follow the diagnosis.

3. **Treatment goals** are the broad statements of what the client wants to achieve in therapy; they must relate to the diagnosis.

4. **Objectives** are the steps taken to achieve the goals. Just as the goals directly relate to the diagnosis, so too do the objectives.

5. **Interventions** are the clinical therapeutic techniques the counselor plans to use with the client. These must be evidence-based interventions appropriate for the diagnosis, such as cognitive behavioral therapy (CBT) for anxiety, dialectical behavior therapy (DBT) for borderline personality disorder, or exposure therapy for phobias. The counselor must be adequately trained to provide any chosen interventions.

6. **Timeline** refers to the projected amount of time expected to meet the objectives.

7. **Method of evaluation** details how the client's progress will be measured.

8. **Tracking progress** includes keeping notes related to the client's achievement of the objectives and goals in the treatment plan. If the client does not show progress, the counselor and client may consider adjusting the treatment plan.

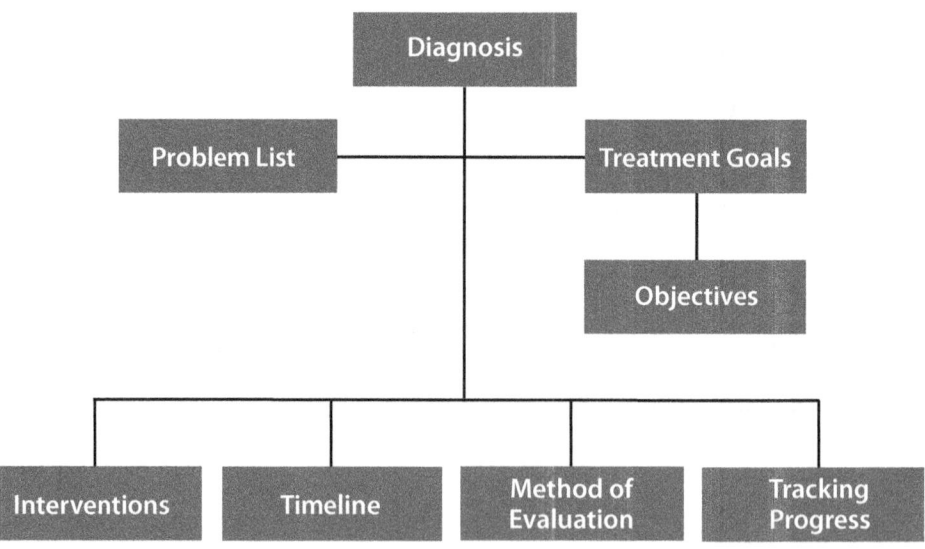

Figure 5.1. Strategizing Treatment Planning

The treatment plan should be reviewed and revised regularly; the schedule and frequency for review depend on both the agency and state regulations. Some states require that agencies providing mental health services review and revise treatment plans formally every thirty days or every four to six sessions. Those reviews must be documented in the client's file. Additionally, some states require an agency's program directors to regularly review client files, sometimes as often as quarterly. This varies based on state law and the type of service provider.

If a state or agency does not provide these guidelines, it is up to the counselor to determine the review schedule based on the frequency of sessions and client needs. It is generally appropriate to review and revise every four to six sessions. Other circumstances may inspire a review and revision of the treatment plan, including

- if the client experiences a crisis;
- a change in diagnosis;
- if a new problem arises;
- if the client solves a stated problem outside of therapy;
- if the client is not making progress with current interventions.

PRACTICE QUESTION

1. Which component of the treatment plan acts as an anchor for directing the rest of the plan?
   A) diagnosis
   B) goals
   C) interventions
   D) timeline

Collaborative Care

Collaboration means working with clients, families, colleagues, and other care providers to support clients in meeting their goals. The goal of **care coordination**, or **collaborative care**, is to achieve safe, effective care through the deliberate organization of client care activities within the interdisciplinary team. Counselors may collaborate with medical staff or other professionals in contexts such as

- inpatient treatment settings;
- outpatient programs;
- schools;
- child protective services;
- the criminal justice system;
- drug courts;
- mental health courts;
- disability services;
- housing case management;
- veterans' services.

Some examples of care coordination include

- sharing knowledge within the health care team (in a clinical setting);
- aligning resources with clients' emotional and social needs;

- setting clients up with community resources;
- reporting on program compliance;
- sharing client progress related to stated goals;
- reporting effects of other interventions, such as medications or case management, that are reported in counseling.

Collaboration with other care providers requires a client's written consent. Ethical conduct requires a counselor to be transparent about what is shared with other providers. Ideally, clients would be involved in any care collaboration meetings, but if they are not, the counselor should tell the clients what information was shared about them. Counselors should also collaborate with other providers and client support systems. A collaborative counselor

- is willing to be mentored, coached, or taught;
- is open to team members' contributions;
- participates in health care meetings to discuss practice issues/care activities;
- reaches out to mentor others and continues self-learning by a willingness to be taught;
- facilitates care delivery discussions and practice decisions;
- optimizes diverse resources and promotes client/family outcomes through inclusivity;
- cooperates in maintaining documentation and reporting;
- participates in discussions regarding ethics and cultural competence;
- educates other providers about the counseling process and the role of the counselor.

During this process, the counselor should collaborate with the client to establish treatment goals and objectives. Clients should be involved in all care decisions.

Clients come to therapy with a presenting problem, but as the counselor conducts intake and assessment, it is important to check in with the client to confirm that he agrees with the diagnosis. This ensures that the counselor is correctly interpreting what the client says. The counselor begins with the end in mind. Important questions to ask the client include the following:

- "How will you know when you are better?"
- "How will you know when the issue is no longer a problem for you?"

These questions give the counselor insight into what the client considers to be the goal and how the client will measure progress. As goals are discussed, the counselor should also outline other services or resources that could help the client achieve his goals.

For example, if the client is depressed because he is in a dead-end job, the counselor might ask him if he feels vocational assessment and training would be helpful. If the client agrees, the counselor can assist with a referral. Ultimately, the client must agree with treatment goals and objectives, or the treatment plan will not be effective.

When determining the treatment plan goals and objectives, an important topic is the integration and maintenance of therapeutic progress. In other words, how will the client and the counselor know that the client is making progress, and what steps can the client take to maintain that progress? Again, this should be an ongoing process.

A counselor's scope of practice is limited to psychological well-being; however, there may be times when a client's psychological well-being is impacted by factors that require concurrent treatment. As a counselor completes a thorough assessment, problems will be identified, including some that are not appropriate for a counselor to address but that impact a client's mental health. **Concurrent treatment** needs may include

- psychiatric medication;
- physical therapy;
- vocational training;
- occupational therapy;
- housing counseling;
- case management;
- medical care.

PRACTICE QUESTION

2. A client asks for a specific type of therapy that one of her friends experienced. During the assessment, the counselor determines that the requested intervention is not appropriate for this client's diagnosis. How should the counselor respond?

    A) do the therapy because the client requested it

    B) come up with a diagnosis that fits so the intervention can be done

    C) ignore the client's request and tell her that the counselor chooses interventions

    D) explain why the intervention is not appropriate for the client and suggest one that is

Establishing Goals

Clients come to therapy because they feel helpless to fix a problem on their own. A neutral third party, such as a counselor, provides an objective perspective to help conceptualize what the client is experiencing.

By engaging in thorough assessments, counselors formulate neutral conceptualizations of what their clients experience. Counselors can then help clients sift through the symptoms and their presentations. This process may include identifying

- what situations trigger the most anxiety;
- what the anxiety symptoms feel like;

- what works for making those symptoms subside;
- what might be a cause for the anxiety.

Breaking down the problem into meaningful parts helps demystify what the clients experience and gives them the precursor to hope that the problem can be solved. Finally, the counselor guides clients in formulating a road map of where they are now and where they would like to be in the future. That road map becomes the client's goals for therapy. There are three main reasons to establish goals:

1. Goals offer hope to clients by creating a plan for what they want to achieve.
2. Goal-setting complies with the medical model of care.
3. Goals demonstrate how therapy will help a client with a presenting problem.

Setting Attainable Goals

Within the goal-setting process, the counselor helps clients identify **strengths** and resources that can help them attain their goals. Strengths are found at the individual, relational, social, and environmental levels.

TABLE 5.1. Client Strengths			
INDIVIDUAL	RELATIONAL	SOCIAL	ENVIRONMENTAL
positive self-esteem	supportive parent	belongs to a religious organization	lives close to services
willing to work hard	supportive significant other or friend	makes friends easily	access to the beach

Identifying **strengths** in the goal-setting process reminds clients of the resources that can help them achieve their goals. Some clients forget about these resources as they become overwhelmed by the presenting problem. Goals should be SMART: **S**pecific, **M**easurable, **A**ttainable, **R**ealistic, **T**ime Restricted. SMART goals are useful for clients for several reasons:

- They break problems into manageable pieces.
- Each goal includes actions to be taken.
- They set a client up for success.
- Success fuels hope, so as clients achieve each SMART goal, they feel empowered to pursue the next.
- They help clients track their progress.

Common client goals include the following:

- functional status (financial stability, employment)
- lifestyle factors (diet, exercise)
- relationships (improve communication, establish boundaries)

- coping skills (exercise instead of substances, journaling)
- changing thought patterns (gratitude journals, identifying cognitive distortions)
- managing emotions (controlling anger, allowing oneself to feel sad)

TABLE 5.2. Example of a SMART Goal in Counseling	
Situation	A client worries all the time and excessively ruminates.
Diagnosis	Generalized anxiety disorder
SMART goal	The client will reduce time spent on rumination from most of the day to thirty minutes per day within two weeks by writing in a daily worry journal.

PRACTICE QUESTION

3. A client presents for therapy because she is afraid of flying and must do so in three months to attend a family member's wedding. Due to family circumstances, she cannot skip the event. Which of the following represents a SMART goal?

    A) The client will process events from her childhood to find the root cause of her fear of flying.

    B) The client will participate in exposure therapy.

    C) The client will succeed in exposure therapy exercises once per week for six weeks.

    D) Over three sessions, the client will learn three relaxation skills that she can use to reduce her anxiety about flying from level 10 to level 4 or below.

Types of Goals

Short-term goals fall within a time frame of up to thirty days and build toward long-term goals. A short-term goal might be to download a mindfulness meditation app and use it once per day for a week to manage anxiety symptoms.

Long-term goals have an extended time frame of three months and beyond. For example, if someone has the aforementioned short-term goal, a long-term goal might be to reduce anxiety symptoms by 50 percent within six months based on the Beck Anxiety Inventory scores.

Short-term goals stack up to help the client achieve long-term goals, and all goals must be directly related to the diagnosis. The intake and assessment inform the counselor's collaborative process with the client to establish goals consistent with the diagnosis. For example, if the client presents with the problem of anxiety that interferes with functioning, the counselor might have him take the Beck Anxiety Inventory (described in the section "Reviewing Progress"). Based on the scores, the counselor might ask him which symptoms he would like to work on first to set short-term goals based on his long-term goal of reducing anxiety.

PRACTICE QUESTION

4. A client needs to overcome her fear of flying to attend a family member's wedding in three months. Which of the following is a long-term goal?

    A) use meditation apps once per day for one week

    B) attend all nine therapy sessions

    C) get on the plane and attend the family member's wedding in three months

    D) keep an anxiety journal for thirty days

Reviewing Progress

Counselors understand that assessment and the **review of progress** of treatment goals occur at multiple levels:

- During the session, the counselor checks in with the client regularly to make sure he is comfortable with the intervention.
    - Client feedback will inform the counselor about the usefulness and appropriateness of the intervention as well as the client's reaction to it.
- At the end of each session, the counselor checks in with the client to determine
    - what the client got out of the session;
    - whether it was helpful;
    - what the client might do between sessions to continue the work.
- Every four to six sessions or every thirty days, the counselor reviews the full treatment plan with the client to determine and document his progress.
- Each quarter or preauthorization period, the counselor reviews the full treatment plan with the client to determine and document his progress.
- At the end of the counseling relationship, the counselor and the client review progress and celebrate successes.

Assessment instrument results facilitate clients' decision-making by quantifying their symptoms. The Beck Anxiety Inventory (BAI) and the Beck Depression Inventory (BDI) measure symptoms of two common mental health concerns and are commonly used in mental health settings.

At intake, the client fills one out, and, based on the scores, the counselor and the client decide how to address the symptoms that scored the lowest. That serves as the starting point for goal-setting. (See Chapter 4 for more on assessment.) At the thirty-day review, the client takes the inventory again to determine how the symptoms have changed. If they have changed for the better, the client can see quantifiable evidence of his progress.

If, for example, the client scores very low on the sleeping pattern scale of the BDI at intake, the counselor may discuss with her how a short-term goal should focus on improving sleep. After thirty days of practicing the intervention, the client's BDI shows that the sleep pattern symptom of depression is no longer an issue, thus demonstrating that the intervention was successful.

Multiple **barriers** can affect client goal attainment:
- The client is mandated to treatment and resistant to change.
- The client lied about the problem and/or symptoms.
- The client is ambivalent about making changes to current behaviors.
- The client presents for one problem and does not want help with any others that may contribute to the presenting problem.
- Goals are too broad, vague, or unrealistic.
- Goals are not achievable or coordinated to help the client succeed.
- External factors in the client's life can interfere.
- The wrong intervention is used to help the client achieve her goals.

PRACTICE QUESTION

5. When should a counselor review a client's progress?
   A) on an ongoing basis and at regular review times
   B) at the client's request
   C) when the supervisor requests a review
   D) only at the end of treatment

Client Education

Understanding the Treatment Plan

Counselors use psychoeducation to **educate** clients about the value of complying with their treatment plans. Counseling is an evidence-based practice, and providing clients with psychoeducation helps to demystify the process and empower them to work toward recovery.

Many clients feel overwhelmed and helpless when they present for therapy. **Psychoeducation** helps to validate and normalize their experiences and gives them hope for recovery based on a clear plan. Methods for psychoeducation include the following:
- explaining to clients the purpose of the intake, clinical interview, and assessment process and how these relate to what will happen in therapy
- teaching clients about their diagnosis, what it means, and the evidence-based interventions that result in positive outcomes
- providing clients with a preview of how the interventions will work together to help them succeed with their treatment plans
- explaining how the treatment plan serves as a road map for them to see their progress over time

- following the treatment plan to help both client and counselor determine the effectiveness of interventions
- explaining to clients that treatment plans can be updated at regular review times

PRACTICE QUESTION

6. What purpose is served by educating clients about the value of complying with their treatment plans?
   A) It puts the responsibility of change on the client.
   B) It empowers clients by providing a clear plan for recovery.
   C) It releases the counselor from liability.
   D) It holds clients accountable.

Conditions for Learning

Adult learners have several distinct traits that NCCs should consider while developing client education plans:

- Adult learners are **independent** and **self-directed**. Counselors should actively engage them in the learning process and encourage them to help develop their treatment plans.
- Adult learners are **results-oriented** and **practical**. Counselors should give them information that they can apply immediately.
- Adult learners may be **resistant to change** and will require justification for new behaviors.
- Adult learners may **learn more slowly** than younger learners; however, they may be more skilled at integrating new knowledge with previous experience.

Educational psychologist Benjamin Bloom described three domains of learning:

1. The **cognitive domain** includes collecting, synthesizing, and applying knowledge.
2. The **affective domain** involves emotions and attitudes, including the ability to be aware of emotions and respond to them.
3. The **psychomotor domain** relates to motor skills, including the ability to perform complex skills and create new movement patterns.

When educating clients, counselors should address all three learning domains. For example, a client who is learning about smoking cessation may need to be taught about the negative health impacts of smoking (cognitive domain), how to manage negative emotions related to quitting (affective domain), and how to correctly apply a nicotine patch (psychomotor domain).

To better educate, encourage, and advocate for clients, NCCs should assess clients' sources of **motivation** in the context of managing their health:

- **Intrinsic motivation** is the desire to achieve a goal, seek challenges, or complete a task that is driven by enjoyment and personal satisfaction (like exercising because it is enjoyable).
- **Extrinsic motivation** is the desire to accomplish a goal that is driven by external rewards or punishment (such as exercising to prevent ill health).

Adult clients' **readiness to learn** can be shaped by many factors, including openness to new information, emotional response to illness (for example, denial, anxiety), religious and cultural beliefs, and social support systems. However, just because a client learns the information does not mean her behaviors will change.

The counselor must assess the **functional status** of a client before developing an education plan for him. Doing so ensures that the plan aligns with the client's abilities and capacity to learn. Functional status is evaluated during assessment with the Mental Status Exam.

Mental health literacy is the degree to which an individual can obtain, process, and understand basic information needed to make personal health decisions. Mental health literacy gives clients ownership over their recovery and empowers them to learn the skills necessary to care for themselves. People do not stay in therapy forever, so the more mental health literacy clients have, the better able they are to care for themselves after therapy ends.

Mental health literacy also helps clients communicate their needs to others who are supportive. For example, someone who improves his mental health literacy about his panic disorder can explain to a loved one how to help him if that person is present during a panic attack.

Interventions for clients with low mental health literacy include

- asking clients questions to assess their current knowledge;
- using plain language and short sentences;
- applying the knowledge to the client's situation;
- limiting important points to three or fewer;
- using visual materials, such as videos or models, where possible;
- discussing issues in terms of short periods (less than ten years);
- simplifying procedures and regimens as much as possible.

 DID YOU KNOW?

Client mental health literacy improves as clients become more involved in their own care.

PRACTICE QUESTION

7. A person who struggles with depression explains how his significant other can support him during a depressive episode to help shorten the duration and under what conditions to call his counselor. Which of the following is he demonstrating?

   A) mental health literacy
   B) treatment plan compliance
   C) incompetence
   D) emergency management

Treatment Termination

Discharge planning is the process of planning for the cessation of treatment. In an inpatient setting, it includes planning for the client's exit from services and preparing for aftercare. Discharge planning

- begins at intake;
- considers under what circumstances or conditions treatment will be successful;
- considers the achievement of client goals, including the ability to care for oneself independently, medical equipment or care needed in the home, referrals, available social support, available community resources, and what to do in case of a crisis.

Discharge planning includes **discharge teaching** relevant to the client's treatment plan. Discharge teaching may include

- an explanation of the diagnosis;
- recommendations for aftercare;
- tips for mental health;
- when to consult with a mental health professional if symptoms get worse.

The Termination Process

Counselors must begin with the end in mind. In other words, the termination process starts at intake and assessment. Counselors should explain to clients that counseling is finite and meant to end.

Part of the treatment planning process is estimating the number of sessions required to help clients achieve their goals. When the treatment plan is formulated with the client, the counselor and client agree on how many sessions it will take to complete treatment.

The counselor needs to consider the client's needs as well as how many sessions the client's insurance company will pay for before requiring preauthorization for more sessions. One way the counselor can do this is by asking the client questions such as:

- How will you know you are better?
- How will you know the problem is solved?
- What does recovery look like for you?

Each session should include some time to assess what the client has accomplished thus far toward his goals. As each session passes and the treatment plan review sessions occur, the counselor refers to the number of sessions left and decides with the client how many more sessions are necessary.

Session fading is a technique through which clients may start with one session every week, but as they progress in the treatment plan, they may have a session every other week. This strategy of adding more time in between sessions continues until the client may need only one session every six months until termination.

There are multiple reasons for termination. **Planned termination** may occur for the following reasons:

- The client has successfully completed treatment.
- The client requires a different level of care.
- The counselor is leaving and will not be working in the treatment setting.
- Insurance or the party paying for services will no longer pay.

Unplanned termination is characterized by the following:

- The client no longer shows up for treatment.
- Problems with the therapeutic relationship prompt a referral to another provider.
- The counselor or client experiences an illness or other emergency.
- The client or counselor dies.
- The client is incarcerated (for example, following mandated treatment).

In situations of **counselor-initiated termination**, the counselor decides to terminate the counseling relationship. Common reasons include:

- The counselor is leaving the agency.
- The counselor lacks the expertise to meet the client's specific needs.
- The counseling process is stagnant.
- There is inappropriate conduct involved.

In these cases, the counselor must explain to the client the reasons for termination, document that conversation, and make every reasonable effort to help the client find another provider. If the client refuses the referral, that should also be documented.

In **client-initiated termination**, the client decides to end the relationship. Reasons for this may vary and include the following:

- The client does not like the counselor.
- The client can no longer afford therapy.
- The client does not feel like therapy is helping.
- The client stops attending sessions (unresponsive clients).

When the client terminates the relationship, the counselor should make a reasonable effort to determine the cause for the termination and document it as well as make a reasonable effort to refer the client to another provider.

Counselors should also make a reasonable effort to reach out to unresponsive clients, both administratively to enforce any policies related to missed or canceled appointments and to determine what barriers are keeping the client from participating in therapy. A counselor might be able to address some of these issues to help the client engage with the therapeutic process.

> **HELPFUL HINT**
>
> Allowing for appointments over telehealth platforms or at hours more convenient to the client can reduce premature termination. Some counselors even offer in-home treatment under certain circumstances.

Premature termination occurs when a client stops attending sessions without completing the treatment plan. A counselor should make a reasonable effort to discover why the client terminated prematurely and provide referral information to the client.

Counselors can take steps to prevent premature termination by scheduling appointments in advance, offering reminders, and explaining the counseling process to improve client understanding of the importance of completing therapy.

In some cases, **client resistance to termination** occurs. This may include asking for more sessions, asking for more time, or developing new problems beyond the presenting problem. A client's resistance to termination may indicate unresolved relationship issues. When a client becomes too attached to a counselor, an assessment may reveal additional problems for therapeutic intervention. It may also indicate that the counselor has not established and maintained professional boundaries with the client.

An **exit interview** is a final evaluation of the client's experience and includes:

- determining the client's progress through treatment and a review of what she learned;
- assessing the client's experience in therapy;
- evaluating the counselor's performance;
- discussing how the client can address future issues on her own;
- determining conditions under which the client might return to counseling;
- reviewing what a client can do if she experiences a crisis;
- discussing aftercare options, such as support groups, peer support, and community resources;
- celebrating the client's accomplishments;
- scheduling a check-in session by phone or in person in three to six months.

> **DID YOU KNOW?**
>
> Most states have regulations that outline the requirements for discharge planning and termination, including what efforts must be made to reengage client-initiated or unplanned terminations and how those efforts must be documented.

PRACTICE QUESTION

8. A client is progressing in the treatment plan and feeling better. The counselor suggests reducing sessions to once every two weeks, and possibly once a month thereafter. What process is likely occurring here?

    A) unplanned termination

    B) session fading

    C) client resistance

    D) premature termination

Transitions in Group Membership

Transitions in group membership depend largely on the type of group. Some, like open psychoeducational or support groups, have a purpose that is not dependent on the relationships among group members. In open groups, membership changes frequently, and little attention is required for the members to adjust.

In closed groups, however, the therapeutic process depends significantly on the relationships among group members. Most closed groups have a session limit. For example, the group may meet for ten sessions and be finished at that point. For finite groups, termination is built into the group intervention, with the last sessions devoted to processing the members' feelings about the group ending, discussing if and how the members want to continue their relationships, celebrating accomplishments, reviewing the effectiveness of the group, giving ideas for how to continue using the skills they learned, and saying goodbye. There is also a review of the confidentiality rules that group members agreed on and how they apply after the group ends.

Other groups fall somewhere in between open and closed groups. The counselor facilitating the group needs to pay attention to the quality of relationships that develop among members and, if a member leaves, devote time to process how people feel about that. In cases where the group decides to ask someone to leave, the remaining members might need time to process what happened.

PRACTICE QUESTION

9. Which of the following types of group therapy would be MOST impacted by the unplanned departure of a group member?
    - **A)** an open support group for people struggling with addiction
    - **B)** a psychoeducational group about parenting skills
    - **C)** a closed group about processing childhood trauma
    - **D)** a twelve-session open anger management group

Follow-Up after Discharge

Follow-up with clients after discharge can be important for evaluating the efficacy of treatment for the client as well as the therapeutic process, customer service, aftercare, and education. Approaches for this include the following:

- **Efficacy of treatment evaluations** ask the client to evaluate the counselor and the treatment process after therapy has concluded. These evaluations may provide clients an opportunity to be more honest with their feedback because they are no longer receiving services.
- **Customer service evaluations** provide feedback about the clinic and administration.
- **Aftercare follow-up** may include providing referrals to resources for community-based groups, mental wellness events, or information on what to do in case of relapse.
- **Education** follow-up can include tips for maintaining good mental health or promoting mental wellness events.

Short-term follow-up tends to occur between one and four months after the client completes treatment. Examples of short-term follow-up include

- efficacy of treatment evaluations;
- customer service evaluations;
- aftercare recommendations.

Long-term follow-up takes place six months or more after the client completes treatment. Examples of long-term follow-up include

- efficacy of treatment evaluations;
- education;
- community events;
- newsletter items.

Follow-up techniques may include

- inviting the client to a follow-up session via text, email, or letter six months after termination;
- reaching out to the client in a phone call, email, letter, or questionnaire;
- sending clinic newsletters to clients.

PRACTICE QUESTION

10. Which follow-up practice would counselors find helpful for improving their therapeutic techniques?

- **A)** a treatment evaluation sent thirty days after client discharge
- **B)** a customer service evaluation to rate the clinic's service
- **C)** an educational newsletter that goes out to clients every six months
- **D)** a community resource guide sent to clients after discharge

Answer Key

1. **A)** Everything in the treatment plan must address the diagnosis.

2. **D)** The treatment intervention must be an evidence-based intervention appropriate for the client's diagnosis.

3. **D)** The goal is specific (learn three skills), measurable (reduce anxiety from 10 to 4), attainable (client chose level 4 as reasonable), realistic (not expecting zero anxiety), and time restricted (within three sessions).

4. **C)** The time frame for this goal is three months, which makes it a long-term goal. Short-term goals tend to include time frames of thirty days or less.

5. **A)** Reviewing client progress occurs at multiple levels, including at each session and at regularly set intervals.

6. **B)** Clients are empowered when they learn about how treatment plans will help them recover and the value of complying with these plans.

7. **A)** Mental health literacy is the ability to understand the basic information needed to care for oneself and make decisions. This person demonstrates his understanding of his depressive disorder and tells his significant other how to help him.

8. **B)** In session fading, a client progressing in the treatment plan reduces the frequency of sessions until termination.

9. **C)** Among the members of a closed group processing trauma, relationships are a significant part of the group process.

10. **A)** Clients may be more honest about the counselor's performance when they are no longer receiving services.

6 | Areas of Clinical Focus: Mood and Anxiety

Emotional dysregulation describes the state of expressing oneself in a socially dysfunctional manner secondary to an inability to internally differentiate emotions. Mood disorders and anxiety often distort an individual's ability to process emotions.

Internally distorted emotions impede a person's ability to gauge social context and appropriately express themselves. Often the perceptions of people experiencing emotional dysregulation are skewed such that they feel they have no control over their expressions.

The inability to perceive internal feeling states, whether disordered or not, tends to both create measurable symptoms and serve as a barrier to treatment. Societal norms of living distractedly and mindlessly tend to keep people from realizing that they are struggling with disordered anxiety or worry.

Measurable symptoms as defined in the *Diagnostic and Statistical Manual of Mental Disorders (DSM)* are simply maladaptive coping skills or misguided attempts to regulate emotions. Depending on the symptoms, the grouping may be termed *disordered*.

Anxiety and Stress

Anxiety and Obsessive Thoughts

While the terms *anxiety*, *stress*, and *worry* are often used interchangeably in colloquial parlance, it is important to parse these terms out to better understand clients' experiences and provide them with the appropriate words to label their feeling states:

- **Worry** refers to thoughts that are often perseverative and project a negative outcome.
- **Stress** often accompanies worry and is described as the perceived experience of increased adrenal response:
  - physical agitation

- tightness in the chest
- elevated heart rate (tachycardia)
- quickening of the breath (tachypnea)
- **Anxiety** refers to the combined experiences of ruminating thoughts and psychomotor stress.

These feeling states of stress, worry, and anxiety are often overwhelming. When combined and experienced over an extended period, certain psychological and physical effects are often measured.

A diagnosis of **generalized anxiety disorder (GAD)** includes criteria of prolonged and pervasive worry and anxiety that impede daily functioning. Specifically, a person must experience at least half a year during which the majority of days are wrought with worry and anxiety.

The *DSM-5* requires that an adult have a minimum of three of the following symptoms to satisfy the requirements for a diagnosis of GAD. Children need to have one symptom:

1. restlessness, feeling keyed up or on edge
2. being easily fatigued
3. irritability
4. muscle tension
5. sleep disturbances (difficulty falling or staying asleep or restless, unsatisfying sleep)

Traditional methods for treating GAD include the following:

- **Cognitive behavioral therapy (CBT)** focuses more exclusively on core thoughts and beliefs that are the cause of ruminating thoughts and uncontrollable worry.
- **Dialectical behavior therapy (DBT)** focuses on increasing functioning in terms of interpersonal relationships.
- **Solution-focused brief therapy (SFBT)** involves bringing attention to clients' internally held strengths and developing these into skills to solve their problem behaviors.
- **Motivational interviewing (MI)** brings clients into an actionable mindset to motivate them to change their behaviors.

See Chapter 1 for more on therapeutic interventions.

While efficacy depends greatly on therapeutic alliance, all models address the emotional dysregulation and negative thought patterns of GAD. Both CBT and DBT aim to address and change limiting belief systems by teaching clients skills to regulate emotion through mindfulness and relaxation techniques first. Regulating emotion through relaxation skills alleviates the first line of symptoms (physical), which then gives space for targeting disordered cognitions.

HELPFUL HINT

Dialectical behavior therapy (DBT) is an effective treatment for personality disorders.

DID YOU KNOW?

Motivational interviewing (MI) is often used for substance abuse treatment.

In conjunction with talk therapy models, pharmacologic interventions effectively treat GAD. These interventions include

- selective serotonin reuptake inhibitors (SSRIs);
- serotonin norepinephrine reuptake inhibitors (SNRIs);
- benzodiazepines.

Obsessive-compulsive disorder (OCD) is perhaps most effectively treated with cognitive behavioral therapy. The layperson's understanding of OCD is that of a person who is particular about organization and cleanliness, but OCD actually requires a two-part diagnosis:

1. intense perseverations on unwanted intrusive thoughts
2. compulsive behaviors that function in response to the unwanted thoughts

A person with OCD often believes that these obsessive behaviors will alleviate the anxiety associated with the rumination on intrusive thoughts. However, the behaviors do not improve functioning, decrease anxiety, or curtail intrusive thoughts. The behaviors are often rigid and repetitive. In fact, they decrease the person's ability to function by taking time away from social interactions and work/family obligations.

Clients with OCD often benefit from high dosages of SSRIs to decrease the level of neurological underpinnings that can cause intrusive thought patterns. In conjunction with medication, behavioral modifications and exposure therapy can be implemented through CBT or other models. These interventions allow clients to break their habituated and rigid patterns of behavior while challenging the cognitive distortions that allow them to continue using their maladaptive coping skills.

When someone's intrusive thoughts are memories of past experiences, specifically traumatic experiences, a counselor may consider a diagnosis of **post-traumatic stress disorder (PTSD)**. Certain memories can trigger physiological reactions that cause a person to dissociate, including

- near-death experiences;
- sexual violence;
- serious injury.

These dissociative reactions are called *flashbacks* and are a hallmark of a PTSD diagnosis. Individuals experiencing PTSD are debilitated by their attempts to avoid the triggers that cause their flashbacks.

To address PTSD, a counselor must address the physiological dysregulation before focusing on the emotional and cognitive distress:

- Interventions such as CBT or DBT with a trauma focus must include a commitment to work on distress tolerance or relaxation skills.
- Without decreasing hyperarousal and physiological symptomology, the brain cannot function at the more executive levels necessary for emotional and cognitive reprocessing.

HELPFUL HINT

A PTSD diagnosis differentiates between intrusive thoughts and flashbacks.

DID YOU KNOW?

Treatment models such as EMDR address the neurological underpinnings of a PTSD diagnosis while simultaneously treating negative cognitions and emotional dysregulation.

PRACTICE QUESTION

1. Which of the following is NOT a diagnostic criterion for GAD?
   A) compulsive rituals performed in an attempt to control obsessive thoughts
   B) difficulty concentrating
   C) perseverative negative thoughts that anticipate negative outcomes (worry)
   D) sleep disturbance

Fear and Panic

While the hyperarousal experienced in PTSD is a result of a tangible external trigger, individuals experiencing panic disorder, social anxiety disorder, and separation anxiety disorder have physical anxiety responses that are triggered by internal stimuli. The common thread among these three diagnoses is the fear around an invisible, often irrational threat.

The treatment model involves the same therapeutic interventions and often the same pharmacology as GAD; however, the approach involves a greater focus on affect regulation. Individuals with these disorders, who often experience unpredictable fear and panic, benefit from learning how to identify their internal feeling states. These skills include

- labeling feelings;
- reporting on the severity of distress (for example, using the subjective units of distress scale [SUDS]).
- working on distress tolerance skills to use when feelings become overwhelming.

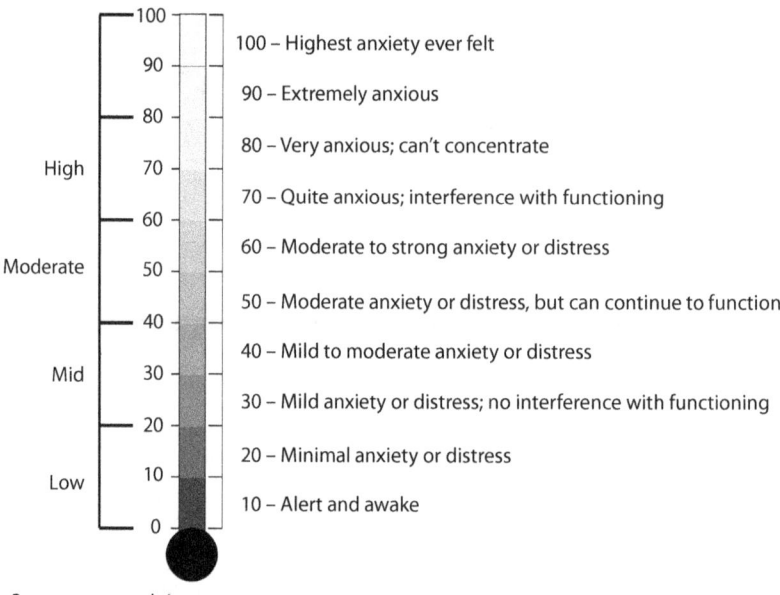

Source: www.mdpi.com

Figure 6.1. SUDS Scale

Using DBT distress tolerance skills in crises can be effective when stress becomes overwhelming and panic sets in. **Panic disorder** is characterized by sudden attacks of overwhelming panic along with constant anticipatory fear of experiencing an attack. Because these attacks are not related to external stimuli, they feel random and uncontrollable to the individual experiencing them.

To be diagnosed with panic disorder, clients must have a minimum of four of the thirteen physical symptoms present during their panic attacks. Additionally, they need to have one month of persistent worry of more panic attacks OR have made significant changes to their behaviors to try to avoid future panic attacks. Their symptoms cannot be caused by drugs and/or alcohol, nor by other mental health concerns. Symptoms associated with panic disorder include

1. palpitations, pounding heart, or accelerated heart rate (tachycardia);
2. sweating;
3. trembling or shaking;
4. sensations of shortness of breath (dyspnea) or smothering;
5. feelings of choking;
6. chest pain or discomfort;
7. nausea or abdominal distress;
8. feeling dizzy, unsteady, light-headed, or faint;
9. chills or heat sensations;
10. paresthesia (numbness or tingling sensations);
11. derealization (feelings of unreality) or depersonalization (being detached from oneself);
12. fear of losing control or "going crazy";
13. fear of dying.

Often, people with panic disorder change their lives to try to avoid having attacks but are unsuccessful. When they come for treatment, CBT/DBT and psychopharmacology are tried-and-true interventions.

Social anxiety disorder presents a similar set of issues wherein the trigger for anxiety is irrational and does not necessarily stem from adverse experiences in the person's past. Typically, there are limiting beliefs and negative cognitions at the root of these anxieties. Clients with social anxiety experience emotional dysregulation in response to feeling watched or judged by others in social settings. Treatment for social anxiety can include

- exposure therapy;
- affect regulation;
- cognitive reprocessing.

Separation anxiety disorder is characterized by chronic worry about real or imagined separation from major attachment figures. The level of emotional dysregulation and distress that individuals experience at even the thought of separation is both developmentally inappropriate and disruptive to some major area of their life. As with social anxiety and panic disorders, therapies to improve emotional regulation, such as CBT and DBT, can help the individual break unhealthy perseverations and obsessive thought patterns.

Family Systems Therapy and other interventions that involve the attachment figure in question are also useful for separation anxiety disorder. If a client presents with a need for family work, the counselor should discuss making a referral. If a client has been working with a counselor for a significant time as an individual, referring her to another practitioner for family work may be in her best interest. Serving as both an individual and family counselor can create dynamics within family sessions that threaten alliance and outcome.

Clients can engage their families in the necessary work by including them in individual therapy to complete assessments or facilitate difficult conversations. In this way, the counselor can empower clients while continuing to maintain the therapeutic relationship. Counselors can also coach their clients to have these conversations at home through role-play during sessions.

PRACTICE QUESTION

2. Which of the following BEST describes panic disorder?
   A) emotional dysregulation in response to feeling watched or judged by others in social settings
   B) being debilitated by flashbacks
   C) attacks of overwhelming panic and constant anticipatory fear of experiencing an attack
   D) chronic worry about real or imagined separation from major attachment figures

Stress

Many effective tools for stress management are widely available thanks to technological advances and cultural interest in mental health and self-care. Typically, **stress management** refers to increasing behaviors or skills that can be implemented throughout the day or at designated times to alleviate the symptoms of stress.

Stress management can help decrease elevated levels of cortisol. Decreasing cortisol is achieved by activating the parasympathetic nervous system and has the following outcomes:
- improved sleep
- prevention of heart disease
- immune system boost

Relaxation techniques tend to center around cultivating the following:
- deep breathing skills
- mindfulness
- meditation practices
- somatic relaxation (such as progressive muscle relaxation)

PRACTICE QUESTION

3. Clinicians can help clients decrease stress by teaching and coaching them to use skills such as

   A) labeling feelings.

   B) DBT distress tolerance.

   C) progressive muscle relaxation.

   D) all of the above.

Mood Disorders

Depression

Depression refers to the state of feeling chronically negative both in mood and cognition. Negative mood includes feelings like

- sadness;
- hopelessness;
- emptiness.

Some examples of negative cognition include

- feelings of self-blame;
- negative self-talk.

Along with negative internal states, individuals with depression also experience physical symptoms that tend toward disparate expressions of either retardation or agitation. These physical symptoms can look like

- an inability to move quickly;
- general fatigue;
- oversleeping;
- physical agitation;
- feeling unable to rest;
- experiencing insomnia.

Major depressive disorder (MDD) and persistent depressive disorder (dysthymia) are differentiated by episodic versus persistent states of depression. In **major depressive disorder (MDD)**, symptoms are experienced for over two weeks and impair daily functioning. An individual needs to have a minimum of five of the following nine symptoms to meet the criteria for MDD:

1. depressed mood most of the day, nearly every day
2. diminished interest or pleasure in all or almost all activities
3. unintended weight loss or gain
4. insomnia or hypersomnia
5. psychomotor agitation or retardation
6. fatigue or loss of energy

7. feeling worthless or having inappropriate guilt
8. inability to concentrate or being indecisive
9. recurrent thoughts of death, suicidal ideation without a plan, a suicide attempt, or a plan to commit suicide

A diagnosis of **dysthymia** (sometimes known as persistent depressive disorder) requires an episodic length of a minimum of two years in adults. Dysthymia can be diagnosed in children and adolescents who experience depressive symptoms most days for at least one year.

Both dysthymia and MDD have numerous specifiers listed in the *DSM-5* that are used to better describe an individual's symptom features to guide providers toward more effective treatment. As a result, conditions such as postpartum depression (PDD) and seasonal affective disorder (SAD) have been incorporated into either a dysthymia or an MDD diagnosis. Under the *DSM-5*, PDD is now MDD/dysthymia with peripartum onset, and SAD is now MDD/dysthymia with seasonal pattern.

Psychopharmacological treatment recommendations vary depending on symptomology dimensions in depression. For example, when symptoms include psychotic features, antipsychotic and antidepressant cotreatment is recommended. In addition to pharmacological interventions, CBT is an effective treatment for MDD. This therapy can improve emotions by changing automatic thoughts and replacing them with healthier thought patterns.

Counselors should be aware that several disorders are comorbid with MDD. According to the *DSM-5*, disorders that are known to occur at the same time as MDD include

- substance use disorders;
- panic disorder;
- obsessive-compulsive disorder;
- anorexia nervosa;
- bulimia nervosa;
- borderline personality disorder.

It is important in all diagnoses—particularly in individuals presenting with depression—to rule out substance abuse as a cause for mood dysregulation:

- The use of amphetamines and other stimulants, as well as some psychedelic substances, can mimic or trigger states of mania.
- Individuals under the influence of depressants such as opioids or benzodiazepines can demonstrate depressive symptoms, such as psychomotor retardation and fatigue.
- Withdrawal from substances can also mimic states of depression.

Bipolar disorders are characterized by extreme changes in mood, concentration, activity levels, and energy. There are three forms of bipolar disorder:

1. **Bipolar I disorder** is characterized by manic episodes of seven days or more and depressive episodes of two weeks or more; hospitalization may be required.

HELPFUL HINT

Individuals presenting with MDD or dysthymia with psychotic features of hallucinations or delusions should be evaluated for bipolar I disorder.

2. **Bipolar II disorder** also presents as a mixture of depressive and hypomanic episodes, but episodes of mania are not as severe as in bipolar I.
3. **Cyclothymia** (rapid cycling bipolar disorder) is characterized by periods of depressive episodes and hypomanic episodes for at least two years (one year in children).

If a client's depression presents with mixed features—which includes states of mania without psychosis and can be congruent to hypomania—the client should be evaluated for both bipolar I and bipolar II disorders. In the case of mixed features, where episodes of depression and mania cycle four or more times within a twelve-month period, the counselor should evaluate for cyclothymia.

A **hypomanic episode** is associated with symptoms that are not as severe as a manic episode. These episodes typically last for about four days, whereas a **manic episode** lasts at least one week.

Hypomanic episodes do lead to changes in behavior; however, individuals experiencing hypomanic episodes do not necessarily need to be hospitalized for their symptoms. On the other hand, a client experiencing a manic episode may need hospitalization. Additionally, people experiencing manic episodes may engage in markedly dangerous behaviors.

TABLE 6.1. Hypomanic Episode Versus Manic Episode

CHARACTERISTICS OF HYPOMANIC EPISODE	CHARACTERISTICS OF MANIC EPISODE
• mild to moderate symptoms	• severe symptoms
• four days duration	• seven days or more duration
• does not need hospitalization	• may need hospitalization
• no functional impairment	• engages in dangerous behaviors

Suicidality in depressed individuals, particularly those affected with bipolar disorders, is both typical and highly concerning. Suicidal ideation is a criterion of depression and should be addressed directly both during intake and treatment without fail. The *DSM-5* states that while having a history of suicide attempts is serious, most individuals who complete suicide do not have failed attempts of suicide. Other factors that can increase a person's risk are

- being a male;
- living alone;
- being single;
- feeling hopelessness;
- living with borderline personality disorder.

Individuals experiencing suicidality have been proven to experience an alleviation of symptoms when they are directly asked about their thoughts around suicide and dying. The myth that talking about suicidal thoughts only makes them worse has been disproved by research and serves only to maintain the shame that increases rates of suicide.

Perhaps a lesser-known fact about suicidality is that those who have successfully created a plan to commit suicide, have decided on, and are in the process of enacting their suicide tend to demonstrate a good mood. Signs to look for include sudden and inexplicable elevation in mood, giving away personal objects of value, disclosure of a specific plan, or complete isolation from any or all areas of life.

Safety plans and safety contracts are often mandated procedures and can be useful tools for broaching disclosure around suicidality. Taking a person-centered, culturally sensitive approach and allowing the individual to express his thoughts and feelings without judgment is the first step to effective treatment. A treatment provider helps the client investigate and identify resources for both internal and external security. An effective treatment method for suicidality is helping the client identify **protective factors**. These may include

- reasons for living;
- life skills;
- coping skills;
- social connections;
- relationships;
- future goals.

PRACTICE QUESTION

4. What is the best way to bring up the topic of suicidality during a counseling session?
    A) not mention it until the client brings it up
    B) talk about how and why suicide is wrong
    C) directly address the client's concerns
    D) call 911

Other Mood Disorders

Several other mood disorders should be noted. **Disruptive mood dysregulation disorder (DMDD)** is a newly named diagnosis from the *DSM-5* created for childhood bipolar-type mood disorder. This diagnosis can only be made with individuals ages six through eighteen:

- Like a bipolar diagnosis, major mood lability and severe emotional dysregulation are described.
- Because depression is often experienced and expressed as anger in children, individuals with DMDD present with irritability and tantrums.
    - There must be at least three outbursts per week.
    - The outbursts must have been occurring for at least a year.

Intermittent explosive disorder (IED) is a diagnosis similar to DMDD within the mood disorder family. A diagnosis used for children, the criteria for IED describe significantly aggressive, destructive, and violent behaviors. The onset of behaviors associated with this diagnosis typically begins in late childhood or adolescence.

An IED diagnosis requires that the individual has verbal outbursts OR a minimum of three behavioral outbursts that involve the destruction of property. The magnitude of the outburst must be extreme for the situation and not be premeditated.

Individuals with this diagnosis can experience distress from their reactions or impairment in their interpersonal and occupational functioning. The outbursts will continue to arise for several years and can be episodic.

Clients with IED benefit from relational therapy and approaches that are mindful of attachment theory. Diagnoses of IED, if untreated, develop into conduct disorder in adolescence and antisocial personality disorder in adulthood.

Premenstrual dysphoric disorder (PMDD) is a diagnosis for those individuals who regularly experience significant emotional dysregulation and symptoms of depression during their menstrual cycle. Potential differential diagnoses for PMDD include

- premenstrual syndrome;
- dysmenorrhea;
- bipolar disorder;
- major depressive disorder;
- persistent depressive disorder.

The onset of premenstrual dysphoric disorder can occur at any point once menarche begins. For many, symptoms worsen when menopause begins. The treatment for PMDD should include consultations with medical professionals including but not limited to an OB-GYN and endocrinologist.

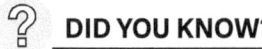

DID YOU KNOW?

As opposed to DMDD, children with IED are less triggered by internal feeling states (mood) and more likely to have significant attachment-related trauma or misalignment.

PRACTICE QUESTION

5. If the same symptoms that describe DMDD in children are found in adults, they would be an indication of which diagnosis?

    A) panic disorder
    B) bulimia nervosa
    C) bipolar-type mood disorder
    D) antisocial personality disorder

Other Issues

Grief and Loss

Grief refers to the state of being that results from experiencing the loss of a meaningful person or relationship. While the ways an individual experiences grief can generally be defined by culture, personality, psychology, and spirituality, people ultimately express grief in intensely personal and varied ways. The widely accepted stages of grief are

- denial/shock;
- guilt/pain;
- anger/bargaining;
- depression;
- acceptance/integration.

It was once believed that these stages occurred in succession; however, people tend to experience these stages in cycles that take various lengths of time and can repeat or restart. For example, an individual may jump from denial to anger, return to pain, move toward acceptance and then back to denial within a day. Or an individual may stay in denial for months at a time and experience other feelings subconsciously or in an otherwise repressed state.

Denial is a protective state that allows people experiencing overwhelming pain to feel a window of tolerance so they can function in their daily lives. However, denial can serve as a subterfuge and facilitate a lack of emotional awareness in other areas of life. Sometimes, those experiencing early stages of grief report feeling "fine" and do not feel they have changed since their loss. Still, spouses or family members may notice changes in behavior (increased isolation or mood lability).

If people in denial are truly struggling to experience and express their feelings, they can become defensive toward situations or people who encourage vulnerability. A safe space can feel like a threat when the feelings being denied are too painful. Denial can become a dangerous pressure cooker of resentment or fear that then motivates maladaptive coping skills or masking behaviors, such as using alcohol/drugs, misrepresenting feelings, and avoiding social connections.

Group therapy can be an effective treatment for those who share a common loss. For example, a group for recently divorced people or for parents who lost children can allow these individuals to process their grief together. Group therapy allows clients to create and maintain relationships in the aftermath of losing important connections.

Isolation results from the masking behaviors associated with denial in the grief process. In isolation, the other stages of grief can become harder to manage. Whether one is dealing with anger, depression, pain, or guilt, connecting with others who are also experiencing similar stages allows those difficult feelings to be acknowledged and mindfully dealt with rather than ignored and perpetuated.

Complicated grief is also known as **persistent complex bereavement disorder (PCBD)** and can be diagnosed when the grieving process significantly impairs the individual's functioning six months after the loss. Persistent complex bereavement disorder can result from a lack of supportive environment; in other words, an environment that promotes isolation and repression will likely extend the process of bereavement.

Traumatic losses, such as the violent death of a loved one, witnessing the death of a loved one, or experiencing multiple deaths in a short period can lead to PCBD. A history of mental illness or substance use can also interfere with the normal process of healing grief, which then results in complications. These complications can include symptoms that are typical in depressive episodes, such as suicidality, emotional numbness, and loss of interest in hobbies.

PRACTICE QUESTION

6. Which of the following BEST describes grief?
   A) Grief is the same for all human beings.
   B) Grief is best dealt with alone.
   C) Grief is easier to process when there is an underlying mental illness.
   D) Grief is the emotional experience that comes after loss.

Developmental and Intellectual Functioning

Intellectual and developmental disabilities (IDDs) encompass a number of disabilities that generally impede a person's ability to

- retain and process information;
- independently solve problems;
- reason;
- perform activities of daily living.

These disabilities result from neurological differences that typically become apparent by the age of two, but they can start any time before the age of eighteen. Some diagnoses that fall under this category are:

- ADD/ADHD
- autism spectrum disorder (ASD)
- cerebral palsy
- Down syndrome
- other genetic disorders

People with IDDs can experience issues with the sensory systems (visual, auditory, olfactory, tactile, and gustatory) and struggle to control their experiences of external stimuli. Noises can feel too loud, lights can seem too bright, and certain food textures/tastes/smells can trigger disgust.

These sensory processing disorders can cause both emotional dysregulation (such as frustration from feeling overwhelmed by stimuli) and difficulties or delays in cognition (for example, formulating thoughts at a slower rate due to distraction).

Adaptive responses to overstimulation and difficulty directing focus can manifest as symptoms of self-stimulatory behavior (stimming) or hyperfocus:

- **Stimming** often includes repetitive movements or vocalizations.
- These symptoms function as a control of stimuli.
- Stimming helps people on the autism spectrum control which sense stimulations are experienced and creates a sense of comfort in familiar feelings.
- Stimming serves to regulate emotions.

Similarly, individuals with ADD/ADHD might focus a conversation on preestablished topics of interest or fixate their attention on one activity for extended periods to avoid being overwhelmed by the input of new information. This cognitive rigidity and perseverative behavior can be observed in people with ASD as well.

People with schizophrenia also experience similar difficulties directing their focus, the difference being that their internal processes (thoughts, feelings, beliefs, and so forth) are experienced in the same way that external stimuli are experienced:

- Hallucinations can be seen as projections of mind, and feeling states and are not differentiable from real visual/auditory experiences.
- The delusional component of a schizophrenic diagnosis functions as an organizational schema to explain the client's reality.

Humans establish theories to explain the phenomena they perceive; for those whose experiences are altered by psychoses and hallucinations, which are not shared by the people or communities around them, conceptualizations of reality are necessarily egocentric and function within uncommon structures of logic.

Intellectual and developmental disabilities that directly impact the nervous system can result in motor control issues, such as difficulties with

HELPFUL HINT

Certain neurological impacts might also lead to seizures.

- speech;
- language;
- dexterity;
- general ambulation.

Affected intellectual aptitude and learning difficulties can be measured through IQ testing, which can qualify individuals for social supports and government programming. Early childhood testing and interventions significantly increase the potential for people with IDDs to function more independently. Therapies can teach adaptive skills and replace maladaptive behaviors to improve outcomes in areas of social life, schooling, and employment. These include

- applied behavior analysis (ABA) therapy;
- speech therapy;
- occupational therapy.

PRACTICE QUESTION

7. Which of the following BEST describes people diagnosed with ADD/ADHD and/or ASD?

    A) They must be diagnosed before the age of two.

    B) They may struggle with regulating sensory stimulation.

    C) They cannot benefit from emotional regulation skills training.

    D) They are incapable of forming close social relationships.

Answer Key

1. **A)** Performing compulsive rituals to control obsessive thoughts is a diagnostic criterion for obsessive compulsive disorder (OCD), not generalized anxiety disorder (GAD). Anxiety disorder may present with either obsessive thoughts or perseverative behaviors, but rituals that are specifically motivated by a misguided attempt to control anxiety are characteristic of OCD.

2. **C)** Panic disorder is characterized by sudden attacks of overwhelming panic and fear of having an attack.

3. **D)** Labeling feelings, dialectical behavior therapy distress tolerance, and progressive muscle relaxation are all techniques counselors can use to help clients decrease stress.

4. **C)** The counselor should directly address suicidality. By naming the observable symptoms and introducing the topic of suicide without hesitation, the counselor is practicing validation by acknowledging the client's experiences and expressions. Validation of often shameful feeling/thought states, such as suicidality, can create a sense of safety and vulnerability. This safe space and intimacy are therapeutic because, although suicidality is an isolating experience, it is alleviated through connection. Feeling safe can also trigger the parasympathetic nervous system and decrease agitation associated with anxiety and depression. Counselors can then begin the process of risk assessment by asking about suicidal thoughts or plans. Counselors should use assessment tools to guide their questions so they can plan for safety using appropriate next steps.

5. **C)** Similar to a bipolar diagnosis, major mood lability and severe emotional dysregulation are described. Because children often experience and express depression as anger, individuals with disruptive mood dysregulation disorder (DMDD) present with irritability and tantrums.

6. **D)** Grief is best described as the emotional experience that comes after loss. People manifest, process, and experience grief differently.

7. **B)** People diagnosed with ADD/ADHD and autism spectrum disorder (ASD) often struggle to regulate sensory stimulation.

7 | Areas of Clinical Focus: Family and Relationships

Families are an intrinsic part of our cultural fabric. The traditional nuclear family consists of a mother, father, and children; however, our understanding of family has shifted quite a bit over time. Today, single parenthood is common and accepted, as are families in which two parents are the same gender. In other families, grandparents or other relatives may serve as the primary caregivers of children.

Historically, a **couple** was defined as a man and a woman in a romantic relationship. Today, we understand couples to be two people in a romantic relationship, regardless of gender identity. Some couples may open their relationship to other people, such as in a **polyamorous** relationship.

Marriage is a union between a couple that grants them certain privileges and responsibilities. The main legal advantages include tax benefits and the right to make end-of-life decisions should a partner become incapacitated.

In the United States, the Defense of Marriage Act was ruled unconstitutional in 2013, paving the way for the Supreme Court's ruling in 2015 that same-sex marriage is legal and must be recognized by all states. Since then, anyone of any gender can marry whomever they please under the law.

Relationships

Social Interactions and Support Systems

Social support systems are an integral part of a healthy functioning life and are comprised of the people a person can turn to with emotional, physical, or spiritual needs. Social support systems may include

- friends;
- family members;
- practitioners;
- religious congregations;
- clergy;

- mentors;
- teachers;
- neighbors;
- other community members.

Family of origin and close friends make up the majority of most people's support networks. Church congregations, clergy, mentors, teachers, neighbors, and other community leaders may make up part of the wider network of a person's support system.

Strong support systems are ideally rich in depth and breadth, with a variety of people who can offer different levels of support. People with a robust social support network can more easily deal with life challenges, such as financial difficulties, health issues, or relationship problems.

Counselors can help clients understand their current social systems and how they function by examining their systemic patterns of interaction. One way counselors do this is through the use of a genogram.

A **genogram** is a tool used by counselors and mental health professionals to help clients make sense of their family relationships so they can better understand where patterns of healthy and unhealthy behaviors are arising. Genograms have many different forms, but most have several elements in common, for example

- squares represent men;
- circles represent women;
- lines between shapes represent relationships.

Some genograms can be simple, like the one in Figure 7.1., while others can be more complex, with different types of lines representing different elements of a relationship. For example, zigzag lines might represent a hostile relationship, while dotted lines might represent estrangement.

Another tool for describing relationships is an ecomap. Instead of focusing on individual relationships like genograms do, **ecomaps** explore broader systems

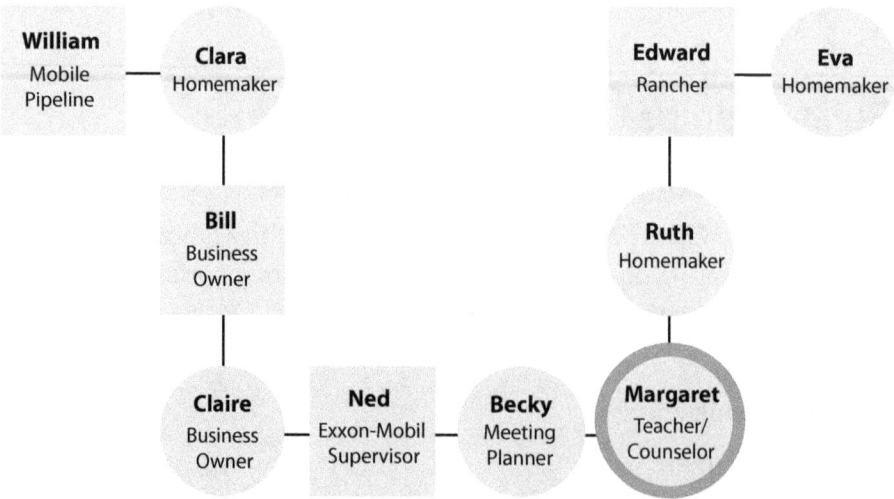

Figure 7.1. Genogram

in a person's life. Small systems like the immediate family, sibling relationships, and extended family might be included on an ecomap. But ecomaps also focus on other systems, such as

- academic obligations/school environment;
- community or professional organizations;
- work/career relationships;
- religious communities;
- legal obligations.

An ecomap reveals the influence that external systems have on a client. For example, a client who is attending university and struggling in her classes might attribute her stress to the university system. This may influence other systems, such as family relationships. As with a genogram, different types of lines and shapes can be used to customize the ecomap to each individual's experience.

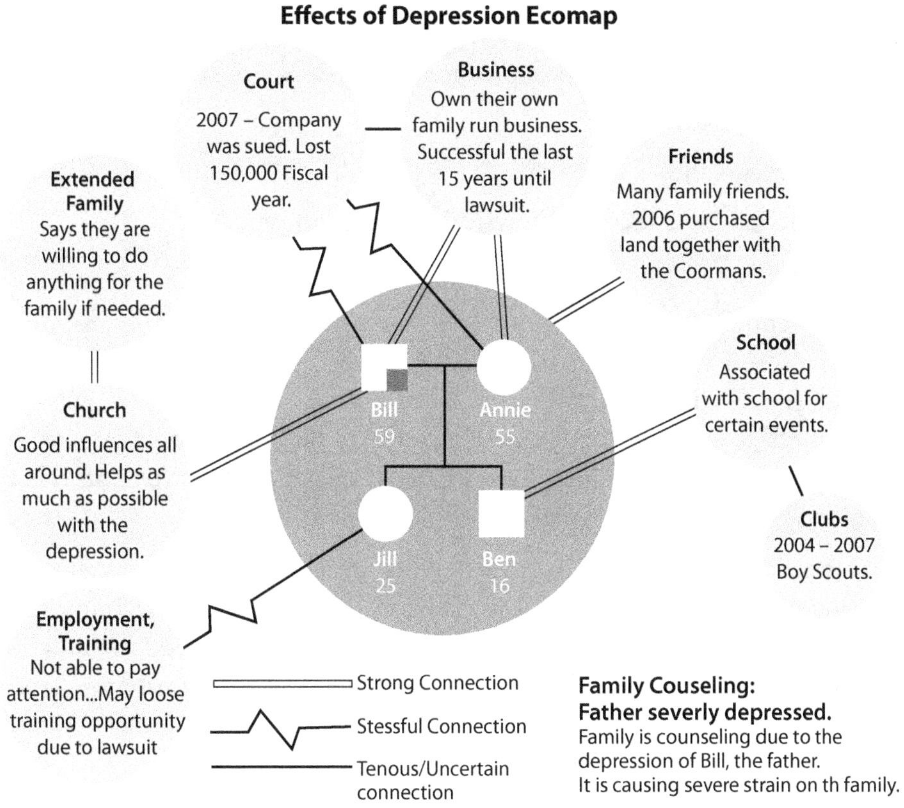

Effects of Depression Ecomap

Court
2007 – Company was sued. Lost 150,000 Fiscal year.

Business
Own their own family run business. Successful the last 15 years until lawsuit.

Friends
Many family friends. 2006 purchased land together with the Coormans.

Extended Family
Says they are willing to do anything for the family if needed.

Church
Good influences all around. Helps as much as possible with the depression.

School
Associated with school for certain events.

Clubs
2004 – 2007 Boy Scouts.

Employment, Training
Not able to pay attention...May loose training opportunity due to lawsuit

Bill 59, Annie 55, Jill 25, Ben 16

= Strong Connection
∿ Stessful Connection
— Tenous/Uncertain connection

Family Couseling:
Father severly depressed.
Family is counseling due to the depression of Bill, the father. It is causing severe strain on th family.

Figure 7.2. Ecomap

Some clients have very poorly developed support systems. This is especially common among adults who experienced abuse as children, since their family ties may be tenuous. Individuals with weak support systems are at high risk for feelings of loneliness and depression. **Loneliness** and depression can lead a person to retreat even further from society despite craving social interaction. Counselors should encourage clients struggling with loneliness to work on the following:

- strengthening existing support systems
- expanding new support systems

- taking on new hobbies
- joining communities with like-minded individuals

The counselor may discover unhealthy **interactional patterns** that stem from the client. For example, a client who habitually breaks up with his girlfriend after two to three months might be avoiding intimacy and vulnerability. Some approaches to use with this client may include

- learning to identify intimacy fears,
- developing coping strategies to self-soothe when faced with anxiety over intimacy.

Some relationships may take on a specific pattern known as codependency. **Codependency** is a type of relationship dynamic in which a partner enables the other partner's destructive habits, such as addiction, immaturity, or irresponsibility. The enabling partner may take on a role of self-sacrifice and feelings of responsibility for others' actions and behaviors, and thus may experience boundary issues and enmeshment. People who are codependent tend to have

- high rates of anxiety or depression;
- compulsions;
- hypervigilance;
- experiences of recurrent physical or sexual abuse;
- possible addiction issues.

Codependency patterns are typically rooted in childhood issues, often among children who were parentified or whose feelings were ignored or punished. When the child grows up, he might ignore his own feelings and deny himself, feeling that he does not deserve to be treated well. People who are codependent may even have been expected to care for their parents due to addiction or mental health issues.

Counselors working with clients who are codependent may start by exploring childhood patterns and working to identify how those impact the client's current life. From there, issues such as developing healthy boundaries, sharing one's feelings, and building self-esteem can be introduced to allow the client to work toward better relationships.

HELPFUL HINT

In their relationships, individuals who are codependent may help their partners maintain unhealthy behaviors by enabling them, despite insisting that they want the behavior to end. Typically, this is motivated by a desire to be needed by their partner.

PRACTICE QUESTION

1. Tammy and Fred have been married for over twenty-five years and are seeking counseling for Fred's alcoholism. They describe their relationship as very close and say they could not live without each other. Despite that, Tammy expresses exhaustion and disappointment with Fred's frequent drinking and subsequent poor behavior. On further questioning, the counselor learns that Tammy is the only one who does the grocery shopping and purchases all the alcohol for Fred, despite insisting that it is all his doing. What is the BEST response?

    A) recommend that Fred immediately enter a detox and rehab program to get his drinking under control

- B) pull Tammy aside and screen for domestic violence to see if Fred is forcing her to purchase the alcohol
- C) recommend that Fred begin doing the shopping with Tammy to make sure she does not purchase more alcohol
- D) broach the possibility that Tammy might be maintaining Fred's behavior by purchasing the alcohol for him

Dating and Marriage

For many people, **dating and marriage** are important parts of a fulfilling life. At the same time, they pose challenges. Some common disagreements that can arise in dating and marriage concern

- finances/the use of money;
- sex;
- the division of household labor;
- levels of trust.

Ultimately, the root of most relationship issues can be traced back to communication problems. Unspoken expectations, unkind language, and difficulty discussing feelings can all make healthy communication about difficult topics nearly impossible. Counselors should work with clients on identifying their communication styles and practicing building healthier communication habits.

Despite a desire to remain in one committed relationship, many people do end up remarrying or entering into more than one long-term relationship in their life. **Remarriage** can come with its own unique set of challenges, including

- a larger network of people involved in the relationship (for example, children, ex-partners, co-parents);
- a renegotiation of family boundaries;
- getting used to sharing a space again.

As with all relationships, counselors should work with remarried couples and families to practice healthy communication, respect of boundaries, and ways to increase love and acceptance within the family unit.

PRACTICE QUESTION

2. George (fifty-eight) and Mary (fifty-four) are widows who recently remarried. They both have adult children who visit often. Tensions have started arising among the children: George's children complain that Mary takes up too much of George's time, and Mary's children do not like how George's children treat her. How can the counselor help?
    - A) ask the children to work it out among themselves as adults
    - B) encourage Mary's children to continue standing up for their mother
    - C) advise the couple to separate themselves from the children for a while to strengthen their bond as newlyweds
    - D) work with the family on identifying the main sources of conflict and practicing healthy communication and boundaries

Relationship Conflict

Communication problems are often the root of many sources of discord in relationships. Learning effective communication techniques to demonstrate care and respect for a partner in times of disagreement can smooth over many stressful interactions. Some of the most common unhealthy communication patterns are described in Table 7.1.

TABLE 7.1. Unhealthy Communication Patterns			
PATTERN	**DESCRIPTION**	**EXAMPLES**	**IMPACT**
"You" statements and directives	• Directives tell the other person what to do. • "You statements" focus on the partner instead of the speaker.	• "You are so rude to me." • "You need to be a better listener." • "You are lazy/sloppy/ irresponsible." • "You have to meet my needs."	Nobody likes being told what to do. Using "you" language conveys negativity and criticism toward the receiving partner and does not actually communicate how the behavior is making the speaker feel or what the speaker would like done differently.
Universal statements	Universal statements often include the words *always* or *never*, *everyone*, *usually*, or *again*.	• "You always interrupt me." • "You never put your clothes in the laundry." • "Everyone says you are lazy." • "You forgot to pick up the mail AGAIN."	These types of statements tell a partner that there is no room for any other kind of behavior from her, which can be hurtful and shut down communication. Such critical statements focus on *who* the listener is as a person, not *what* behaviors the speaker would like addressed.
Personalization	This technique focuses on *who* the person is, instead of what they are doing that is problematic.	• "You are such a jerk." • "You are really stupid."	In the first example, it could be that the speaker is feeling hurt by something the listener said. By choosing to personalize the statement, the speaker loses focus on the undesired behavior (the listener's unkind words). Such statements perpetuate hurt and prevent intimacy and vulnerability.

PATTERN	DESCRIPTION	EXAMPLES	IMPACT
Invalidation	This occurs when one partner expresses a hurt, desire, want, or need, and the partner dismisses or undermines these feelings.	• "Why are you so upset about this?" • "I don't see what the big deal is." • "This happened to me before; I didn't cry about it."	Having a vulnerable thought or feeling ignored, dismissed, or belittled drives a wedge between partners and communicates to the hurt person that his feelings do not matter to his partner.

Counselors can work with their clients to identify which unhealthy communication patterns they are engaging in and help them replace these with more effective communication patterns. Healthier communication patterns include

- focusing on "I" statements;
- focusing on communicating feelings;
- demonstrating love and respect throughout the conversation (for example, through words or even small actions, like holding hands).

Intimate partner violence (IPV) occurs when one or both partners in a relationship engage in physical violence, sexual violence, stalking, or psychological aggression against the other:

- Globally, about one in three women will experience IPV in their life.
- Men can also experience IPV, though less is known about the statistical frequency.

The violence rarely decreases, making IPV a very dangerous situation. In fact, the violence typically increases over time and can lead to the death of the person experiencing the violence.

Abuse tends to follow a very predictable cycle of tension, outburst, honeymoon period, and calm. As tensions arise and emotions get heated,

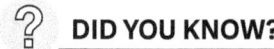

DID YOU KNOW?

Invalidation is an extremely harmful communication pattern in a relationship because it typically occurs after a moment of vulnerability on the other partner's part.

HELPFUL HINT

Universal statements are typically used with "you" statements.

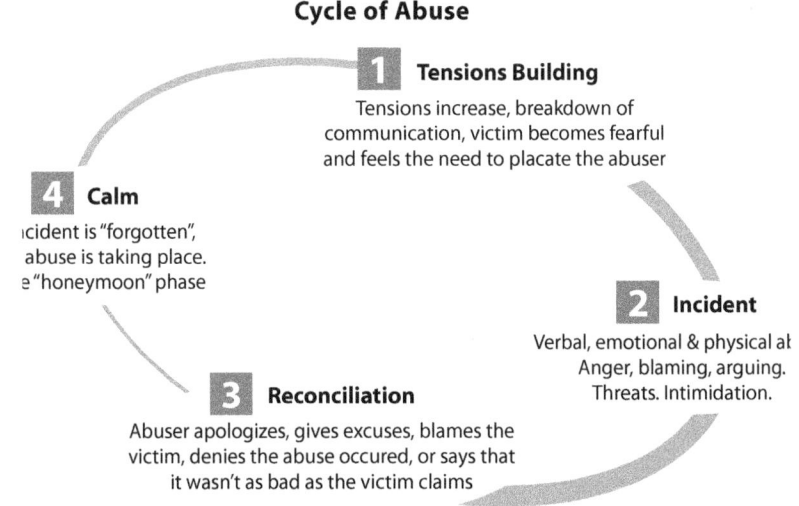

Figure 7.3. Cycle of Abuse

incidents with various levels of verbal and physical abuse, sexual coercion, and psychological abuse arise.

After the incident, the attacker will often be contrite: she may apologize, promise to make it up to the other person, or even agree to go to counseling or other treatments. Then there is a period of calm when there are no incidents, leading the person experiencing the abuse to fall into a lull of false security.

Counselors working with people experiencing IPV must keep an open door of communication and encourage their clients to develop a safety plan. Client **safety plans** could include

- moving money to a separate account;
- seeking employment or skill development;
- having a safe person with whom the client can move in if a decision to leave is made.

People who experience abuse may take years to leave their partner—if they ever do. Certain factors that prompt someone to stay in an abusive relationship include

- financial dependence;
- shared children;
- a hope that the relationship will improve.

Divorce is the legal dissolution of a marriage. Divorce is a high-stress time in a client's life, typically involving the ending of a years- or even decades-long relationship in which all of one's financial assets are tied up with another person. The emotional, financial, and logistical stresses of divorce can be overwhelming.

Counselors can work with clients to build up their support systems to help cushion the pain of a divorce, develop coping skills outside of the relationship, and learn how to live alone after many years of sharing a life.

PRACTICE QUESTION

3. Denise and her husband, Tony, have come to counseling to seek help with their relationship. They report fighting constantly and having difficulties resolving issues. During intake, Tony remarks, "This won't help anyway; Denise never listens to anyone." What negative communication pattern is Tony engaging in?

   A) "you" statements

   B) universalization

   C) personalization

   D) invalidation

Childhood and Family Issues

Family composition can take many forms:
- Some families consist of single parents.
- Grandparents sometimes take the role of parents.
- Other relatives may be primary or secondary caregivers.
- Cousins may be raised in the same household.
- Families can also include stepparents and step- and half-siblings.

Cultural background may significantly influence the family composition. For example, many Asian families live with grandparents in the home who serve as patriarchs and may also provide an important role in caregiving and teaching cultural traditions. Counselors should assume an attitude of cultural humility and learn from clients how their unique family systems function at their best in order to support them within their own cultural values.

Not every family is based entirely on biological kinship. A person's **family of origin** might be the family he lives with. People who were adopted, who live with foster parents, or who move out to be on their own may consider other significant people to be their family. Regardless of where people live, their family of origin can have a significant influence on their outlook on life, their values, and how they interact with the world.

Family member interactions vary widely from family to family. Exploring these themes can be enlightening, especially for adult clients who may be struggling in areas such as intimacy and healthy romantic relationships. The following questions can help clients better understand their own behaviors:
- What did their parents' relationship look like?
- Was it loving and communicative, or abusive?
- What were the parent-child dynamics like?
- How were children viewed in the family?
- What about gender roles?
- Were there healthy boundaries in the family or minimal boundaries?

The Family Life Cycle

The **family life cycle** is typically divided into six stages, each with its own **stage-critical tasks**:

1. **Leaving home**: developing self-identity, differentiating from family
2. **Marriage**: adjustment to and development of a satisfying married life, adjusting to a new kin network, navigating family planning
3. **Families with young children**: adjusting to the high needs of infants and toddlers, creating a satisfying family life for all members
4. **Families with adolescents**: encouraging academic success and planning for their future, balancing freedom with responsibility

5. **Launching children**: supporting young adults as they navigate careers, college, and relationships
6. **Families in later life**: coping with loss, living alone, adjusting to retirement

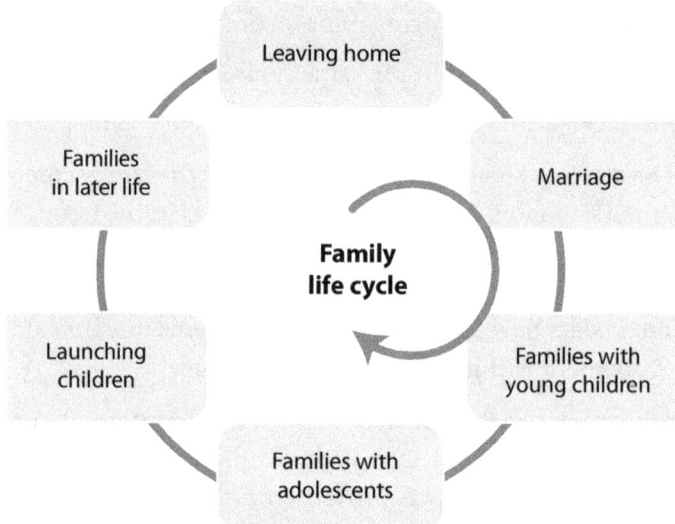

Figure 7.4. Family Life Cycle Stages

A counselor should know which stage in the family life cycle the client is in. That way, the counselor can determine what key areas the client is likely to be struggling with and what areas he needs to succeed in to feel accomplished and ready for the next stage.

Extended families can offer a wealth of resources and joy; they can also contribute to family friction. When couples or young people diverge from the rest of the family's values, it can disrupt family norms and cause friction. Clients who are struggling with extended family relations may benefit from identifying boundaries to keep within their family and how to honor them in a way in which they are comfortable.

PRACTICE QUESTION

4. Marta (twenty-six) and her fiancé, John (twenty-eight), have been having some difficulties with their family relations. Marta's family is very religious and wants their wedding to be held in the Catholic church. While John is an atheist and does not wish to be wed in a church, Marta is ambivalent about a church wedding. How can the counselor help them?

   A) help the couple identify the pros and cons of either acquiescing to the family or doing what they prefer
   B) explain to John the importance of integrating with his new family
   C) encourage the couple to compromise
   D) work with Marta on setting better boundaries with her family

Children and Parenting

Parenting and co-parenting can be difficult processes, especially when parents have different ideas about how to raise kids. For example, one parent may take a more relaxed approach, while the other has a more active style.

Inconsistency in the home environment can create childhood stressors and leave kids feeling confused and out of control. Wherever there is confusion or ambivalence, parents need to discuss the issues with each other and let the kids know what the expectations are for the family.

Co-parenting (joint parenting with an ex-partner) can present its own unique set of challenges. Since the children are staying with each parent separately, co-parents may not be aligned in parenting style or rules. Short of legitimate concerns of abuse or neglect, co-parents need to trust each other with their children's care and work to let go of less significant issues, such as one parent allowing a later bedtime or more sweets. Counselors can help their clients by working on

- recognizing the importance of their children having strong and healthy relationships with both parents;
- learning to let go of control over how their child is parented when at the other parent's house.

Many parents come to counseling to seek help with children's **behavioral problems**. This can include behaviors like fighting in school, defiance in the home, refusal to do homework, or elevated sibling rivalries.

Sometimes a child's behavior may be unpleasant but is ultimately age appropriate and not a significant cause for concern, such as when a four-year-old experiments with "naughty" words. Consistency is a big part of working with children with behavioral issues, and counselors may need to work extensively with parents to improve consistent and measured responses to behavioral issues. Parents must not become emotionally reactive themselves when their child is misbehaving; instead, they should be a source of calm and measured expectations.

A common reason parents may bring their child into counseling is because the child is experiencing **bullying**. In the past, bullying was seen as a normal part of childhood, but it is now recognized as a phenomenon that can have a lasting negative effect on a child's well-being and self-worth. Bullied children are often targeted because they appear vulnerable—they may have few friends and already experience low self-esteem. Counselors can work with children on how to improve confidence and self-esteem, which can make attacks less threatening, as well as how to seek out positive peer friendships in the classroom or other settings.

Some children—especially those who are very young—may go through periods of **separation anxiety** when apart from their families:

- In very young children (under age three) this is a normal developmental stage.
- If the anxiety is overwhelming even at school age, intervention may be necessary.

Separation anxiety may be triggered by

- a stressful life event;
- stress or separation anxiety on the part of the parent.

Children who experience distress at separating from their parents often imagine that something bad will happen to them or their parents when they are not together, leaving them alone in the world. In some children, the anxiety can be so severe that they are distressed at the idea of going to school or playing alone with other kids. Counselors can help children by

- practicing cognitive behavioral therapy (CBT) techniques to manage emotions;
- involving the parents in helping to support the child with her anxiety.

Child development issues, such as autism spectrum disorder, attention-deficit hyperactivity disorder (ADHD), and learning disabilities, can be very stressful for parents. Getting a diagnosis, learning about treatment, and advocating for a child is an involved process that can wear parents thin. Counselors can support clients by

- helping them manage their own stress using techniques like CBT and developing positive coping strategies;
- connecting parents with services and providers in schools and communities, which can ease the burden of care.

💡 **HELPFUL HINT**

See Chapter 6 for more information on intellectual and developmental delays.

A wide support system of friends, family, and neighbors can also help decrease the stress associated with raising children who have developmental delays.

PRACTICE QUESTION

5. Deborah is a single mom to Chloe (age nine). Deborah was recently in a car accident and had to stay in the hospital overnight. Ever since the accident, Chloe has been clinging to Deborah's side. She cries easily and refuses to stay with her grandparents alone even though she used to love going to their house on weekends. How can the counselor help Chloe?

   A) Chloe and Deborah can engage in family counseling to learn coping skills for separation anxiety.

   B) Chloe should be referred to a child specialist for PTSD.

   C) The counselor should inquire if there is possible abuse going on with the grandparents.

   D) The counselor should observe if Deborah has been neglecting Chloe since the accident.

Blended Families and Adoption

Adoption is the process of parents raising a nonbiological child as if that child were their own biological child. Adoption can occur within families (such as kinship adoptions from grandparents or aunts and uncles), or it can take place with someone who is not a relative:

- Some adoptions are informal (never legally recognized). This may happen within extended families.
- In other adoptions, the caregivers go through a legal process to become the legal parents of the adoptee.

Despite the many benefits of adoption, it can be a fraught process for adoptees. There are seven core issues that are common among adoptees:

1. **Loss**: the loss of one's birth parents, relatives, and perhaps even culture/language
2. **Rejection**: feelings of abandonment that trigger feelings of rejection by the birth family
3. **Guilt and shame**: internalizing that the adoption was their fault, that they were given up because they were "too difficult" or not good enough
4. **Grief**: the grief of losing one's birth family, which is closely tied to loss
5. **Identity**: cultural, medical, and biological identities that come into play; integrating the past identity of an adoptee with his present identity
6. **Intimacy**: the emotional issues surrounding adoption that may cause a child to withdraw in an effort to self-protect
7. **Mastery/control**: a feeling of helplessness and a sense that the adoptee's life is out of her hands

HELPFUL HINT

It is important to provide an open and nonjudgmental space for adopted children to process their feelings.

Parents and caregivers can support their adopted children through these challenges with open communication and understanding. Caregivers should allow the child to feel all of his feelings and ask lots of questions, even uncomfortable ones, such as "Why did my mom give me up?" Counselors working with families may focus on supporting parents in how to best provide high levels of emotional support.

Blended families form when parents bring children from previous relationships into a new marriage or partnership. Some common challenges in blended families include

- sibling rivalries;
- adjusting to new people who may take up parents' attention;
- conflict with ex-partners;
- parenting style differences.

Any conflict between adults must stay between the adults; the children should not be brought into the disagreements. This can cause unnecessary pressure to "take sides" and may even cause the child to turn against a birth parent.

Sibling rivalries and needs for attention are often closely linked. Finding ways to create special time with each child, including stepchildren, in addition to group family activities can help ease the transition when bringing two families together.

PRACTICE QUESTION

6. Anna is a nine-year-old girl who was adopted into her current family when she was three. Recently, she has begun having outbursts around bedtime, refusing to listen to her parents, and frequently shouting, "You're not my real mom!" The parents are distraught and do not know how to approach the issue. What should the counselor do?

    A) recommend that Anna reconnect with her birth mother

    B) counsel Anna's parents around setting firmer boundaries with bedtime

    C) teach Anna's parents ways to empathically reflect Anna's feelings about her adoption

    D) recommend that Anna's father take over bedtime for a few weeks

Abuse and Violence

Abuse can occur in any family and lead to lifelong emotional challenges for individuals who experience abuse:

- **Physical abuse** involves the use of physical force against a person. In addition to hitting or beating, this type of abuse includes shaking a person, holding someone underwater, or throwing things at someone.
- **Sexual abuse** includes coercive sex or sexual acts, taking pictures of the person without permission, exposing minors to pornography, or behaving sexually with minors. It can be done through the use of force or violence, threats, drugging, or emotional manipulation.
- **Emotional abuse** includes belittling language, name-calling, bullying, withholding love and affection, or telling the person that he is worthless or will never amount to anything.

Family abuse can happen between adults in a family, between older and younger siblings, or between parent and child. Some common warning signs of abuse include

- bruises or injuries that are not well explained;
- burns, especially patterned burns that cannot be explained;
- patterned injury marks as from a belt or other object;
- unattended medical issues;
- children expressing fear or dislike of their parents;
- high fight-or-flight response to being touched;
- bruising, bleeding, or pain around genitals;
- pregnancy or STDs;
- sexually acting out at a young age;
- speech problems, emotional development delays;
- depression, low self-esteem;
- poor academic performance;
- unexplained physical pain, such as headaches or stomachaches;

- poor hygiene;
- missing a lot of school;
- being underweight;
- hoarding.

Domestic violence is not reportable unless the child has witnessed the abuse. Regardless of reporting, the counselor can—and should—continue to stay involved with the family and assist with safety planning, building parenting skills and emotion regulation, and assisting with any next steps that may need to be taken if an investigation is opened.

 HELPFUL HINT
Counselors have a legal and ethical obligation to report any suspected child abuse or cases in which children witness domestic violence. It is not the counselor's duty to investigate to confirm child abuse—only to report it to the appropriate authorities.

PRACTICE QUESTION

7. Which of the following scenarios would require a counselor to make a child abuse report to the state?

    A) Freddie was pushed by a peer at school and has a bruise; he says he is afraid of the kid who hit him.

    B) Marco (eight) has been pinching his mom every day when she picks him up from school; he says his mom is mean and does not like him.

    C) Suzie reports feeling sad and scared because she can hear her parents yelling sometimes after she goes to bed at night.

    D) Angie tells the counselor that her stepdad likes to take pictures of her in her bathing suit when they are alone.

Answer Key

1. **D)** Tammy and Fred's relationship is highly codependent. Bringing awareness to the dynamic can help both partners recognize patterns and begin to make changes in their relationship.

2. **D)** Helping the family work on their communication and set expectations and boundaries early in the marriage will benefit the entire family unit in the long run.

3. **B)** Words like always or never indicate universalization, which can pigeonhole someone and prevent positive growth in the relationship.

4. **A)** Marta and John are beginning their married relationship and would benefit most from practicing making decisions together based on their own values and dynamics. This may be a time to set a boundary with the family, or it may be a time to be flexible—it is not clear based on the information.

5. **A)** Family therapy to learn about separation anxiety and develop coping skills can help treat the symptoms of separation anxiety.

6. **C)** Anna is likely experiencing identity issues and feelings of loss surrounding her adoption. Reflecting Anna's feelings and putting them into emotion-based language can help Anna better process her emotions and feel safe opening up to her adoptive parents.

7. **D)** While all of the situations would benefit from monitoring for possible indicators of abuse, option D is the only clear indicator of an abusive situation.

8 Areas of Clinical Focus: Physical Intersections

Physical Health

The physical health of clients can take a significant toll on their emotional well-being, and vice versa. Clients may seek assistance from a counselor to manage stress or anxiety when they are actually stressed because they have significant medical bills or have been out of work due to an injury. Conversely, stress and trauma can *lead* to significant health concerns, including

- gastrointestinal issues;
- hypertension (increased blood pressure);
- poor sleep.

Though these problems are closely related, a counselor's approach might vary depending on the root cause of the issue:

- Clients experiencing excessive stress that is directly related to physical health issues would benefit from ample opportunities to express their feelings on the extent of their health concerns and psychoeducation on how mental health is related.
- Clients experiencing physical health issues related to their mental illness would benefit from in-depth discussion of the mind-body connection.

Treatment goals may focus on building coping skills, such as mindfulness, perspective-taking, and physical exercise.

CONTINUE

PRACTICE QUESTION

1. Olivia tells her counselor that she has been irritable and crying for weeks, struggles to get out of bed, and no longer has any interest in her favorite hobbies. The counselor asks when these symptoms started, and Olivia says, "Three weeks ago, just after I learned of my cancer diagnosis." How should the counselor diagnose Olivia?

    A) major depression
    B) no diagnosis is necessary
    C) anxiety disorder
    D) adjustment disorder with depressed mood

Sleep

Sleep is an essential part of healthy living. People spend about one-third of their lives sleeping, so problems with sleep will have a significant impact on other areas of a client's life.

Sleep cycles are made up of four stages that can last from 90 to 120 minutes. Once one sleep cycle ends, the next cycle begins. People's bodies respond differently to each of the sleep stages.

Clients with sleep problems should be assessed for any medical causes before being screened for mental health concerns. Among individuals with non-medically related sleep issues, insomnia is the most common complaint:

- **Insomnia disorder** is marked by struggling to fall asleep or stay asleep, or waking up earlier than intended, with a negative impact on one or multiple areas of functioning.
    - The sleep disturbance needs to be present for a minimum of three months, for at least three days each week.
    - It can be a symptom of many other mental health disorders, including most mood disorders.

Treatment for insomnia begins with understanding the cause of the insomnia. Practices such as keeping a sleep diary can help clients pinpoint patterns in their sleep to discuss in sessions. Some clients may have developed poor sleep habits that may be contributing to their insomnia.

People who sleep excessively may have **hypersomnolence disorder**. This is characterized by

- naps during the day;
- extended periods of sleep overnight;
- struggling to fully wake up when they are awakened unexpectedly.

The self-reported excessive sleepiness needs to occur for a minimum of three months, at least three times each week. As with insomnia disorder, the change in sleep behavior negatively impacts clients' functioning and causes distress.

Some clients may exhibit **sleepwalking disorders**, characterized by episodes of activity during sleep, such as walking, talking, and even doing menial tasks.

People with sleepwalking disorders have no memory of getting up. Sleepwalking disorders can also cause distress in daily functioning.

Providing psychoeducation on good sleep hygiene may be beneficial for clients. Doctors recommend

- making the room as dark as possible;
- lowering the temperature of the room at night;
- limiting screen time before bed;
- limiting exciting activities before bed.

Many sleep-related disorders are medical conditions, and clients with these conditions should be referred to a sleep specialist. These include the following:

- **Narcolepsy** is extreme sleepiness marked by the need for excessive napping throughout the day. It is typically confirmed with a sleep study and electrocardiogram (ECG) to observe rapid eye movement (REM) sleep patterns.
- **Sleep apnea** refers to obstructed breathing, which can cause snoring and moments when breathing stops. Clients are very sleepy during the day due to disturbed sleep.
- **Restless leg syndrome** is a condition that causes the legs to move constantly when a person is trying to sleep, which inhibits the ability to fall asleep.
- **Medication-induced insomnia** is caused by a variety of substances and medications that disturb sleep through many different avenues.

PRACTICE QUESTION

2. Lydia is a twelve-year-old client whose parents brought her to the counselor because she is not doing well in school. Her teachers say that she has not been turning in her assignments and falls asleep in class. Lydia's parents have noticed that it is increasingly difficult to wake her up in the morning, and they are worried it is impacting her education. What is the FIRST course of action the counselor should take?

    A) tell the family to wait six months before treatment because it is common for middle school children to require more sleep

    B) screen Lydia for any medically induced sleep conditions, such as narcolepsy or restless leg syndrome

    C) ask Lydia and her parents to keep a sleep diary

    D) ask Lydia if anything has been bothering her lately at school

Aging and Retirement

As people age, new problems present themselves in life. Among **older adult** clients, **retirement** is often a top concern. Client concerns typically include

- financial worries;
- fear of boredom or isolation;

- anxiety in processing that they are in the final stages of their lives.

Key elements of treatment for older adult clients include helping them

- name and understand their concerns;
- begin a plan to address these concerns;
- seek family support.

Working with older clients often involves **end-of-life** care and management of **terminal illnesses**. Just like when family members grieve the death of a loved one, people experience grief over the knowledge of their own mortality as well. Some clients may be deciding whether to pursue further treatment or enter hospice.

Many caregivers of older and dying clients also seek counseling to manage the stress of caregiving. Often **caregivers** are taking care of a close relative, such as a parent. The stress of the day-to-day needs of caregiving, along with emotional struggles, especially if relationships were poor, can be overwhelming for many caregivers. In treatment, it can be beneficial to discuss the following with caregivers:

- working on coping skills to manage stress
- self-advocacy in seeking out respite and support
- exploring feelings of grief in all areas

 DID YOU KNOW?

For many clients, exploration of spirituality and religion is an important part of their end-of-life treatment. See Chapter 9 for more on spirituality and religion.

PRACTICE QUESTION

3. Frank is an eighty-two-year-old client seeing a counselor as part of his hospice team. Frank tells the counselor that he knows he is dying and has accepted this. His only regret is how he raised his son, with whom he has a strained relationship. How should the counselor respond to Frank?

   A) tell Frank that his son loves him very much

   B) call Frank's son and tell him that his father is seeking forgiveness

   C) ask Frank what he would say to his son if he were here right now

   D) encourage Frank to focus on the positive parts of his life

Other Disorders

Trichotillomania is a disorder characterized by excessive hairpulling. To be diagnosed with trichotillomania, the client must be pulling his hair out excessively to the point that there may be bald patches or the hair stops growing back. The client must also have made several attempts to stop the hairpulling, and this behavior must cause some level of mental distress. People engage in hairpulling for a variety of reasons, including

- to deal with negative emotions;
- to experience positive emotions (a feeling of "release" when pulling);
- to address boredom.

People with trichotillomania often experience intense shame or embarrassment regarding their behavior, especially if it is severe enough to cause hair loss or bald patches. They will typically try to hide the behavior or do it in private, and may use makeup, clothing, or wigs to conceal any noticeable hair loss. If left untreated, trichotillomania can cause people to avoid social activities, may lead to permanent skin or hair damage, and, for people who excessively eat their hair, can even cause digestive tract issues.

HELPFUL HINT

Research on effective treatment for trichotillomania is limited. Current best practices include talk therapy modalities, such as habit reversal training, cognitive behavioral therapy, and acceptance and commitment therapy.

Body dysmorphic disorder (BDD) is a mental illness that causes an individual to be preoccupied with and excessively focused on problems with specific body parts. These preoccupations can cause a person to be so concerned with his appearance that it takes up all of his time and energy and can significantly disrupt his day-to-day life. People with BDD may exhibit the following behaviors:

- constantly checking the mirror
- excessively grooming or picking their skin
- talking at length about the perceived flaws in their body
- seeking constant reassurance from friends and family about their physical appearance

People with BDD often believe that others are as fixated on their perceived flaws as they are and commonly believe their flaws to be much more significant than they really are, with little ability to challenge that belief. Like trichotillomania, treatments for BDD include habit reversal training, cognitive behavioral therapy, and acceptance and commitment therapy:

- In **habit reversal training**, clients learn how to identify what triggers them to engage in a harmful behavior. They then work on replacing that behavior with less destructive ones.
- **Cognitive behavioral therapy (CBT)** focuses on distortions or beliefs clients have about their body or behaviors, including identifying emotional triggers for the behaviors. Specifics include
  - challenging the automatic negative thoughts and finding ways to reframe them;
  - learning about how emotions, thoughts, and feelings are all interconnected;
  - developing coping mechanisms to limit hairpulling, excessive body checking, skin picking, or rumination.
- **Acceptance and commitment therapy (ACT)** focuses on self-acceptance and discourages acting on the urge.

The most common medications for BDD are selective serotonin reuptake inhibitors (SSRIs), which are typically used to treat depression and anxiety.

CONTINUE

PRACTICE QUESTION

4. A client expresses to his counselor feelings of general anxiety and emotional distress. During the intake appointment, the counselor notices the client picking his skin to the point of bleeding. He has scabbed-over wounds on his arms and face. The counselor asks him about the skin picking, and he says that he is trying to smooth out his skin so that it is not so uneven. The client is likely experiencing

   A) drug addiction or withdrawal.
   B) trichotillomania.
   C) obsessive compulsive disorder.
   D) body dysmorphic disorder.

Substance Use Disorders and Eating Disorders

Substance Use Disorders

Substance use disorders are characterized by the excessive use of mind-altering substances to a degree that the user's life, relationships, and/or work are negatively impacted. People with substance use disorders, also known as addiction, cannot control their substance intake, even when they try to limit it or quit entirely.

People are often exposed to substances through recreational use; in other cases, habit-forming medications that have been prescribed by a doctor are misused. Some substances are easier to become addicted to than others. Common symptoms of substance use disorder include

- needing more of the substance to reach a euphoric state ("get high");
- withdrawal symptoms when trying to quit;
- an inability to quit despite trying to do so;
- having urges to use the drug or substance that can't be ignored;
- spending more money than desired or can be afforded on the substances;
- neglecting work or family obligations due to substance use;
- engaging in risky behaviors while on the substance or in an attempt to obtain the substance (for example, stealing or driving under the influence).

 HELPFUL HINT

Street drugs present the greatest risk for people seeking opioids since they are often laced with other substances and not measured accurately, which can lead to emergent reactions and overdoses.

TABLE 8.1. Commonly Misused Substances

USES	SHORT-TERM EFFECTS	LONG-TERM EFFECTS
Alcohol		
• common uses: to relax, socialize, or lower inhibitions in social settings • risks: misuse to cope with negative emotions or mental health issues	• lowered inhibitions • increased reaction time • diminished judgment • dehydration • nausea • dry mouth • disrupted sleep	• increased risk of severe organ damage, especially liver • memory problems • risk of withdrawal symptoms, including hallucinations and seizures • stopping heavy use without physician supervision can be fatal
Opioids		
• common uses: prescribed analgesics (e.g., morphine, codeine, fentanyl, methadone, oxycodone) • risks: seeking out illicit opioids (heroin, manufactured pills), especially once prescriptions are completed	• endorphin release, invoking euphoria • muffling of pain receptors (analgesic effect)	• diminished ability for the body to create endorphins naturally, leading to greater dependence • possible to become addicted very quickly • may experience withdrawal symptoms very easily
Sedative-Hypnotics		
• common uses: prescribed antianxiety medications (e.g., alprazolam [Xanax], diazepam [Valium]); medications to treat insomnia (e.g., zolpidem [Ambien]) • risks: misuse to cope with negative emotions or mental health issues	• drowsiness • confusion • sleepiness • slurred speech • memory problems • dyspnea	• risk of withdrawal symptoms, including seizures • stopping treatment without physician supervision can result in seizures or delirium

continued on next page

TABLE 8.1. Commonly Misused Substances (continued)

USES	SHORT-TERM EFFECTS	LONG-TERM EFFECTS
Stimulants		
• common uses: prescribed treatments for ADHD, narcolepsy (e.g., methylphenidate [Ritalin], dextroamphetamine [Adderall]) • risks: seeking out illicit stimulants (e.g., cocaine, methamphetamine)	• increased alertness • decreased appetite • insomnia • agitation • hypertension • irregular heartbeat	• tolerance (requiring more of the drug to feel the effects) • irrational behavior, especially when seeking out the substance • paranoia • hallucinations • skin picking • psychotic symptoms • angina and heart damage
Marijuana		
• common uses: increasingly socially acceptable and legal in many states; like alcohol, used to relax, socialize, or lower inhibitions in social settings • risks: similar to alcohol; include misuse to cope with negative emotions or mental health issues	• euphoria • increased appetite • memory impairment • paranoia • hallucinations	• dependence • withdrawal from activities • spending excessive amounts of money on the substance • behavioral changes • abandoning friendships • decreased motivation in life

Working with clients seeking recovery from addiction requires boundaries. For example, an intoxicated client can be nonattentive, defiant, or dangerous. Sessions should be conducted while clients are sober. In addition, counselors should be alert for signs of **withdrawal** from substances, which can be a medical emergency. Symptoms of withdrawal include

- vomiting;
- tremors;
- increased heart rate (tachycardia);
- anxiety;
- sweating;
- insomnia;
- fatigue;
- seizures and delirium tremens (in extreme cases).

Clients complaining of these symptoms may benefit from medical assistance while undergoing withdrawal, such as a referral to a detox facility or inpatient treatment.

PRACTICE QUESTION

5. A fifty-seven-year-old man has been meeting with a counselor to address his alcohol dependence. Over the past few weeks, he has cut down on his drinking and arrives at his scheduled appointment sweating. He states he has been vomiting, and he has a noticeable tremor in his hands. What should the counselor do?

    A) call 911, even if the client refuses to consent, as he is likely detoxing and may experience seizures or possibly death

    B) explain the possible dangers of alcohol withdrawal and collaborate with him to decide whether to seek medical help

    C) encourage him to withstand the uncomfortable symptoms for a few days, as they will likely pass after the painful process of detox

    D) encourage him to decrease his alcohol intake more slowly, as he will be less likely to suffer such serious withdrawal symptoms

Other Addiction Issues

Process addictions may not involve the consumption of mind-altering substances, but the signs and symptoms of addictive behavior are surprisingly similar. Some symptoms are

- lying about one's behavior;
- spending exorbitant amounts of money or time on the behavior;
- being unable to stop the behavior;
- the behavior negatively impacting relationships.

Gambling addiction involves a compulsive need to gamble, often with increasing sums of money, property, or other items of value. Gambling addiction can include playing cards, lottery tickets, online gambling, casinos, and more.

Shopping or spending addiction is the compulsive need to purchase items. Everyone shops, but it becomes a problem when the spending is impacting one's life, or when one is using shopping to deal with or manage negative emotions or create positive emotions.

Unlike gambling or even shopping, **gaming addiction** does not typically involve the vast consumption of money, and unlike gambling, winning a game is related to skill and practice, not luck. Nonetheless, some people game at such a high rate that it impacts their day-to-day lives and may negatively affect relationships or even their ability to hold down a job.

Work addiction is often not recognized because dedication to work is socially valuable and seen as good by society. However, things can go too far when work is the only thing people can think about, when they are letting their work take precedence over their physical and mental health, and when they are overly emotionally tied to their work-related successes and failures.

Apart from gambling (which is listed as gambling disorder in the *DSM-5*), the addictive behaviors listed here are not clinically diagnosed disorders. Nonetheless, they are behavioral challenges that may negatively impact clients' daily lives.

PRACTICE QUESTION

6. Shana is a twenty-one-year-old female client seeing a counselor for the first time. She is struggling financially, which is causing her stress and anxiety. During intake, she mentions that she enjoys online poker to de-stress and will spend hours every week playing. Shana says that she earns money through gambling and always comes out ahead. What is the best way to respond to Shana?

    A) "That sounds like an interesting job."

    B) "I'm glad to see that you have some coping mechanisms for your stress."

    C) "Do you ever find that you can't stop playing, or try to stop and can't?"

    D) "Online poker is addictive, and you should stop immediately."

Addressing Addiction Issues

Treatment for addiction falls into two main types:

1. evidence-based treatment
2. alternative treatments

Cognitive behavioral therapy (CBT) is an evidence-based treatment model and one of the most commonly used for treating addiction. This treatment focuses on the mind-body connection and teaches clients to understand the relationships among their thoughts, feelings, and behaviors. Clients with addiction practice learning how to identify any cognitive distortions they are engaging in that are contributing to their substance use or process addiction.

Dialectical behavior therapy (DBT) is an evidence-based treatment that was developed to help people with borderline personality disorder manage their emotions. For individuals with addiction, DBT helps teach mindfulness, which increases emotion regulation and builds distress tolerance. Clients learn to identify what triggers them to want to use harmful substances and discover alternative coping mechanisms to avoid destructive behaviors.

Twelve-step programs emerged in the 1930s. These are nonprofessional peer-based support groups supported by members' donations, making them a viable option for people with limited financial means. They encourage total abstinence. Most twelve-step programs emphasize

- interpersonal connections, particularly through attending meetings;
- spirituality or a connection with a higher power;
- self-improvement by working the twelve steps with a sponsor (a nonprofessional person in recovery).

Alcoholics Anonymous (AA) is the most well-known twelve-step program, but there are others, like Narcotics Anonymous (NA), Cocaine Anonymous (CA), and more.

Many people in recovery have found success with the twelve-step model, but some people are not comfortable with it. Criticisms of the twelve-step model include its emphasis on spirituality and total abstinence. Still, these programs can offer important social benefits for people seeking support in making positive changes in their lives. For many clients, they may work well in tandem with other interventions.

> **DID YOU KNOW?**
> There are twelve-step groups that address issues outside of substance use; these include Sex and Love Addicts Anonymous (SLAA) and Codependents Anonymous (CoDA).

PRACTICE QUESTION

7. Andrew has been seeing his counselor for several weeks for treatment of his prescription opioid addiction. He has identified insomnia as a trigger for his pill usage and has learned several coping skills to try when he feels the urge to take pills. This week he shows up late, is surly, and tells the counselor that he is thinking of quitting treatment. What is the BEST response from the counselor?

   A) "You are free to go; this treatment is not court-mandated."

   B) "What's making you think of quitting?"

   C) "Your behavior change indicates that you are using again."

   D) "You would benefit from a twelve-step program instead of counseling."

Eating Disorders

Eating disorders are characterized by abnormal eating patterns to the point that they impair physical health and social well-being. Many people with eating disorders compare their symptoms of maladaptive eating to those with addiction, including cravings and compulsions.

Binge eating disorder (BED) is characterized by overeating over short periods to the point of being too full, even when one is not hungry:

- People with BED typically report eating alone during their binges and experiencing feelings of shame and disgust about their eating habits.
- The recommended modalities for people with BED are CBT and DBT; the goal is to learn to identify emotional triggers that cause a person to want to binge and to develop alternative coping skills that are not food-related.

Anorexia nervosa (AN) has the highest death rate of all mental health disorders. People with AN restrict their energy intake to the point that they lose dangerous amounts of weight:

- Energy restriction can occur through dieting, fasting, and excessive exercise.
- It can also occur through cycles of bingeing and purging in the form of self-induced vomiting or by taking laxatives and diuretics.

- People with AN have a distorted body image and believe themselves to be overweight, or they are unaware of how dangerous their current weight loss is.
- People with anorexia have high rates of suicide as well as hospitalization due to organ failure, dehydration, and other problems.
- Treatment for AN begins with medical supervision to bring the client's weight back up to within normal ranges.
- A team approach is the best way to treat AN.
  - A team approach might involve doctors, dietitians, and family therapy.
  - Family therapy is the only evidence-based mental health treatment for AN.

Bulimia nervosa is marked by cycles of bingeing and purging to avoid the overeating that contributes to weight gain.

- While people with BN are highly concerned with their weight, they will usually stay within normal weight ranges and may even be overweight.
- As with AN, a team approach using the expertise of physicians, dietitians, and family counselors can provide important treatment options for those with bulimia nervosa.

Other specified feeding or eating disorders (OSFED) is a catch-all diagnosis reserved for clients whose eating disorders do not fit into an existing diagnosis. Treatment for OSFED is similar to those used with other eating disorders: using a multidisciplinary approach is ideal.

Pica occurs when an individual eats nonnutritive and nonfood substances, such as chalk or paper. A diagnosis is made when this behavior occurs for a month or longer and is neither culturally supported nor a social norm. People with pica may benefit from medical intervention since cravings could indicate the lack of an essential nutrient.

PRACTICE QUESTION

8. Claire is a high school student referred for treatment by her school counselor. She has been losing weight all semester, and she is now so thin that her clothes no longer fit her. Last week, Claire fainted in gym class. When her teacher gave her an energy bar, Claire refused to eat it. She tells the counselor that she just wants to lose a few pounds, and her teachers are overreacting. Which of the following is the BEST response by the counselor?

    A) consult with Claire's parents and insist that they hospitalize her immediately

    B) begin individual therapy with Claire to work on her body image issues

    C) refer Claire back to the school counselor since the behaviors are only being observed at school

    D) convey to Claire's parents the importance of family therapy to help Claire

Gender and Sexuality

Gender Identity

Gender identity is a person's individual sense of their gender as male, female, something in between, or something completely different. **Gender identity** refers to how people see their gender and how they feel, regardless of their biological sex.

Sex is a label based on genitalia, typically as observed by doctors at birth. People can be male or female, or, rarely, intersex (a rare genetic condition causing a person to have gametes with both male and female characteristics).

While most people's gender identity tends to be congruent with their biological sex, some people's will not. When someone's gender identity is incongruent with their biological sex, it can cause distress for those individuals and prompt them to express their gender in a way that is more in line with how they feel internally. For many people, these feelings can be confusing and distressing, and they may seek out counseling to help them clarify and better understand their feelings.

Significantly distressing feelings regarding gender identity incongruence that last for at least six months describe **gender dysphoria**, a psychological condition found in the *DSM-5*.

When someone's gender identity is persistently incongruent with their biological sex, this is known as being **transgender**. People who are transgender may choose to **transition** how they present their gender publicly to live in more alignment with their gender identity. Transitioning can be social or physical and may include the following:

- changing one's name
- using different pronouns
- dressing in a different manner
- changing behaviors

Physical procedures may include

- hormone replacement therapy;
- primary or secondary sex affirmation surgeries.

Transgender people may seek out counseling for assistance in better understanding their condition, deciding how much they want to physically and socially transition, and when they want to start publicly transitioning.

Some people who are transgender, especially those who do not "pass" well (in other words, those whose appearance does not seem to match their biological sex), may experience sexual harassment, bullying, and isolation from family members or others. These clients may be more vulnerable and need additional therapeutic support.

PRACTICE QUESTION

9. Emily began seeing a counselor about six months ago for treatment for anxiety and relationship difficulties. Through CBT and mindfulness practices, Emily reports that her symptoms are more manageable, and the counselor is considering making discharge plans. But in her most recent session, Emily expressed having questions about her gender identity and wants to explore that in sessions. What is the BEST course of action?

   A) Since Emily's symptoms are improving, she can be discharged from services and may return later if more issues come up.

   B) Emily should be challenged on her gender concerns; she may be avoiding discharge by fabricating symptoms.

   C) Emily should be referred out to a gender specialist.

   D) The counselor should explore with Emily the nature of her gender identity concerns and begin developing a treatment plan for the new presenting issue.

Sexuality

Sexuality is an important part of a healthy adult life. When someone struggles with **sexual functioning**, it can be a troubling condition. Sexual dysfunctions can include issues such as

- premature ejaculation;
- delayed ejaculation;
- inability to orgasm;
- low libido;
- physical pain associated with sex.

Sexual functioning problems can have a number of causes including

- poor health;
- depression;
- stress;
- physical injury.

Clients struggling with sexual functioning may experience feelings of shame or confusion, inferiority, and stress surrounding the difficulties. For clients seeking to manage or improve their sexual functioning, a focus on managing stress and mental well-being is essential, as libido and sexual health are closely related to stress.

Some women may experience a condition known as **genito-pelvic pain/ penetration disorder**. In this physical condition, the muscles of the vaginal wall tighten so excessively as to make penetrative sex impossible or extremely painful. It also causes anxiety about performing penetrative sex. Though this is a physical condition, the causes are largely psychological and have to do with anxiety surrounding penetrative sex. These anxieties may stem from

- previous traumatic sexual experiences;
- cultural or religious attitudes toward sex;

- medical concerns;
- relationship problems;
- general difficulties with sexual arousal.

Treatment focuses on discovering the root cause of the anxiety and addressing it in tandem with relaxation practices, a temporary ceasing of penetrative sex, and a focus on arousal, exploration of the body, and emotional connection with one's partner to decrease anxiety and increase feelings of comfort, safety, and relaxation.

Pornography use is a controversial subject within the psychology field. It is currently not classified as a disorder in the *DSM-5* because researchers say that excessive porn use does not involve excessive risk-taking or an increased tolerance, two elements that are essential to an addiction diagnosis. Nonetheless, pornography use can cause problems in relationships, especially under certain circumstances:

- when partners are not in agreement about usage
- when one partner is hiding the behavior
- when it is being used to avoid intimacy

Despite some claims that pornography use can drive a wedge between couples, evidence points to excessive or problematic pornography use (such as hiding the use) as being a symptom of relationship problems, not the cause. Couples looking to address pornography usage in therapy benefit from learning how to openly communicate with each other about sensitive sexual subjects without judgment.

PRACTICE QUESTION

10. George and Carla are seeking help with their relationship. They have been having intimacy issues for months, and it is taking a toll on their relationship. George has erectile dysfunction and is not able to perform sexually when they attempt intercourse. When speaking to the counselor privately, George says that he feels emasculated and that he is not a good partner to his girlfriend. How should the counselor respond?

  A) invite Carla to explain to George how she feels about their lack of intimacy

  B) refer George to a physician for his erectile dysfunction

  C) help the couple move toward acceptance of a sex-free relationship

  D) encourage the couple to explore non-penetrative ways to be intimate together

CONTINUE

Answer Key

1. **D)** Although Olivia's symptoms are consistent with major depression, her cancer diagnosis presents a clear stressor. Treatment should focus on processing the news, adjusting to it, and practicing acceptance of her reaction to the cancer diagnosis.

2. **B)** Adolescent children need plenty of sleep, but Lydia's amount of sleeping is excessive. The first step would be to rule out any medical conditions that would require a physician's care. Any suspicion of a medical cause should trigger a referral to a sleep specialist.

3. **C)** Many people seek reconciliation and forgiveness at the end of life. Without knowing the nature of the relationship, it is hard to say if Frank's son will visit or not. Even just saying the words out loud or writing them on paper can provide some relief and a feeling of closure for clients seeking reconciliation.

4. **D)** A client experiencing body dysmorphic disorder has obsessive thoughts about bodily imperfections and flaws and repeats certain behaviors to try to improve these perceived flaws. Though drug addiction and obsessive compulsive disorder (OCD) can include body picking as a symptom, the reason behind the body picking (attempts to improve one's appearance) is the key distinguishing factor for a body dysmorphic disorder (BDD) diagnosis.

5. **B)** Certain medical risks, like vomiting and shaking, are associated with alcohol withdrawal. In severe situations, seizures, hallucinations, and death are possible. Extreme withdrawal requires medical intervention. Vomiting and tremors do not necessarily indicate a medical emergency, but they do indicate alcohol withdrawal. The counselor should explain the possible risks of alcohol withdrawal to the client and discuss whether he wants to seek medical treatment.

6. **C)** One sign of addiction is an inability to stop the behavior, even when a person tries very hard to do so. By asking Shana if she has tried to stop playing online poker, the counselor is screening to see how intense her gambling addiction is.

7. **B)** It is possible that Andrew relapsed and is ashamed, or it may be that he is dealing with a highly stressful life event that led him to relapse, and he sees no point in continuing treatment. Explaining what happened in his own words is an important first step in being able to explore the connections among events in his life, his thoughts and feelings, and his behaviors. He might still benefit from attending a twelve-step program, but that does not mean he should discontinue counseling.

8. **D)** Family therapy is the only evidence-based mental health treatment for anorexia. Hospitalization may be necessary for Claire at a later time if her prognosis is severe enough, but it is rarely recommended to begin with the most invasive treatment.

9. **D)** Counselors have a duty to treat clients to the best of their abilities. Gender questions are within the purview of counselors, and if clients present with those concerns, the counselor should screen for symptoms and develop a treatment plan with clients based on their goals and therapeutic best practices.

10. **D)** Sex and intimacy are important elements of a healthy relationship, but stressing about performance can exacerbate performance issues. Removing the expectation of penetrative sex can relieve some of the performance pressures George is feeling and may help the couple regain some closeness and intimacy with less stress.

9 | Areas of Clinical Focus: Social Issues

Career and Finances

Career trajectories influence lifestyle, income, life satisfaction, work-life balance, and retirement and can therefore be a driving force in encouraging individuals to seek counseling. Counselors should be prepared to support people in developing career goals and helping them find the best career fit. Several theories of career development are useful in counseling.

Career Development Theories

Social cognitive career theory (SCCT) is based on Albert Bandura's research on social learning theory, which emphasizes self-cognition and social processes. This theory addresses the learning aspects of career development and how goals can shift and adjust over time based on positive or negative feedback from the environment. There are three main components of SCCT:

- self-efficacy
- outcome expectations
- personal goals

Self-efficacy refers to an individual's perception of her ability to complete tasks or execute certain behaviors. People can demonstrate high or low self-efficacy in different areas. For example, a person might feel that he is very good at communicating with people but struggles with complex math and analysis. Personal success is seen as the biggest factor in developing self-efficacy. According to SCCT, self-efficacy is driven by the following:

- personal accomplishments
- social persuasion (others telling a person that she is good at a particular task)
- vicarious experiences (seeing other people perform those same tasks)
- an individual's physical state (not being anxious when performing the task)

Outcome expectations are what a person believes will happen when a task is completed. As with self-efficacy, outcome expectations are typically built through experience and the observation of others. People with high self-efficacy about their job performance would expect certain positive outcomes, such as

- approval from others;
- tangible benefits (a raise or promotion);
- better working conditions.

Finally, **personal goals** are the decisions an individual makes to pursue specific activities to achieve future outcomes. Personal goals can help propel people forward in their careers even when there are long gaps between external benefits, like promotions or raises. In SCCT there are two types of personal goals:

1. **Choice goals** are related to decision-making, such as choosing a new career path or field of study.
2. **Performance goals** tend to be more concrete and measurable, such as pursuing an A in a class or a promotion at work.

According to SCCT, personal goals are related to outcome expectations and self-efficacy. This is because the level of a person's talent in her field will shape the kinds of goals she pursues, and her success or failure in achieving those goals will likely influence future self-efficacy and expected outcomes.

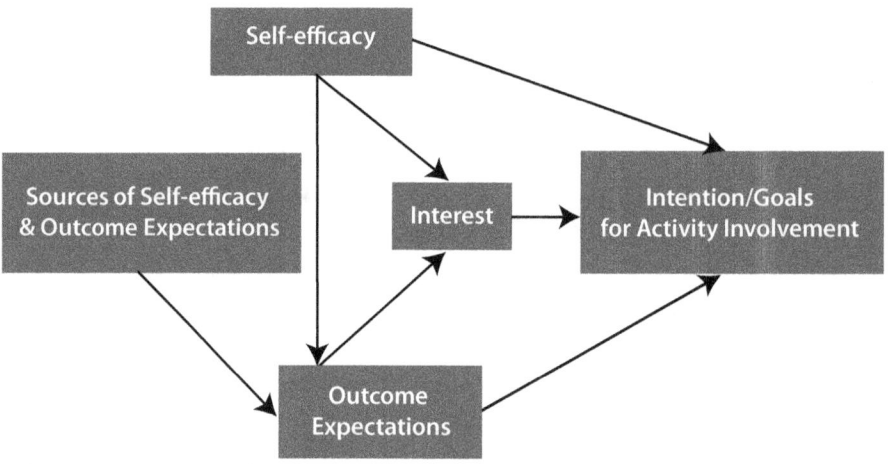

Figure 9.1. Social Cognitive Career Theory

Trait-factor theory is based on the idea that careers are best matched to people's individual traits and skills. This theory is particularly useful because the process of career development between client and counselor is broken down into stages. Educator Frank Parsons believed that three components were essential for successful career development:

1. accurate self-assessment of one's talents or proclivities and interests
2. accurate understanding of the current labor and job markets
3. fair judgment of the relationship between one's skill set and the need for it in the labor market

Individuals who are capable of accurately assessing their skills, interests, and the needs of the current labor market would find a job that leverages their skills. Parsons believed that workers who focus on tasks for which they have the highest aptitude would be the most successful.

Parsons developed a seven-stage counseling system to help people determine the best career path. This system can be used by counselors in guiding clients through career development and choice-making.

 DID YOU KNOW?

Trait-factor theory was developed by **Frank Parsons**, who many consider to be the father of the career counseling movement. His theories are still used today to help people discover their ideal career paths.

TABLE 9.1. Parson's Seven-Stage Counseling System	
Personal data	The client and counselor together generate a list of traits and characteristics about the client, especially as they relate to career development.
Self-analysis	The client individually reflects on traits and tendencies that might impact his career. These can be positive, negative, or neutral. Some examples are being goal-oriented, task-oriented, results-driven; working better in groups or autonomously, etc.
The client's own choice and decision	Successful career development must ultimately be client-led. While the counselor can offer ideas, guidance, and feedback, the focus must always be on client goals.
Counselor's analysis	The counselor's role is to help clients both reflect on their stated choices and determine if they are in line with their other stated goals. For example, clients who say they want to be in a leadership position but don't want to work more than thirty hours a week might need to reflect on which goal is more important to them.
Outlook on the vocational field	Career counselors should understand current career trends, expectations, and skill norms to help clients match their skills and goals with available jobs.
Induction and advice	Both counselor and client will work best if the focus is objective and goal-directed, with a clear eye on the possibilities and limitations in the field and within the client's skills and abilities.
General helpfulness	The counselor helps clients adjust to their chosen positions, reflect on these, and make any needed adjustments.

Psychologist John Holland developed a theory of personality and occupation, known as **RIASEC**, to help people determine their best career fit. According to RIASEC, people are best suited to career environments that match their personalities. He theorized that there are six main personality types that correlate to career types:

- **r**ealistic
- **i**nvestigative
- **a**rtistic
- **s**ocial
- **e**nterprising
- **c**onventional

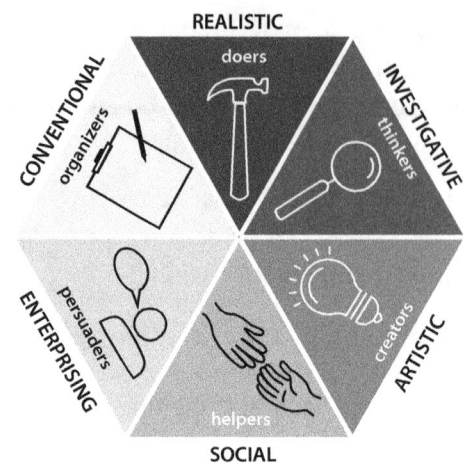

Figure 9.2. The Holland Hexagon (RIASEC)

TABLE 9.2. RIASEC Personality Types and Correlating Career Types

CATEGORY	TRAITS	PREFERENCES/ VALUES	TYPICAL CAREERS
Realistic	pragmatic, concrete	• animals, tools, machines • appreciate practical things they can observe in their environment, such as plants and animals, equipment, or tools	trades such as plumbing, electrical work, and carpentry, or environmental work such as agriculture, wildlife preservation, veterinary care, etc.
Investigative	academic, cerebral	• math, science, logic, reasoning • avoid sales and jobs requiring persuasion	academia (especially STEM careers), engineering, research
Artistic	creative	• acting, dance, music, writing, art • independent, expressive • value creative output in themselves and others	fine arts, graphic design, writing, film/media
Social	personal, service-oriented	• outgoing, amiable, extroverted • value relationships	teacher, counselor, health care professional, sales

CATEGORY	TRAITS	PREFERENCES/ VALUES	TYPICAL CAREERS
Enterprising	persuasive/ leaders	• skilled at convincing others of the value of their ideas, products, or plans • perceive themselves as ambitious and high-energy with good people skills • may shy away from analytical or scientific thinking, preferring to think "big picture"	business, politics, leadership positions
Conventional	organized, reliable	• enjoy working with numbers, records, or machines; thrive on order, set tasks, and do not mind repetition • rely on external plans to set their work into motion	bookkeeping, CPAs, data analytics, secretarial work, project management, and other task-oriented and highly organization-reliant positions

PRACTICE QUESTION

1. Which of the following elements is a key component of Bandura's social cognitive career theory?

    A) personality assessments

    B) job market analysis

    C) self-analysis

    D) self-efficacy

Financial Concerns

Many clients seek out counseling to address financial stress and even seek guidance on improving financial habits. Some of the main financial concerns include

- managing debt;
- loss of income;
- increased expenses due to life events, such as injury, children, or retirement.

While money management is unlikely to be the primary focus of counseling sessions, understanding the most common financial stressors and accompanying mental health concerns is essential to best support clients who are facing financial difficulties.

 DID YOU KNOW?

About 80 percent of Americans have some kind of **debt**; the median debt amount carried is nearly $90,000. The likelihood that counselors will encounter clients with debt is very high.

A counselor must understand the origin of a client's debt to effectively discuss the issue. Does the client have student loan debt that she is slowly chipping away at? Or are there spending issues, such as charging bills to credit cards? In some cases, the spending issues might be more significant and related to addiction, such as shopping, gambling, or drug addictions. These may require more serious intervention with a referral to an addiction clinic.

Some clients may benefit from referrals to debt counseling. Others may benefit more from exploring coping mechanisms. Counselors can work with clients to

- avoid excess spending;
- shift existing habits;
- reevaluate their life priorities.

Income loss is another significant financial stressor and can occur in different ways:

- job loss
- cutbacks in hours
- being furloughed
- inability to work due to illness or disability
- a partner's job loss
- loss of benefits (for example, EBT benefits, social security, or child support)

These losses in income streams often coincide with stressful life events. Illness, injury, job loss, and other life changes can be significant stressors that clients may need help navigating and processing emotionally. Counseling may target

- coping and self-care skills;
- building up or relying on existing safety nets;
- working on finding ways to increase the income stream.

Counselors are not typically equipped to handle all the nuances of navigating social welfare systems, so referring clients to an agency skilled in assisting with financial issues may be helpful in these cases.

Certain common **life events** can also have stressful financial implications:

- having a baby
- getting married
- becoming injured or disabled
- preparing for retirement

Some life changes might be expected (for example, retirement), whereas others might be unexpected. The counselor should create space to help clients express the emotions that arise with these life changes. Equally important, the counselor should collaborate with clients to develop concrete solutions to their financial challenges.

Financial stressors can trigger a variety of mental health symptoms and exacerbate existing stress. Exploring these concerns with clients is essential to successfully navigate life's stressors. Counselors should screen for certain concerns, including

- grief;
- relationship problems;
- anxiety;
- depression;
- eating problems (too much or too little);
- physical complaints (for example, upset stomach, headaches, muscle tension);
- sleep difficulties (too much or too little).

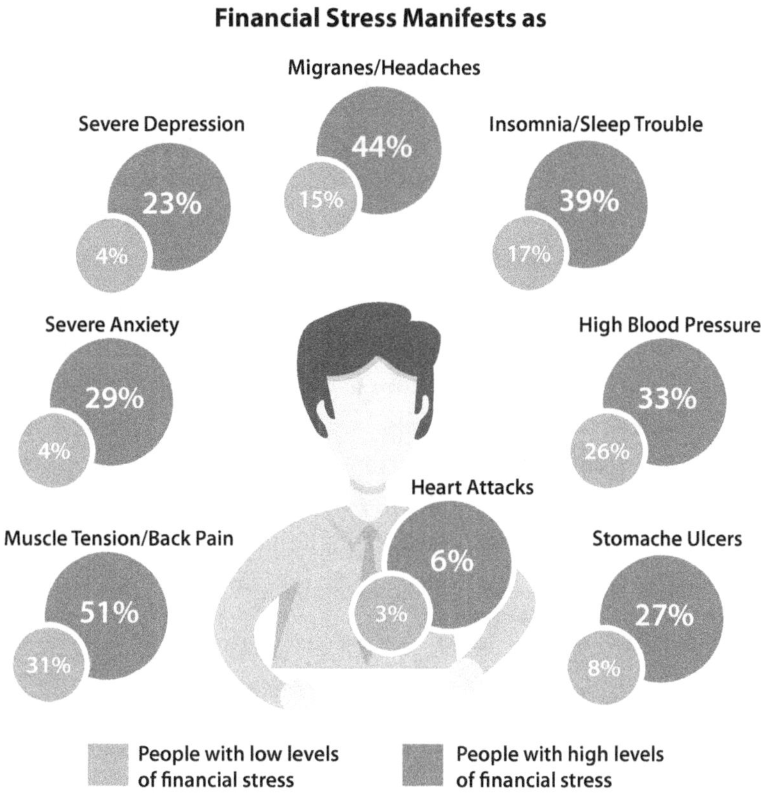

Financial Stress Manifests as

- Migranes/Headaches: 44% / 15%
- Severe Depression: 23% / 4%
- Insomnia/Sleep Trouble: 39% / 17%
- Severe Anxiety: 29% / 4%
- High Blood Pressure: 33% / 26%
- Muscle Tension/Back Pain: 51% / 31%
- Heart Attacks: 6% / 3%
- Stomache Ulcers: 27% / 8%

People with low levels of financial stress | People with high levels of financial stress

Figure 9.3. Physical Impacts of Financial Stress

Poverty can have a significant impact on mental well-being. Individuals living in poverty are twice as likely to report symptoms of depression as those who are not living in poverty. The constant stressors of not having enough money can impact sleep, overall well-being, and financial decision-making.

The impacts of living in chronic poverty are often not fully alleviated even when a person gains upward mobility. Many people who grew up in poverty continue to struggle in adulthood with feeling secure and stable in their finances, which may drive them to make emotion-based financial decisions.

PRACTICE QUESTION

2. Linda is a thirty-two-year-old single mother with significant credit card debt. She comes to counseling seeking support for managing life stressors related to her financial difficulties. How should the counselor begin treatment?

    A) refer out to a professional who is qualified to provide financial counseling

    B) conduct a review of Linda's spending habits and debt-to-income ratio

    C) explore which stressors are of the highest concern for Linda

    D) screen Linda for anxiety and depression

Culture, Religion, and Spirituality

Culture and Oppression

Cultural competence is key to providing excellent counseling care. **Cultural competence** means treating clients as experts in their own lives and personal stories.

To be culturally competent is more than simply knowing basic facts about a person's culture or being aware of certain norms. Developing cultural competence is an ongoing process that involves seeking guidance from the client, from supervisors, and doing external research on cultural norms for clients in treatment. Understanding cultural norms is an important starting place for any counselor, but it is not the end of the conversation.

Additional factors are important to consider when approaching client care in a culturally competent manner. **Level of acculturation** refers to how comfortable clients feel in the dominant culture as opposed to their culture of origin. For example, a client from Mexico who has only been in the US for two years is going to have very different life experiences and cultural norms from a client born in Mexico who has lived in the US for most of her life. A client's level of acculturation and how he interacts with the dominant culture is impacted by

- the level of acculturation of the client's family;
- the primary language spoken in the home;
- the culture of the client's partner or spouse.

Research shows that genuine cultural competence can lead to high-quality therapeutic care. Counselors can exhibit cultural competence in several ways:

- demonstrating a warm and open attitude
- showing genuine interest and curiosity about the client's culture
- using humor to engage with mistakes or misunderstandings to ease any tension that may arise
- asking good-natured and humble questions to show care and a willingness to learn

Counselors must be particularly mindful of issues related to culture and oppression:

- **Racism** is the belief that certain races are superior to others.

HELPFUL HINT

Acculturation is different from **assimilation**, a negative process of forcing people from non-dominant cultures to abandon or suppress their culture. Acculturation is a natural process that happens over time and does not necessarily involve abandonment of one's values or cultural norms.

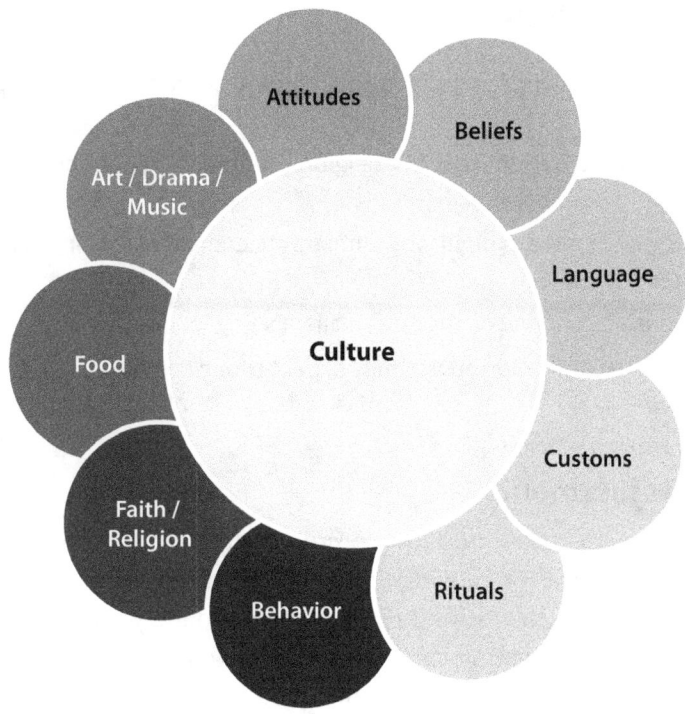

Figure 9.4. Cultural Competence

- **Discrimination** occurs when someone or a group of people are treated unfairly based on immutable characteristics, such as race, ethnicity, age, gender, sexual orientation or gender identity, or religion.
- **Oppression** is a situation in which people are governed or controlled unfairly or in a cruel or harsh way, often based on immutable characteristics.

Current events often make their way into the counselor's office. It is likely that clients, especially clients who are people of color, are experiencing distress due to racism, police brutality, microaggressions, and more. Witnessing people being targeted by racist attacks can cause individuals to remember their own experiences of racial discrimination. Racially motivated attacks—whether physical or verbal—are degrading and humiliating experiences for the survivors. A counselor must be present and practice active listening when navigating these sensitive topics with clients.

Counselors are called on to be anti-racist in their practice and overall work. Providing quality care to individuals from all walks of life with particular attention to those who are most vulnerable is essential to that practice. Competent counseling for individuals from diverse backgrounds in particular requires the counselor to educate herself on the role of systems and their impacts on clients' lives.

Furthermore, counselors can enact anti-racist counseling by practicing cultural respect and curiosity, maintaining a learning attitude, and advocating for increased access to quality mental health resources for people of all races, ethnicities, ages, sexualities, and abilities.

 HELPFUL HINT

Some counselors may have personally experienced racism and discrimination; others may have never endured racial attacks or microaggressions. Self-disclosure should be used with discretion in these situations: keeping the focus on the client's experiences is the top priority.

PRACTICE QUESTION

3. Which of the following is an example of cultural competence in a therapy session?

    A) explaining to a client that her religion is oppressing her because of her gender

    B) asking a client to explain why immigrants come from their country to the United States

    C) expressing surprise or shock at a client's English proficiency

    D) inviting a client to discuss family expectations surrounding his bar mitzvah

Cultural Adjustment

Cultural adjustment issues are most common when people move to very new cultures, for instance when moving to a new country or using a new language. However, even moving to a new city in one's home country can trigger a cultural adjustment period. Navigating the norms, expectations, and ways of life can be both exciting and challenging, and many people may seek out counseling for their experiences if they need additional support. Cultural adjustment occurs over four stages as described in Table. 9.3.

TABLE 9.3. Four Stages of Cultural Adjustment
Stage 1: Honeymoon/Tourist Stage
When someone first moves to a new location, everything can seem exciting and new. There are new foods to try, places to see, and people to meet. It is common for people to feel excited and hopeful during this stage, envisioning what their new life will be like. This stage can last from a few days to several weeks.
Stage 2: Distress/Crisis Stage
Problems begin here. Learning the language may be difficult, adjusting to different cultural norms and expectations can be an issue, and challenges start cropping up. In this stage, homesickness may take over, and it is common for people to compare their new lives with their previous circumstances. Challenges such as language barriers, gender relations, deference for authority, social norms such as tipping, use of curse words, food availability from one's home location, and many other issues can compound and create significant stress and homesickness in individuals. This phase typically starts a few weeks or months into the move and can last several months.
Stage 3: Reintegration Stage
Several months to a year after the move, feelings of crisis may start to subside. As people become more used to the norms and expectations in their new home, they can relax and navigate more situations with ease. They begin to reintegrate aspects of their old lives into their new lives (such as cooking favorite childhood meals) and can laugh off minor cultural frictions. Their new location still feels "new," but thoughts of being an outsider or feelings of loneliness or intense homesickness begin to subside.

Stage 4: "Home" Stage
People have fully integrated themselves into their new environment and culture. Language barriers have eased, and their understanding of cultural norms in the new environment has heightened. They can bring aspects of their old home and environment into their new location. Problems or challenges in the new location are not perceived as negatively as before and are instead accepted as part of the way of life. The new location begins to feel like home.

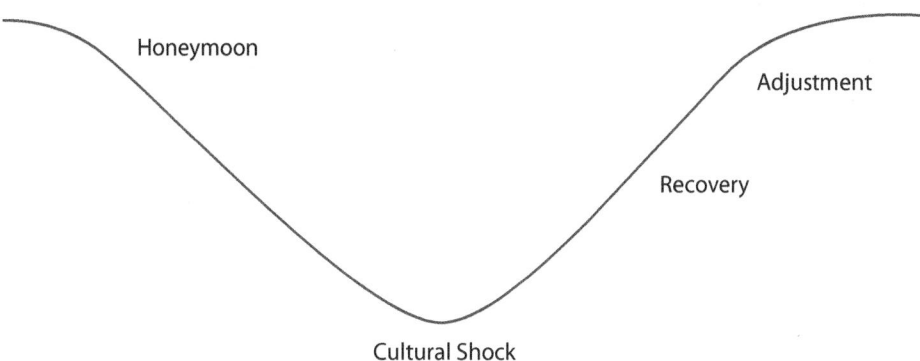

Figure 9.5. Cultural Adjustment

Not every person goes through all four stages of cultural adjustment. Some people remain at Stage 2, Distress/Crisis, for extended periods. This phenomenon, known as **culture shock**, was originally described by anthropologist Kalervo Oberg. People experiencing culture shock may display

- heightened negative emotions about their new location;
- anger and annoyance at various aspects of their new environment;
- a lack of interest in integrating into the new environment;
- a strong preference for norms from their home environment.

If left untreated, these negative emotions can lead to anxiety and depression, self-isolation, and physical symptoms such as upset stomach, poor sleep, and aches and pains. Counselors with clients experiencing significant culture shock should help them determine what specific triggers are causing their difficulties. It could be that they have not made friends yet, or perhaps there are specific norms in their new environment that are particularly challenging for them compared with their home environment. For example, someone coming from a more conservative country might struggle to adapt to the more open dating culture in the United States.

Counselors should work to understand the client's home culture to validate the difficulties of the transition. It is important to monitor symptoms to ensure that the cultural adjustment does not develop into more significant mental health concerns, like anxiety and depression.

Some clients may feel insecure about making mistakes when practicing their new language. If this worry is significant enough, it can prevent them from socializing in their new location. For these clients, working on building self-esteem and confidence can help improve their ability to practice the local language more often, which will help immensely with adjustment issues. Connecting with fellow expats can also be an important way to ease into the transition. Finally, psychoeducation on the norms of cultural adjustment can be a reassuring conversation for people who have not traveled before and may be unfamiliar with the concept of cultural adjustment.

PRACTICE QUESTION

4. Which of the following is the first stage of cultural adjustment?
    A) "Home" stage
    B) Honeymoon/Tourist stage
    C) Reintegration stage
    D) Distress/Crisis stage

Religion and Spirituality

Religion and spirituality can be very important parts of some clients' lives. **Spirituality** can include formal religious practices, such as prayer and worship, but can also encompass broader concepts, such as sense of self and purpose, values, community, forgiveness, and mental well-being.

Spirituality has been found to have positive impacts on people's lives: It can offer a framework or set of values for how to live one's life and foster self-esteem and self-worth. It can also encourage positive outlooks and ways of interacting in the world, such as expressing compassion, generosity, forgiveness, and inner peace. Clients who are experiencing spiritual difficulties might report issues such as

- a feeling of emptiness or a lack of purpose in the world;
- negative outlook on life;
- excessive judgment of themselves or others;
- excessive anxiety;
- loneliness and isolation.

In the past, it was considered inappropriate to discuss spirituality with clients. Practitioners felt it was unprofessional, were concerned about differences in beliefs, or wanted to avoid controversy in the counseling room. However, research has found that incorporating religious or spiritual practices that align with the client's values can have a positive impact on the therapeutic process.

Counselors can encourage clients to incorporate religion and spirituality into therapy sessions and to continue beneficial practices outside the session. Depending on the client, these may include

- meditation;
- mindfulness techniques (like deep breathing);

- values exploration (such as mood boards);
- developing personal rituals or practices;
- complementary health approaches (for example, yoga);
- prayer and reading spiritual texts (religious or otherwise) related to their faith practice.

A counselor should ensure that religious or faith-based practices are client-led. The counselor should also have a high level of cultural competency. For example, counselors who are not qualified to perform a certain service (like teaching yoga) should not do so; however, they may encourage their clients to try a yoga class if the clients are medically capable. A nonreligious counselor can still encourage a religious client to refer to comforting religious texts when he is feeling anxiety and can even have him read them in session, allowing him to take the lead.

When using spiritual practices with clients, the counselor needs to separate her personal spiritual or religious beliefs from those of the client. It is inappropriate to proselytize or push one's personal beliefs onto clients; however, encouraging clients to explore their own spiritual beliefs, practices, and values can be an enriching and rewarding tool in a holistic therapeutic practice. Again, any spiritual or religious exploration should be client-led.

Values exploration may be neutral or centered in religious and spiritual beliefs. Everyone has values and beliefs about what is important in life, how the world works, and what it means to be a good person. For people who are experiencing a big change in life, revisiting or clarifying their values in a therapeutic environment can encourage them to make decisions based on what is most important to them.

 HELPFUL HINT

Approaches to spirituality can vary widely. While some people find spiritual benefits from tarot cards, doing creative activities, or listening to music, others are more traditional and attend services or practice a faith. Exploring areas that have been spiritually meaningful to you as a counselor can help prepare you for spiritual discussions with clients.

Navigating Religious Values Conflicts

Some clients seek counseling because they are experiencing values conflicts regarding religious norms and expectations. These **values conflicts** may be external and causing discord with family members (for example, a person who is no longer religious and is being pressured to continue attending church by family members) or within themselves (for example, a gay person who belongs to a faith practice that does not accept the LGBTQ community). Whatever the source of the conflict, the approach will be similar.

First, it is important to approach the issue with an open and nonjudgmental attitude. The goal is to help the client explore his own values, not impose the counselor's values on the client. Developing a strong rapport that allows room for open communication and trust between the client and counselor is essential for values conflict work. Second, the counselor must understand what the exact conflict is, the source of the conflict, and how the client feels about it. For example, a married couple comes from different religious backgrounds. One wants their children to be baptized in the local church; the other wants the children to come to their own decisions. To navigate the conflict, the counselor and client must be able to identify these different desires and understand any outside pressure (like family or cultural expectations) that may influence decision-making.

Finally, the counselor and client can explore different options for how to proceed. Consider the example of the married couple:
- What will the outcome be if the client insists on the baptism?
- How will it impact the client's life?
- How will the client feel about the decision?
- What about waiting and letting the child decide?
- Are there options that haven't been considered, such as baptism in a different church, an alternate religious ceremony, or waiting for a year or two before conducting the baptism?

The counselor's role is to help clients explore the various options and help them decide for themselves what choice to make to resolve the conflict.

While religion and spirituality can have many positive impacts on one's life, spiritual abuse can occur as well and create negative impacts. **Spiritual abuse** is a broad term that encompasses religious and spiritual beliefs to control, coerce, shame, humiliate, or terrorize people.

The use of shame and guilt is one of the most common tools of spiritual abuse. It can be used against people to pressure them into giving money, control their behavior (such as who they socialize with or marry), or dictate how they should dress. It can even influence the career they choose. Spiritual abuse can be used to manipulate someone's emotions or silence their questions. Appeals to authority may be used to enact spiritual abuse as well (for example, a faith leader who has to personally give permission before people are allowed to date or marry).

Spiritual abuse can include insulting people's spiritual beliefs, forcing people to act in ways that violate their spiritual beliefs, or, in the case of parents, not allowing their children to make their own spiritual decisions.

People who have experienced spiritual abuse need support and a safe space where they can explore the pain of their experiences and take the time to realign their spiritual values free of coercion or guilt. The validation counselors can provide regarding the pain associated with spiritual abuse can be an important step in the healing process for these clients. Working from a trauma-informed perspective can be a key part of providing competent care for clients who have experienced spiritual abuse.

PRACTICE QUESTION

5. Ethan is a new client who has just moved out of his parents' home to attend college. Ethan was raised Catholic and is still a devout believer. Now that he is in college though, he has begun having sex with his new girlfriend. Ethan is very anxious about this because he believes it is a sin. What is Ethan experiencing?

   A) spiritual abuse
   B) a values conflict
   C) spiritual growth
   D) an existential crisis

Answer Key

1. **D)** Self-efficacy, outcome expectations, and personal goals are the three main components of Bandura's social cognitive career theory (SCCT).

2. **C)** Therapy is always focused on what the client sees as her presenting problem and the area on which she would like to work. By asking Linda what her biggest concerns are, the counselor prioritizes the client's perspective on her life and encourages engagement with the therapeutic process.

3. **D)** Cultural competence means letting the client be the expert of his culture and experiences. Asking a client to describe a cultural experience in his own words shows cultural competence.

4. **B)** The Honeymoon/Tourist Stage is the first stage of cultural adjustment. For many people, it can feel similar to being on vacation or a honeymoon.

5. **B)** A values conflict is when a person is acting in a way that conflicts with his values, has conflict with other people in his life because of differences in values, or is feeling personal distress over the lack of alignment between his behavior and his beliefs.

10 Human Growth and Development

An understanding of human growth and development is essential for any counselor. This chapter reviews theories of human growth and development.

Elements of Developmental Psychology

Lifespan Development and Behaviorism

Development begins at conception and continues throughout a person's lifetime. **Developmental psychology** studies the ways in which people change over time. Because most developmental change occurs during childhood, that is the emphasis of this field.

- **Cephalocaudal development** refers to the concept that human development and growth start at the head and move down. The head is the first to grow, and then the body grows to fit the size of the head.
- **Heredity** is the passing on of genetic traits from parents to their offspring through genes, chromosomes, and DNA.
- **Hereditability** refers to the possibility that a trait or condition can be passed from parents to offspring and to the portion of a trait that can be explained via genetic factors.

There are several significant debates in developmental psychology. Does biology or environment have a greater impact on human development? Psychologists have determined that both play a significant role.

Every person has certain biological traits that shape their personality traits. For example, research has found that some people have neurons that are sensitive to over-stimulation. These people tend to be introverts (in fact, as a general rule, introverts have these neurons).

However, some of these people are raised in ways that help them overcome this sensitivity to an extent—perhaps their parents required them to engage in lengthy conversations with other adults frequently—leading them to become extroverts.

The concept of **power of the environment** centers around the fact that humans do not live in a vacuum. Rather, they are influenced by people, places, ideas, and conditions in the world around them.

Empiricism is the theory that all data comes from the senses or through measurable observations or quantifiable data. Empiricism is a forerunner of behaviorism, which theorizes that developmental changes are quantitative, and experience creates knowledge.

> **DID YOU KNOW?**
>
> John B. Watson coined the term *behaviorism* in 1913.

Behaviorism is the psychological theory that all human behavior is learned through the various forms of conditioning that people encounter from experience. It can be measured and changed by modifying behaviors. The psychologist **B.F. Skinner** was often referred to as the "father" of behaviorism. He believed that all behavior is learned and therefore all behavior can be shaped through operant conditioning.

Applied behavior analysis (ABA) is a method of behavioral therapy. Most often used with children with autism spectrum disorders, ABA can also be applied to a variety of issues that require a purely behavioral intervention. The therapy uses the principles of conditioning to gradually change behaviors.

Organismic theorists look at human development and personality as a total experience where developmental changes are qualitative and require a holistic perspective.

PRACTICE QUESTION

1. A sixteen-year-old male presents for therapy with symptoms of schizophrenia. During the intake, the counselor learns that his grandfather and paternal uncle had similar symptoms, though they were never officially diagnosed. This indicates that schizophrenia is what?

    A) heritable

    B) cephalocaudal

    C) empirical

    D) organismic

Motor Sensory Development

The greatest changes in sensory, motor, and perceptual development happen in the first two years of life. When babies are first born, most of their senses operate in a similar way to those of adults. For example, babies are able to hear before they are born; studies show that babies turn toward the sound of their mother's voice just minutes after being born, indicating they recognize the mother's voice from their time in the womb.

The exception to this rule is vision. A baby's vision changes significantly in its first year of life; initially it has a range of vision of only eight to twelve inches and no depth perception. As a result, infants rely primarily on hearing; vision does not become the dominant sense until around the age of twelve months. Babies also prefer faces to other objects. This preference, along with their limited vision range, means that their sight is initially focused on their caregiver.

While babies' senses might be similar to those of adults, their ability to interpret sensory inputs is very different. They must learn to **perceive** or interpret the sensory information they receive. This occurs as they interact with their environment and their caregivers, and as they age.

Eleanor Gibson conducted an experiment in which she created a "visual cliff" by extending a Plexiglass ledge off a wooden table. All babies looked to their mothers for guidance when they approached the cliff; older babies refused to cross it regardless of their mothers' expressions. Gibson posited that while all babies could see the cliff, the older babies had a more complex perception of it because of their more advanced development and their experiences with crawling (and falling).

Figure 10.1. Gibson's Visual Cliff

In early psychology, babies were not believed to have any innate motor skills; the brain was considered to be **tabula rasa**, or a blank slate. However, later research revealed that all humans are actually born with certain reflexes which then later disappear. These include **rooting**, turning the head and opening the mouth in search of food when the cheek is touched; **sucking**, moving the mouth to draw milk from a nipple; **grasping**, the tight clenching of anything placed on a baby's palm; the **Moro reflex**, a startle reflex in which a baby throws its arms out and pulls them back in; and the **Babinski reflex**, when a baby's extends its big toe when the bottom of the foot is touched.

These reflexes fade through the process of **maturation**, the biological process of aging. Maturation is also a key component of other motor development: a baby cannot perform certain skills until its body has properly matured. For example, no matter what a parent tries to do, a six-month-old baby cannot run or jump.

PRACTICE QUESTION

2. Which of the following senses is most different at birth as compared to adulthood?

    A) sight
    B) smell
    C) hearing
    D) taste

Attachment Theory

In 1953, psychologist **John Bowlby** posited his attachment theory to explain the nature of the relationship between caregiver and child. Bowlby argued that in infancy, babies form an **attachment**, an enduring emotional bond to a particular figure, usually the primary caregiver.

Whereas psychologists previously attributed attachment to the association between being fed and the caregiver, Bowlby noticed that babies often maintained a strong attachment to their mothers, even when they were not the ones doing the feeding. So he theorized that attachment is actually evolutionary in nature, developed for an infant's survival.

Having someone who will provide that care allows babies to then use them as a base to explore their world, returning to them when they feel threatened. Attachment is not about food, but about care and responsiveness to needs. Thus, attachment is essential to development as a prototype for future relationships; disruption of attachment leads to difficulties in adulthood. He identified the ages of 0 – 5 as a critical period for the development of attachment.

In the early 1970s, **Mary Ainsworth** empirically proved Bowlby's attachment theory through her experiment titled "the Strange Situation." Ainsworth conducted an experiment where she first had mother and baby in a room, then introduced a stranger. The mother then left, leaving the baby alone with the stranger for a few minutes. After this, the mother returned and the stranger left. Then the mother left the baby alone in the room, after which the stranger returned, followed shortly thereafter by the mother (and the stranger left again). Ainsworth concluded that babies exhibited three types of attachment, related to the care provided by the attachment figure:

1. **Secure Attachment**: In this case, the baby is very secure in its relationship to the attachment figure. The baby uses this figure as a base for exploration and is soothed easily by them when upset. The baby is unhappy to see them go but calms quickly when they return. Ainsworth found that secure attachment resulted from a caring and attuned caregiver.

2. **Ambivalent Attachment**: In this case, the baby exhibited extreme fussiness and clinginess. The baby was unhappy when left alone with the stranger but was not easily soothed by the caregiver. This resulted from an inconsistent level of responsiveness from the caregiver.

3. **Avoidant Attachment**: In this case, the baby was completely detached from the caregiver. The baby explored the room without any orientation toward the attachment figure and responded equally to the caregiver and the stranger.

PRACTICE QUESTION

3. A baby who cries when approached by a stranger, but who calms quickly when held by her primary giver, is exhibiting which of the following?

   A) conditioned response

B) ambivalent attachment
C) avoidant attachment
D) secure attachment

Baumrind's Parenting Styles

Diana Baumrind developed the theory of parenting styles based on her interactions with children and their parents. Underlying Baumrind's theory is the idea that children need both structure and warmth. Baumrind theorized three main parenting styles, which are described in Table 10.1.

TABLE 10.1. Baumrind's Parenting Styles

STYLE	DEFINITION
Authoritarian	- focused on structure - parents often described as strict - limited freedom, warmth, or love toward children - no explanations provided to help children make choices
Permissive	- little structure - children allowed to do what they want - offers children more warmth and love - few boundaries - indulges children
Authoritative	- balanced version of the authoritarian and permissive - considered the ideal mode of parenting - boundaries, limits, and structure balanced with warmth and love - rules and the consequences for breaking them understood by children - children's knowledge that they are loved even when making bad choices

PRACTICE QUESTION

4. Michelle is fifteen and in therapy for anxiety. When asked to describe her parents, she calls them "drill sergeants." Which parenting style does this indicate?

    A) authoritative
    B) authoritarian
    C) permissive
    D) involved

Harlow's Maternal Deprivation Theory

Harry Harlow is most known for his experiments with **rhesus monkeys**, which explored the effects of maternal deprivation and attachment. His theory was that the bonding process between mother and infant requires not only attachment but also **contact comfort**, or the tactile sensation of comfort. In the experiment, he separated baby monkeys from their mothers at birth and put them in cages with two different artificial "mothers."

- One of the fake mothers was made of wire and provided the monkeys with food.
- The other mother was wrapped in soft cloth but did not offer food.
- Harlow found that the baby monkeys spent most of their time with the soft mother.

In a variation of this experiment, Harlow introduced a frightening stimulus. Again, the babies sought comfort from the soft mother. Finally, when the monkeys developed into adults, those with artificial mothers had more social problems with other monkeys compared to the ones who grew up with their real mothers.

PRACTICE QUESTION

5. What did Harry Harlow's experiments with monkeys reveal about mother-infant attachments?
    - **A)** Baby monkeys need food to grow strong.
    - **B)** Baby monkeys need contact comfort for healthy development.
    - **C)** Having a mother makes no difference to development.
    - **D)** Contact comfort is not necessary for monkeys.

Cognitive and Language Development

The study of cognitive development looks at the ways in which people—mostly children—think about and evaluate the world, and how that changes over time. The most significant figure in cognitive development is **Jean Piaget**.

Piaget theorized that children view the world through **schemata**, cognitive rules for interpreting the world which are developed based on their experiences. When they encounter new information or have a new experience, they either incorporate it into their existing schemata, called **assimilation**, or—if the new information is contradictory or does not fit—they adjust their schemata based on the new information, called **accommodation**. The balance between assimilation and accommodation is called **equilibration**.

For example, all of the men in a girl's life may have short hair. She then believes that all men have short hair. If she encounters a young boy with short hair, she will assimilate the information into the existing schema: all males have short hair. If, however, she encounters a man with long hair, her first reaction might be surprise, confusion, or even amusement. She will then accommodate the information by adjusting her schema: most men have short hair, but some have long hair.

Piaget's Stages of Cognitive Development

Piaget identified four stages of cognitive development:

Sensorimotor Stage (birth – age 2): In this stage, a baby's behavior is governed by its senses, and its schemata are based on its reflexes. Most significantly, during this time babies develop **object permanence**, the understanding that, even if an object is outside of their perceptual range, it still exists. If a four-month-old baby is fussing for his father's keys, the father need only put the keys away, and the baby will forget they exist.

Preoperational Stage (ages 2 – 7): The most important development during this stage is **language**. Children learn to use symbolic schema—through speech, drawing, letters, and numbers—to represent real-world objects. Their memories are developing and there are able to use their imaginations. However, they still cannot understand more complex ideas like cause and effect, time and comparison. A three-year-old pours her milk over her dinner plate in an attempt to understand cause and effect. During this stage, children are also completely **egocentric**; they cannot think beyond their own worldview. Children in this stage demonstrate **centration**, focusing on a singular aspect of a situation or object without noticing other elements of it.

Concrete Operations (ages 8 – 12): During this stage, children begin to develop logical thinking. They understand the passage of time and can comprehend that an action causes a certain reaction. Piaget identified **conservation** as the biggest developmental leap during this stage. Children in this stage can understand that the properties of an object stay the same even when its shape changes. For example, they understand that a rope is still a rope whether it is stretched out long or wrapped into an intricate knot. Another important step is developing the **concept of reversibility**, the idea that an action can be undone.

Formal Operations (age 12 – adulthood): In this final stage, humans develop abstract reasoning and consider ideas and objects in their mind without physically seeing them. For example, they are able to formulate a hypothesis about what will happen in an experiment before ever running the experiment. People are also able to engage in **metacognition**, thinking about *how* they think. While this is the final stage, Piaget argued that not everyone reaches this stage; some remain at the concrete operations stage.

In recent years, critiques of Piaget's theory have emerged. For one, Piaget's primary research subjects were his own children; he lacked a diverse group of research subjects, and his judgment may have been clouded. Furthermore, psychologists believe that many children go through Piaget's stages more quickly than he posited.

Other psychologists question the validity of stages in general. These psychologists support the **information-processing model**, which follows the same development path as Piaget's but in a continuous manner, rather than in stages.

 HELPFUL HINT

Remember, *conservation, concept of reversibility,* and *Concrete Operations* all start with the letter C.

PRACTICE QUESTION

6. A group of students are discussing the best ways to study for an upcoming exam. This is an example of which of Piaget's stages of development?

   A) Concrete Operations stage

   B) Formal Operations stage

   C) Preoperational stage

   D) Sensorimotor stage

Vygotsky's Cultural-Historical Theory

An alternative theory, the **Cultural-Historical Theory** of cognitive development, was posited by **Lev Vygotsky**. Vygotsky believed that society and culture were critical in a child's cognitive development. Vygotsky's work is based on the assumption that children learn about their culture—and how it interprets and responds to the world—through their formal and informal interactions with adults.

For example, a child is reading a book with her mother about animals that live in the forest. The mother points out the squirrels in the trees and the deer munching grass. In this way, the child learns how her culture classifies and talks about animals.

He also assumes that for cognitive growth to take place, children need both challenging tasks and room to play. Challenging tasks force children to stretch cognitively, making new connections and furthering their understanding. However, in order for this to be most effective, they need an adult—or anyone with more knowledge and experience than them—to **scaffold** their learning, by helping them through the process of acquiring the new skills.

Returning to the mother and child, the child is now trying to complete an animal puzzle. The mother scaffolds this process by encouraging her work, asking guiding questions, and helping her place a few pieces until she is able to do it on her own. Vygotsky called this learning area—the area between what a child can do without help and what she can do with help—the **zone of proximal development (ZPD)**.

PRACTICE QUESTION

7. The term *scaffolding*—providing a student guidance and support from an adult or peer, as appropriate, and eventually fading away from the support—came from which of the following theories?

   A) Lev Vygotsky's zone of proximal development

   B) Howard Gardner's multiple intelligences theory

   C) Albert Bandura's social learning theory

   D) Erik Erikson's theory of psychosocial development

Language Development

Adults—and even children—cannot remember a time when language and thinking were separate. Once language is acquired, the two processes are completely intertwined.

But how does language develop? Researchers have found that, regardless of the language a baby is learning, all babies go through the same stages of acquisition. Around four months, babies begin to babble, practicing the sounds of the language (or languages) that they hear regularly. Around their first birthday, the babbling turns into single words, like "book." By eighteen months, babies begin to bring together their single words into two-word phrases with clear meaning but no syntax. So "book!" becomes "Mommy book!"

Syntax begins to develop as the child advances into forming three- and four-word phrases. At first, young children often misapply or overuse grammatical rules, a process called **overgeneralization**.

For example, knowing that one uses the suffix "-ed" to create the past tense, a child in the **telegraphic** phase might say, "Daddy throwed the ball," not understanding that it does not apply to every word. This is corrected through modeling: when adults or older children use correct grammar so that the younger child can model their mode of speaking.

There is debate over the actual process of language acquisition. Psychologists who study behavior have argued that language is acquired through a process called conditioning. Essentially, this means that when children properly use language, they receive praise and positive feedback (which may even be just receiving an item they request) from their parents or caregivers. This then encourages them to use the language in the same way again.

Cognitive psychologists argue, however, that people deprived of this kind of parental conditioning are still able to develop language. **Noam Chomsky** put forward the **nativist theory of language** which states that each person is born with a language acquisition device inside of them. This device allows for language acquisition unless it is interrupted or damaged during a critical period. Current researchers have concluded that language is acquired both through behavior modification and through natural development in that critical period.

PRACTICE QUESTION

8. Which of the following is an example of overgeneralization in language development?

   A) "Mommy, I eated all of my vegetables!"
   B) "Mommy, monkey."
   C) "Baby cracker eat."
   D) "Book!"

Lifespan Developmental Theory

Piaget, Vygotsky, Bowlby, and Ainsworth focused primarily on infancy and early childhood in their theories, as this is where the majority of developmental change happens. Other psychologists, however, developed theories examining development across the entire lifespan of a human.

Erikson's Psychosocial Development Theory

The most well-known lifespan developmental theory is **Erik Erikson's psychosocial development theory**. Erikson was trained in the psychoanalytic school of psychology, so his theory is based in that rather than in evidence-based research. However, it has still heavily impacted psychology as a whole, particularly the treatment and schooling of children.

Erikson theorized that development occurs in eight stages with each stage centered on a specific social conflict. The manner in which the conflict is resolved impacts who the person ultimately becomes.

- Stage 1 (age 0 – 1): Trust versus Mistrust

Babies determine if they can trust their caregivers. If they can, as adults, they will appreciate the value of relationships and interdependence. If they cannot, they will remain untrusting and disconnected.

- Stage 2 (age 1 – 3): Autonomy versus Shame and Doubt

Toddlers attempt to exert their will over their own bodies. This manifests itself through activities like potty-training and learning to dress themselves. If toddlers are able to develop a level of independence, as adults they will have a strong sense of autonomy. If not, they will be plagued by feelings of shame and self-doubt.

- Stage 3 (age 3 – 5): Initiative versus Guilt

This is also known as the "why?" stage. Children develop curiosity and a desire to exert control over their environment as well (because they feel they have some control over themselves and trust in the adults around them). If this initiative is encouraged, they will have a strong sense of curiosity and purpose going forward. If not, they feel guilt and avoid future curiosity.

- Stage 4 (age 6 – 11): Industry versus Inferiority

This is the beginning of a child's formal education. If they feel that they are as good academically and socially as their peers, they will develop confidence. If not, they will develop an **inferiority complex**, a generalized feeling of incompetence and performance anxiety.

- Stage 5 (age 12 – 18): Identity versus Role Confusion

During adolescence, the primary social task is to discover one's most comfortable social identity. All teenagers, then, try on different roles. If they find their identity, they will have a stable sense of self. If not, they will encounter an **identity crisis**, a period of profound identity confusion.

- Stage 6 (age 19 – 40): Intimacy versus Isolation

Young adults must develop loving relationships with others while balancing their work needs. Success leads to strong, lasting relationships; failure leads to isolation and loneliness.

- Stage 7 (40 – 65): Generativity versus Stagnation

Individuals in middle adulthood strive to create something that will outlast them—through raising children or engaging in meaningful work. Those who succeed feel fulfilled and accomplished. Those who do not, endure a **midlife crisis**, becoming disengaged with the world or trying to change the direction of their lives. They may change their identities or attempt to exert more control over those around them. The fear of death is greatest in this period.

- Stage 8 (65 – death): Integrity versus Despair

As individuals near the end of life, they will reflect to determine whether they are satisfied with their life choices. If they are, they will develop wisdom. If not, they will experience despair.

PRACTICE QUESTION

9. According to Erikson, toddlers who develop a sense of control over their own bodies will experience which of the following as adults?

    A) trust
    B) industry
    C) autonomy
    D) identity

Theories of Moral Development: Kohlberg and Gilligan

Lawrence Kohlberg took another perspective in examining human development, developing **Kohlberg's theory of moral development**. He became interested in the question, "How does the ability to reason in ethical situations change?"

To answer this question, he posed several dilemmas to people of varying ages. The most well-known of these is the **Heinz dilemma**: A man must decide if he should steal a drug that he cannot afford in order to save his wife's life. Based on the responses he collected, Kohlberg articulated three levels of moral development, each composed of two stages.

TABLE 10.2. Kohlberg's Three Levels of Moral Development		
STAGE	**AGE RANGE**	**DESCRIPTION**
Pre-Conventional Level		
1: Obedience/Punishment	Preschool	Focus on avoiding punishment: Heinz should not steal the drug because he might get caught and put in jail.

continued on next page

TABLE 10.2. Kohlberg's Three Levels of Moral Development (continued)

STAGE	AGE RANGE	DESCRIPTION
Pre-Conventional Level (continued)		
2: Self-Interest/Reward	Elementary School	Focus on rewards instead of punishment; goal is to maximize benefits to oneself: Heinz should steal the drug because having his wife live would make him happy.
Conventional Level		
3: Interpersonal Accord	Middle School	Focus on being perceived as a "good" person and being liked: Heinz should steal the drug because he will be seen as a hero.
4: Law and Order	High School	Reliance on perceived fixed rules of conduct (e.g., learned from parents, peers): Heinz should not steal the drug because stealing is wrong.
Post-Conventional Level		
5: Social Contract	High School/Young Adulthood	Understand that legally right and morally right are not always the same; laws are for majority benefit and may conflict with best interest of the individual: Heinz should steal the drug because, while theft is illegal, the protection of life is more important than the protection of property.
6: Universal Principles (only achieved by some)	Adulthood	Self-defined and protected ethical principles: Heinz should steal the drug because life must be preserved at all costs.

There are many critiques of Kohlberg's research. The primary criticisms are that the situations were fictional and unfamiliar for many of the participants. The participants ranged in age from 10 to 16, and so had no frame of reference for making a decision about saving a dying wife.

Carol Gilligan critiqued Kohlberg for his bias. All of the participants in the original study were male, and when girls were tested later, they demonstrated slower moral development. However, Gilligan argued that there is a difference in moral development based on gender, and Kohlberg's stages only articulate the development of male morality.

In her 1982 book *A Different Voice*, Gilligan posited that male morality is based on absolute abstract ideas, with justice being the fundamental moral principle. Female morality is based on specific, individual situations with caring for others being the fundamental moral principle.

Later researchers have also questioned Gilligan's gender distinctions, and this debate continues.

PRACTICE QUESTION

10. Which of the following is NOT a critique of Kohlberg's moral development theory?

   A) He chose to examine a cross-section of participants rather than complete a longitudinal study.

   B) The study articulated a gender difference in moral reasoning that does not exist.

   C) His ethical dilemmas were artificial.

   D) Ethical decision-making can differ significantly in real-world versus hypothetical situations.

Daniel Levinson's Four Major Eras Theory

Daniel Levinson posited theories of adult development and divided them into four eras, or stages. He wrote about his ideas in two well-known books:

- *The Seasons of a Man's Life* focused on the life span that men experience.
- *The Seasons of a Woman's Life* chronicled the life span unique to women's experiences.

Both books expanded on the four major eras theory:

- Preadulthood (childhood and adolescence) is a stage of development characterized by dependence on adults.
- Early adulthood occurs after age twenty-two, but the transition period takes place between seventeen and twenty-two.
  - This stage is characterized by solidifying one's identity; understanding how one fits into the world; and changing family relationships, culminating in pursuing a career and family.
- Middle adulthood occurs after age forty, but the transition period takes place between forty and forty-five, which is when most people experience the midlife crisis.
  - The **midlife crisis** is a period when people question the trajectory of their lives.
  - Levinson considered it a positive event that inspires change if it is needed; without it, a person can feel stagnation toward the end of life.
  - The midlife crisis occurs regardless of class.

- Later adulthood occurs after age sixty-five, with the transition period between sixty and sixty-five. This is the stage of life when people transition out of their careers, into retirement, and often look back on their lives.

PRACTICE QUESTION

11. Tamara is forty-two and comes to therapy to discuss her anxiety and depression. During the interview, she reveals that her children are grown, and she does not know what to do with herself. She spent most of her time as a stay-at-home mom homeschooling her children, and now she has nothing to do, no purpose, and she feels lost. What might Tamara be experiencing?

    A) midlife crisis

    B) major depressive episode

    C) separation anxiety

    D) stress

William Perry's Four-Stage Theory of Intellectual and Ethical Development in Adults

William Perry developed a four-stage theory of intellectual and ethical development in adults. Perry's theory focuses on the cognitive and moral development of college students as they engage in higher learning and become more independent. He believed that students needed to go through each stage (described in Table 10.3.) to become effective at critical thinking skills.

TABLE 10.3. Perry's Four-Stage Theory of Intellectual and Ethical Development in Adults

STAGE	DEFINITION
Dualism	There is one right answer; a student just needs to find it.
Multiplicity	There is no right answer, but someone in authority must figure out the answer.
Relativism	One can prove any answer with enough evidence.
Commitment	One is open to independently learning and exploring for answers.

PRACTICE QUESTION

12. A college student who defers to the experts on a subject might be in which stage?

    A) dualism

    B) multiplicity

    C) relativism

    D) commitment

James W. Fowler's Theory of Faith and Spiritual Development

James W. Fowler was a theologian, minister, and human development professor who established the stages of faith development throughout the life span.

- **Stage 0: undifferentiated (primal) faith (0 – 4 years, infancy):** A baby does not feel faith, per se, but experiences feelings of trust and assurance that can grow into faith or neglect, the latter of which will lead to lack of faith.
- **Stage 1: intuitive-projective faith (two – seven years, early childhood):** A child develops the sense of right and wrong and learns faith stories without true understanding.
- **Stage 2: mythic-literal faith (childhood):** A child develops the sense of fairness associated with religious beliefs. The schema is simple: doing good deeds results in good things, and doing bad deeds results in bad things.
- **Stage 3: synthetic-conventional faith (adolescence):** An adolescent begins to identify with a belief system and form a sense of faith.
- **Stage 4: individuative-reflective faith (young adulthood):** Young adults explore faith further, often encountering conflict in their beliefs or developing a greater appreciation for them.
- **Stage 5: conjunctive faith (mid-thirties):** An adult comes to understand that faith is beyond basic religious beliefs.
- **Stage 6: universalizing faith (midlife):** Adults live out the tenets of their faith and are not bothered by differences in religious traditions.

PRACTICE QUESTION

13. Which stage of faith is associated with fairness and justice in its simplest forms?

    A) stage 0: undifferentiated
    B) stage 1: intuitive-projective faith
    C) stage 2: mythic-literal faith
    D) stage 3: synthetic-conventional faith

Robert Kegan's Six Stages of Life Span Development

Robert Kegan expanded on the work of Jean Piaget and theorized six stages of development based on how people create meaning, which grows throughout the life span. In counseling, **meaning-making** is the process of evaluating life events for their existential value. In particular, it means processing an event to find the good that comes from it that may not be readily apparent.

TABLE 10.4. Kegan's Six Stages of Life Span Development

STAGE	AGE RANGE	DEFINITION
Incorporative	infancy – 2	A child is completely dependent on the mother or primary caregiver.
Impulsive	2 – 6	A child is guided by pursuing what she wants and giving in to impulses. Behavior is guided by rules and consequences.
Imperial	6 – adolescence	A child is more influenced by his relationships and whether others approve of him or not. Empathy develops, but much of how a child thinks of himself comes from the opinions of others.
Interpersonal	adulthood	Adults create mutual, interdependent relationships.
Institutional	adulthood	Adults exhibit autonomy and self-expression.
Interindividual	adulthood	Adults focus on intimacy and genuine relationships that contribute to identity.

In counseling, the ***holding environment*** refers to the space that a counselor creates for a client that includes safety and nonjudgment. It is an attitude and approach that allows clients to express what they need to. Thus, the counselor "holds" the space for clients, so they feel safe in the relationship.

PRACTICE QUESTION

14. Robert Kegan's life span development stages focus on which aspect of human development?

   A) physical growth

   B) spiritual development

   C) relationships

   D) meaning-making

Personality

The study of personality is essentially the study of what makes a person who they are. This is a complicated question, but one that is fundamental to psychology.

There are four general approaches to answering this question: psychoanalytic, trait, social-cognitive, and humanistic.

Freud's Psychoanalytic Theories and Criticism

The most well-known **psychoanalytic** psychologist is **Sigmund Freud**. Freud believed that personality was set in early childhood. According to Freud, the stages of development were:

1. oral
2. anal
3. phallic (Oedipal/Electra complex)
4. latency
5. genital

If a child progressed through the stages of development without a problem, they would be well-adjusted. If, instead, the child experienced an unresolved conflict at a certain stage, they would develop a **fixation**, or become stuck at that stage; this conflict would affect their adult personality.

For example, if an individual experienced a conflict in the first stage—the oral stage—he may develop an oral fixation and need to constantly have something in his mouth.

In addition to his developmental theories, Freud theorized that the personality was composed of three parts:

- **Id**: The unconscious or unknown mind that operates on instinct. Emotions reside here as these are instinctive and not actively created by the individual.
- **Ego**: Existing partly in the unconscious mind and partly in the conscious mind, the ego follows the **reality principle**, and it negotiates between the id and the limitations of the environment.
- **Superego**: The superego is a person's conscience, determining right from wrong. It can influence the ego to account for moral considerations.

While extremely popular, Freud's theories face significant criticism. They are not based upon empirical evidence, and the nature of many of his structures (e.g., the id) make them unprovable. His theories also have no predictive power. While they can be used to explain why someone acted the way that they did, they cannot predict how someone will act in the future. Freud is also criticized for overemphasizing early childhood and sex and for being offensive to women (e.g., he claimed all women have penis envy).

On the opposite side of Freud is Alfred Adler's **individual psychology**. Diverging from Freud's pessimistic view of humanity, Adler had an inherently optimistic view, arguing that people are all ultimately striving for success or superiority. If a person enjoys success—meaning that they contribute to the community benefit while maintaining their personal identity—their personality is unified. If not, or if the person strives for superiority (personal gain without real regard for others), they will be ultimately unfulfilled.

PRACTICE QUESTION

15. When accidentally rear-ended by another car, Mark becomes enraged and attacks the other driver. How would Freud explain Mark's actions?

  A) Mark's id was determining his actions.

  B) Mark's super-ego was determining his actions.

  C) Mark's ego was determining his actions.

  D) Mark's actions were the result of negotiations between his ego, his id and his superego.

Trait, Social-Cognitive, and Humanistic Theories

Trait theories describe personalities by identifying main traits or characteristics. Characteristics of an individual's personality are considered stable and motivate their behavior. **Nomothetic theorists** argue that the same set of traits can be used to describe all personalities. For example, Hans Eyesenck posited that a transection of an introversion-extraversion scale (essentially how shy or outgoing one is) originally created by **Carl Jung** and a neuroticism scale (how anxious or fearful one is) could classify all personalities.

Idiographic theorists, on the other hand, argue that one set of traits cannot be used to describe everybody. Instead, people should be defined by the few traits that best define them, which can vary from person to person.

The primary criticism of trait theory is that it assumes that personalities are stable, when in fact people might behave very differently depending on the situation. For example, someone might be extremely talkative and social among their family, but shy and reserved in public.

According to social-cognitive theories, personality is the result of a combination of environment and patterns of thought. **Albert Bandura**'s theory of **reciprocal determinism** posits that personality results from the interaction between the person (their traits), the environment, and the person's behavior. For example, a person might be naturally optimistic, but become less so after a series of disappointments and failures.

Julian Rotter's **locus of control theory** posits that personality is determined by whether one feels in control of what happens to them. Those who have an internal locus of control—those who feel in control of their lives—tend to be healthier and more engaged, while those with an external locus of control—those who feel luck or destiny controls their lives—tend to be less successful.

Humanistic theorists challenge the **determinism**—the idea that personality is determined by past events—innate in other personality theories. Instead, they argue that people are able to exercise free will to determine their own destinies.

According to humanistic theory, an individual's personality is determined by their overall feeling about themselves (called **self-concept**) and the level of confidence they have in their own abilities (called **self-esteem**).

- **Abraham Maslow** argued that people strive to reach **self-actualization**, the maximizing of their own potential. (See page 209 for more on Maslow.)

- **Carl Rogers** posited that people need blanket acceptance, which he called **unconditional positive regard**, from other people in order to self-actualize.

Humanistic theory is criticized for being overly optimistic and vague. For example, it is difficult to measure if someone has reached their full potential.

> **HELPFUL HINT**
> See Chapter 1 for more on unconditional positive regard in counseling.

PRACTICE QUESTION

16. Bandura's theory of reciprocal determinism—that personality is the result of the interaction between the individual, their behavior, and their environment—is part of which school of personality theory?

    A) humanistic
    B) psychoanalytical
    C) social cognitive
    D) trait

Motivation and Stress

The reason for an individual's behavior is called **motivation**. Motivations can be either conscious and obvious, or unconscious and subtle. Much of motivation theory is based on research in learning and personality.

Maslow's Hierarchy of Needs

Abraham Maslow theorized that motivation was based on need, but all needs are not equal. He identifies five levels of need from basic biological needs for safety and survival to the need to fulfill life goals and self-actualization.

According to Maslow, each level of need must be fulfilled before the next can be addressed. However, there are examples that contradict this model. For example, Buddhist monks who practice self-immolation (lighting themselves

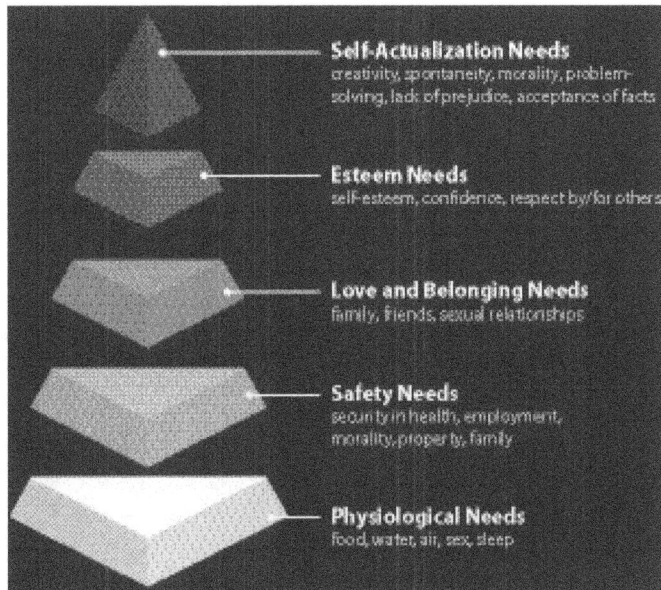

Figure 10.2. Maslow's Hierarchy of Needs

on fire) during the Vietnam War prioritized the need of self-actualization over the need for survival.

PRACTICE QUESTION

17. Which of the following is true of Maslow's hierarchy of needs?
    A) All needs ultimately relate to survival and safety.
    B) All needs must be met simultaneously.
    C) A level of need cannot be addressed until the previous level is met.
    D) Personal relationships are the ultimate need.

Sources of Motivation

Motivation comes from a variety of sources: internal, external, and environmental. The individual attitudes and goals of those people in an individual's life, as well as broader societal attitudes and goals, may serve as motivation for an individual. An example of this **social motivation** would be a student who works hard in school to gain admission to college because of the value society places on a college education.

If, however, that same student sought admission to college in order to master high level skills and to better understand the world, they would be propelled by **achievement motivation**. People who are motivated by achievement continually seek greater challenges.

All motivators can be classified as either **extrinsic motivators**—coming from outside of one's self—or **intrinsic motivators**—coming from within. For example, the person motivated to gain admission to college to get a good job or to be held in high esteem by others is extrinsically motivated. The student who seeks admission to college in order feel a sense of accomplishment or achieve mastery in a particular discipline is intrinsically motivated.

Both types of motivation are effective in encouraging desired behaviors; however, once extrinsic motivators end, so does the behavior. Once the student looking for peer approval gains admission to college, he is more likely than his intrinsically motivated counterpart to perform poorly. Therefore, extrinsic motivators are suitable for short-term behavior goals, while intrinsic motivators are better at encouraging long-term positive behaviors.

PRACTICE QUESTION

18. When Amy fails her math test, she decides it is because the questions were too confusing. This is an example of which of the following types of attribution?
    A) person-stable attribution
    B) person-unstable attribution
    C) situation-stable attribution
    D) situation-unstable attribution

Stress

Any situation that taxes one's coping abilities by threatening—or seeming to threaten—a person's wellbeing is considered **stress**. Common stressors include life changes, external and internal pressure, environmental factors, frustration, and conflict.

Acute stressors are relatively short in duration and have a clear endpoint, whereas chronic stressors are relatively long in duration and have no apparent time limit. Acute stressors have little negative impact and can even be beneficial at times. For example, short-term frustration, the thwarting of the pursuit of a goal, can act as a motivator for further achievement. **Chronic stressors**, on the other hand, have significant physiological and psychological consequences. Hans Selye detailed the body's stress response in his **General Adaptation Syndrome (GAS)** as it applies to all animals:

- **Alarm reaction**: The heart rate increases; blood is diverted away from other body functions to prepare the animal for action. This is also known as the **fight-or-flight response**, as the animal is prepared to either attack or flee.

- **Resistance**: Hormones are released to maintain the state of readiness. In chronic stress, this state is maintained for too long, depleting the body's resources.

- **Exhaustion**: The body returns to a normal state. If the resistance state lasted too long, the body will be more vulnerable to disease and sustain long-term damage. This is why chronic stress is associated with health problems like arthritis, ulcers, asthma, migraine headaches, heart disease, and depression.

Maintaining a resistance state resulting from some kind of stressful event—either acute or long-term (e.g., war, sexual assault, watching someone die, or almost dying themselves) can also lead to **post-traumatic stress disorder (PTSD)**. People with PTSD experience disturbed behavior—including nightmares, jumpiness, and temper flares.

Chronic stress also disrupts attention and inhibits memory. Chronic, or **toxic stress**, related to poverty can even change the chemical makeup of a child's brain, disrupting and weakening its circuits.

The best way to deal with stress is to use **constructive coping mechanisms** like confronting a problem directly, breaking it down into manageable pieces, maintaining flexibility, and remaining aware of one's coping and stress resources. Studies have also shown that maintaining **perceived control**, or the feeling that one is in control of a stressor, reduces the overall stress level. For example, the patient who is given control of his own pain control medication reports a lower overall pain level than the patient who is prescribed doses, even when the amount of medicine received is the same.

CONTINUE

PRACTICE QUESTION

19. Hans Selye developed his general adaptation syndrome to describe which of the following?

    A) personality traits

    B) reactions to stress

    C) memory processes

    D) problem-solving processes

Answer Key

1. **A)** The client's symptoms and history indicate that the disorder was passed on through the generations of his family.

2. **A)** At birth, babies can only see 8 – 12 inches in front of their faces. They do not gain full sight until they are one year old.

3. **D)** The baby's actions demonstrate a strong attachment to the caregiver.

4. **B)** Authoritarian parents impose rules and structure with very little explanation or warmth, similar to how a drill sergeant might enforce order.

5. **B)** The baby monkeys preferred the soft fake mothers even when they did not offer food.

6. **B)** The Formal Operations stage is the final stage. Individuals develop the ability to engage in metacognition, thinking about how they think.

7. **A)** Vygotsky's zone of proximal development describes tasks students can perform with help and gradually learn to do on their own.

8. **A)** Overgeneralization describes the tendency of young children to misapply grammatical rules by assuming that the rules apply universally.

9. **C)** According to Erikson, autonomy emerges when a toddler develops a sense of independence. This occurs in the second stage.

10. **B)** Carol Gilligan critiqued Kohlberg for having a strong male bias in his theory, pointing to the fact that all the original participants were male and his own male perspective on moral reasoning impacted how he evaluated various types of reasoning. Gilligan herself articulated different types of moral reasoning based on gender, which has since been called into question.

11. **A)** A midlife crisis occurs when people question their life's purpose.

12. **B)** The multiplicity stage puts the burden of answers on authority figures.

13. **C)** Children at the mythic-literal faith stage associate good deeds with good outcomes and vice versa.

14. **D)** Kegan's developmental stages consider how people in each stage develop their social understanding, identities, and create meaning in their lives.

15. **A)** The id governs all emotion and impulsive behavior. When attacking the other driver, Mark was being driven solely by his emotions.

16. **C)** Social cognitive theory looks at the ways in which individual thought and overall environment impact personality. Bandura was a prominent social-cognitive theorist.

17. **C)** According to Maslow, the ability to fulfill a need is dependent on the fulfillment of needs lower in the hierarchy.

18. **D)** Amy attributes her failure to the situation of the particular test, making it an unstable attribution and a situational one.

19. **B)** The general adaptation syndrome describes the physiological reaction all animals have to stress.

?? NCMHCE Practice Test

Case Study 1

Intake Session

Age: 16

Sex assigned at birth: female

Gender: feminine

Sexuality: heterosexual

Ethnicity: White

Relationship status: unknown

Counseling setting: outpatient

Type(s) of counseling: individual

Presenting problem: behavioral problems in the family, depression

Diagnosis: F91.3 oppositional defiant disorder, moderate

Presenting Problem

The sixteen-year-old client is brought to counseling by her mother, who says that her daughter's behavior is disruptive to the family and her performance in school has declined significantly in the past six months. The family includes the mother, the father, the client, an older son, and a younger daughter. The mother reports that the client frequently argues with and yells at the mother and father, does not comply with family rules, will not allow her younger sister to be alone at home, and refuses to participate in family activities. The mother describes her daughter as a combination of depressed, angry, and withdrawn; she loses her temper easily and out of proportion to the situation. The mother says she does not understand this behavior because her daughter never used to be this way; she was studious, kind, and playful. The mother states that her daughter's behavior has been so disruptive to the family that last week she sent her to live with her maternal grandparents because the household cannot function with her argumentative behavior. During the session, the client does not speak except when asked direct questions by the counselor. When answering, she does not make eye contact.

Mental Status

The client is well-groomed, neat, clean, and stylish in her clothing choices. She wears her hair styled, and does her makeup tastefully. Her depressed mood is visible in her body language, which is closed and congruent with her flat affect. During the session, she did not make eye contact with the counselor and sat as far away from her mother as she could. The client denied any auditory or visual hallucinations as well as any thoughts or plans of suicide. She has no previous history of mental health problems. She nodded in agreement when asked if she felt depressed. The client reported having no appetite, losing weight, and experiencing difficulty sleeping.

Family History

The client is the middle child of her biological parents with whom she lives. The mother reports that her daughter has never been close with her mother or her father, but that she is close to her siblings. Her older brother, who is eighteen, taught her to play guitar, but recently she does not want anything to do with him. The mother reports that her daughter has been protective of her younger sister, who is nine, and many of the fights are over what the client thinks about her siblings' relationships with their parents. The client moved to her maternal grandparents' home one week ago, and the mother reports that the grandparents say the client stays in her room "all the time" and stopped going to school.

Counseling Session 1

The client comes alone to the next counseling session. The session focuses on establishing rapport with the client, educating her about the counseling process, and gathering more intake data from her directly. The client is well-groomed, stylish, and clean. Her nonverbal presentation is closed, and she rarely makes eye contact with the counselor. When the counselor asks what she thought about what her mother said in the previous session, the client says it was "all bullsh***." She reports fighting with her parents because they think her brother is "a saint," saying, "They never listen to me; they think I am stupid because he is so smart." She says she loves her little sister and wants to protect her. The client states that she feels depressed most of the day, every day, with little interest in doing activities she once liked to do. She used to enjoy playing and writing music, watching anime, writing poetry, drawing, and talking to online friends, but for the past six months, she has felt fatigued and unmotivated to do anything. She says living with her grandparents is nice because they leave her alone, but it makes her sadder and more worried about her sister.

Counseling Session 2

This session occurs two weeks later and focuses on establishing rapport with the client by talking about the things she is interested in. She discloses that she is very artistic and loves anime, drawing, and writing. Once she learned to play guitar, she started to write songs and has recorded several of them. She reports that she does not fit in well at school because she is "so artsy," and her school is a small rural school where most of the kids grew up on farms. As a result, she has a lot of online friends, including a boyfriend whom she has never met. Toward the end of the session, she reveals that her brother came into her room one night six months ago and touched her inappropriately. She woke up and fought back, hitting him in the face and giving him a black eye. They both lied to their parents about the incident. Since then, she wants nothing to do with her brother and worries that he will go after her sister. The rest of the session focuses on how her symptoms are related to the trauma of that event and the burden of keeping the secret. The counselor also discusses with the client the process of reporting the incident to child protective services.

1. How can the counselor fulfill mandated reporter obligations while maintaining the relationship with the client?
   A) The counselor can tell the client that the law is paramount and that the counselor must immediately report the incident with the client's brother.
   B) The counselor can explain the legal requirements to the client, facilitate disclosure to the parents, and make the report with the family present.
   C) The counselor can agree to not make the report in order to protect the client's brother and family relationship.
   D) The counselor can instruct the client to report the incident herself to the authorities.

2. Based on the intake, what does the client's significant behavior change six months prior indicate?
   A) Something happened to the client, or the client started to engage in high-risk behaviors.
   B) The client is a teenager; behavior changes are normal.
   C) The client's social situation has changed.
   D) It is likely that nothing has changed, and the mother is just exaggerating.

3. Why would it be appropriate to conduct a suicide risk assessment with this client?
   A) Suicide risk assessment is required for all adolescents.
   B) The mother indicated it was necessary.
   C) The client underwent a significant behavioral change six months ago.
   D) A suicide risk assessment is not needed.

4. After session 1, what is an appropriate short-term therapeutic goal for the counselor to work toward with this client?
   A) establish a trusting relationship with her
   B) explore the origin of her depressive symptoms
   C) get her back in school
   D) refer her to a psychiatrist for medication

5. After session 2, what is an appropriate short-term therapeutic goal the counselor can work toward with this client?
   A) charge the brother with sexual assault
   B) establish physical and psychological safety
   C) refer the family to family counseling
   D) engage in exposure therapy

6. What could the counselor have said to the client in session 1 to increase trust?
   A) "Based on your mother's report, my diagnosis for you is oppositional defiant disorder."
   B) "Was your mother right about your behavior changes?"
   C) "You didn't say much during the intake session, so does that mean you agree with your mother's observations?"
   D) "Your mother did most of the talking in the intake, but I would much rather hear your perspective of what you're experiencing."

7. How does the client's disclosure in session 2 change the diagnosis?
   A) It makes the counselor suspicious about who is lying.
   B) It suggests that the client's behavior changes are a result of the sexual assault, not due to the proposed diagnosis.
   C) It changes the diagnosis to intermittent explosive disorder.
   D) It does not change the diagnosis.

8. What could the counselor say to show the client that what she says is more important than what her mother reported?
   A) "I sense that your version of events is much different from what your mother reported."
   B) "Should I believe everything your mother says?"
   C) "So what really happened?"
   D) "I don't believe your mother; I think she is lying."

9. How can the counselor summarize the client's relationship with her parents to her in a way that demonstrates empathy?
   A) "You should listen to your parents at all times."
   B) "If your parents are not good for you, you should continue to live with your grandparents."
   C) "It sounds like you feel overlooked and misunderstood by your parents."
   D) "Why can't you just get along with your family?"

10. What stated client strengths could the counselor use to develop healthy coping skills with this client?
    A) art and music
    B) strong personality
    C) family relationships
    D) friends

11. What type of referral might be appropriate after reporting the assault?
    A) substance use treatment
    B) family therapy
    C) couples therapy
    D) vocational therapy

12. Which therapy modality would be appropriate and build on the client's strengths?
    A) acceptance and commitment therapy
    B) Brainspotting
    C) art therapy
    D) CBT

Case Study 2

Intake Session

Age: 45

Sex assigned at birth: male

Gender: masculine

Sexuality: heterosexual

Ethnicity: Hispanic or Latino

Relationship status: married

Counseling setting: outpatient

Type(s) of counseling: individual

Presenting problem: relapse after five years of sobriety

Diagnosis: F15.10 Amphetamine use disorder, mild due to relapse

Presenting Problem

The client and his wife attend the intake session together. The previous week, the client experienced a significant stressor at work, and he used methamphetamine to help him get through his shift. He had been sober for over five years and now has a significant desire to stop. The client was involved in gangs in his teens and twenties, including using and selling methamphetamine and cocaine. When he was twenty-six, he served a short prison sentence for possession with intent to sell. While there, he participated in a recovery program and continued in recovery upon release. He met his wife fifteen years ago, and he promised her he would not go back to that life. They have two young children. The client's wife is tearful in the session, expressing fear that he will return to "his old life." The client appears remorseful and sad. He reports feeling a lot of stress at work, fears losing his job, and says he has been feeling depressed. Other symptoms include difficulty sleeping, lack of interest in activities, and fighting more often with his wife. He has agreed to attend therapy so his wife will not leave him.

Mental Status

The client is well-groomed, wears clean clothes, and demonstrates adequate hygiene. He appears tired, as evidenced by dark circles around his eyes. His affect is congruent with his stated depressed mood; his body language is lethargic, and his speech is slow and at low volume. When discussing his relapse, he appears tearful. The client denies auditory or visual hallucinations as well as suicidal and homicidal plans or intent.

Family History

The client does not talk much about his family of origin except to say that his father died when he was six years old and he grew up very poor. His mother and sister live in another state, and they have not talked much since he went to prison. He considers his wife and children his only family and says he is fairly close with his father-in-law. He has not discussed his relapse with anyone besides his wife and the coworker who got him the drugs.

Counseling Session 1

The client arrives at the second session one week later, looking disheveled and like he slept in his clothes. He reveals that he used drugs again at work. His wife found out and kicked him out of the house. The counselor conducts a safety assessment with the client and engages in motivational interviewing techniques to determine the pattern of triggers related to the relapse and to evaluate the client's current resources. The client reports feeling hopeless and depressed, is having difficulty sleeping, and is angry that he allowed himself to get into this situation. He still goes to work because he wants to provide for his family, but he is afraid his employer will find out about his drug use and fire him. He cries when talking about his family and says they are his top priority. The counselor engages the client in a decisional balance exercise to elicit change talk. There is also discussion about the client's triggers and what he can do in the short term to avoid those triggers. The client agrees to attend NA meetings, look for a sponsor, and discuss attending couples therapy with his wife—he will need her support in recovery.

Counseling Session 2

The client arrives at the third session one week later looking well-groomed, yet sad. He reports going to NA meetings every day, since there is a meeting a block from his work, and he found a sponsor. He struggles with cravings at work but can contact his sponsor through text while on the job, and that helps. He also reports that he requested a transfer at work so he does not have to be around the coworker who can get him meth. His wife has not let him come back home; he is living with his in-laws. He reports that his wife is encouraging but will not go to counseling with him until he is sober for thirty days. This motivates him, as he misses his family greatly. The client talks about feeling down, fighting hopelessness, and struggling to believe he can change. The counselor engages in cognitive techniques to explore where his beliefs about himself come from. The client reveals he was molested by an older cousin soon after his father died. It went on for several years. He feels great shame about this and has not told any other counselors, sponsors, or his wife.

1. Can the counselor see the client and his wife for couples therapy?
   A) Yes, the counselor can help them work through their issues.
   B) No, it would be a dual relationship.
   C) No, the counselor is not qualified to conduct couples therapy.
   D) Yes, as long as it is in the best interest of the client.

2. What additional assessment should the counselor conduct with the client after counseling session 1?
   A) an intelligence assessment to determine the client's capability for change
   B) a suicide risk assessment due to the client's feelings of hopelessness and change in family situation
   C) a career counseling assessment to determine if a different job is appropriate to support the client in his recovery
   D) a marital communication assessment to encourage the reunification of the family

3. How does the client's disclosure in session 2 change the diagnosis?
   A) The client's disclosure does not change the diagnosis.
   B) The counselor should consider depression as a co-occurring disorder.
   C) The client will need to do another intake to be properly assessed for another diagnosis.
   D) Undisclosed childhood trauma suggests a co-occurring trauma-related diagnosis.

4. Which of the following is an appropriate short-term goal for this client at the end of session 1?
   A) sign up for residential or detox treatment
   B) connect with two sources of social support and recovery support, such as NA, within fourteen days
   C) engage in family counseling within fourteen days
   D) search for a new job and apply for at least two within the next thirty days

5. Based on the disclosure in session 2, how could the counselor change the treatment plan?
   A) The plan can address childhood trauma and how it relates to substance use.
   B) The treatment plan does not need to be changed.
   C) The treatment plan can focus on family therapy rather than individual therapy.
   D) The treatment plan can focus only on maintaining abstinence from substances.

6. In what stage of change is the client in during session 1?
   A) precontemplation
   B) action
   C) lapse/relapse
   D) contemplation

7. What could the counselor say to increase the client's level of determination, making it more likely he will take action?
   A) "All you need to do is put in a little more effort if you really want to stay clean; think of your future."
   B) "Relapse can be a normal part of the recovery cycle; we can figure out how to prevent it from happening again."
   C) "If you don't maintain recovery, it is likely you'll lose your family."
   D) "At some point, you need to think about what your kids will think about your addiction and stop thinking only of yourself."

8. What kind of psychoeducation would be helpful to this client after his disclosure in session 2?
   A) the effect of methamphetamine use on the body
   B) statistics about childhood trauma
   C) the impact of childhood trauma on substance use and relationships
   D) laws regarding methamphetamine possession and use

9. What could the counselor have said to the client to show unconditional positive regard for him when he reported relapsing?
   A) "It's time to move on and stop repeating the same patterns in your life. Think about all you could have in your life."
   B) "Making a change in your life will help you feel better about yourself."
   C) "Don't listen to the judgments of others. Only focus on what you want to achieve."
   D) "Your struggle with substances does not define you. Making a bad decision does not make you a bad person."

10. How could the counselor have responded with cultural competence to the client's disclosure in session 2?
    - A) "Telling someone might have made others think you were less of a man; that is a heavy burden to carry alone."
    - B) "Do you feel stigmatized because of what you experienced as a child? You should understand that many people have similar experiences."
    - C) "You could have told your wife; she is supposed to be there for you."
    - D) "You were so young; I imagine it was impossible to fight back, but why didn't you ask another adult for help?"

11. Which of the following interventions might be appropriate for this client?
    - A) DBT
    - B) ACT
    - C) trauma-focused CBT
    - D) group therapy

12. When the client revealed the sexual assault in session 2, what could the counselor have said to bring the client's awareness to the present?
    - A) "How does it feel to disclose this to me?"
    - B) "Why did you tell me about this?"
    - C) "Would telling your wife be appropriate?"
    - D) "How does this affect your relationship with your wife?"

13. Given the client's disclosure about childhood sexual abuse and lack of a relationship with his father, what theory could explain the client's substance use?
    - A) behavioral theory
    - B) systems theory
    - C) cognitive theory
    - D) attachment theory

Case Study 3

Intake Session

Age: 52

Sex assigned at birth: female

Gender: feminine

Sexuality: bisexual

Ethnicity: White

Relationship status: divorced

Counseling setting: women's prison counseling

Type(s) of counseling: individual

Presenting problem: anger management

Diagnosis: F63.81 intermittent explosive disorder

Presenting Problem

The client is mandated to attend counseling within the prison system due to her rage outbursts and fighting with other inmates. The referral report contains a history of her behaviors and includes comments that the client's anger is out of proportion to the situations. When asked about them, the client only provides very short answers, either confirming or denying the information. The counselor asks the client about how she ended up in prison, and she responds that the report says it all. The counselor says that is true, but he would like to hear the client's story in her own words since reports do not often tell the true story. The client stares at the counselor in silence for a time and then tells a short version of her story. The client was arrested for armed robbery five years ago. Although she was working at the time, she did not make much money, and her two children needed things for school. Her boyfriend at the time said he knew of a pawn shop where they could steal things like iPads and laptop computers. He assured her he had inside information and that it would be easy; however, after they broke in, the police came, and they were arrested. Because she had a knife on her person, which she did not use on anyone, she was charged with armed robbery. She could not afford an attorney, and her public defender "was useless." Rather than go through a jury trial, she agreed to a five-year sentence. Not long after her incarceration, she was moved to another facility across the state, so she cannot see her kids, who are living with her mother now. She feels anger and distrust at the system and says she feels "screwed" and targeted "because I'm poor and White." She describes prison as a "rat cage" and the other women as "b^%$es" that she has to keep at bay. Her one friend in jail is also her romantic partner, but she denies being a lesbian. She reports not being able to sleep, feeling on edge all the time, and startling at the slightest noise. The client believes there are groups of women out to get her and the guards do not care. When people come at her, she "goes off the hook"—unplanned—and often gets in fights. When she is put in isolation, she says she can get some "peace and quiet."

Mental Status

The client appears well-groomed and is dressed in prison-issue attire. She makes direct eye contact, with a facial expression that implies defiance. She is guarded, suspicious of authority figures, and does not trust anyone in the system. The client denies auditory and visual hallucinations as well as suicidal ideation. She expresses homicidal intent toward guards and other inmates, but further assessment reveals she has no plans to follow through on those thoughts. She states that if she were to act on any of her thoughts, she would be in prison even longer, which is not something she wants to do because that is what people in the system would like to happen.

Family History

The client reports growing up poor with her mom and younger sister. Her father left the family when she was five, and they never saw him again. Her mom worked all the time, so she and her sister "pretty much raised ourselves." They lived in a trailer in a small rural town, and she was bullied in school for being poor. She learned to fight from an army veteran who lived in the same trailer park and got in fights in high school. She graduated and went to tech school for two years, where she learned the welding trade; however, it was hard for her to find a job in welding because it is "not a woman's job." She met her husband when she was thirty-one; they married and had two kids, but he left when the kids were ten and twelve. They are now fourteen and sixteen, living with her mother in the same trailer she grew up in, and she says she knows "how much it sucks for them." She gets weekly phone calls from her mother, but her kids will not talk to her.

Counseling Session 1

The following week, the client reports that she was in isolation for the past week and is feeling "pretty good." She smiles more this session. The counselor asks her how she is coping. She says that when she gets in a fight, she feels like she "gets it out of her system," and she prefers to be in isolation. The client asks if there is a way the counselor can say that she is "completely nuts," so she can remain in isolation for the rest of her sentence. The counselor describes the physical symptoms of anxiety and invites the client to consider that she experiences anxiety, which comes out as anger. The counselor guides the client in identifying situations that arouse those physical symptoms and rating the severity of the symptoms. The counselor leads the client through a mindfulness exercise to calm her anxiety.

Counseling Session 2

The client arrives at the session visibly angry, as evidenced by her body language and facial expression. She begins talking to the counselor very fast and very loudly. After she was released from isolation, she was involved in another fight, yet she states that she did not start it. During that fight, she hit the other woman so hard that her jaw fractured, and there is an upcoming proceeding to determine if more time will be added to her sentence as a result of that assault. As she tells the story, she paces. Once she finishes, the counselor leads her in another mindfulness exercise to help her calm down, and they process the incident and the next steps.

1. How could the counselor respond if the client asks how much of what they talk about gets back to the prison staff?
    A) that the counselor needs to report everything
    B) that the counselor must operate with a minimal disclosure policy
    C) that it is not the client's concern what goes into the documentation
    D) that the counselor will answer any questions posed by prison administrators

2. Based on the client's reported symptoms, how might the diagnosis change?
    A) Based on the client's childhood, she likely has an attachment disorder.
    B) The diagnosis should consider depression and anxiety, as they are more common.
    C) There may be elements of a heightened threat response.
    D) No diagnosis change should be considered.

3. What other assessment could the counselor use with the client to measure progress?
    A) Hamilton Rating Scale for Depression
    B) Beck Anxiety Inventory
    C) intelligence test
    D) anger management scale

4. What is a short-term therapeutic goal for this client?
    A) learn emotional regulation skills
    B) establish positive social relationships
    C) obtain job skills
    D) reestablish a positive relationship with her children

5. Which type of treatment intervention would MOST effectively target the client's symptoms?
   A) CBT
   B) exposure therapy
   C) EMDR
   D) DBT

6. What can the counselor say to the client to demonstrate an understanding about her fighting?
   A) "It sounds like fighting is a way to protect yourself against emotional hurt."
   B) "Fighting is not the way to solve problems, but I think you're learning that."
   C) "I wonder how much fighting has really helped you."
   D) "I understand, it can feel really good to fight, even if it accomplishes nothing."

7. How can the counselor reframe the client's cycle of fighting and isolation?
   A) by reminding the client that fighting will not solve anything
   B) by explaining that this behavioral cycle gets the client what she wants
   C) by reinforcing prison policies and stating that more time can be added to her sentence
   D) by explaining that continuing to fight will hurt her chances of getting out and being with her children

8. How can the counselor use psychoeducation with this client to probe deeper issues?
   A) to explain the rules of the prison and why the client needs to comply
   B) to discuss theories about prison discipline and its efficacy
   C) to explain the therapeutic process and how counseling works within the prison system
   D) to explain how an insecure attachment style influences relationship skills and emotional regulation skills

9. What did the counselor do during the intake that prompted the client to open up and tell her story?
   A) explained the informed consent process thoroughly
   B) confronted her about her violent behavior
   C) exhibited nonjudgment and established an alliance with the client against the system
   D) smiled and maintained eye contact to show friendliness

10. In session 2, what could the counselor have done nonverbally to defuse the client's anger?
    A) sat in silence and let the client wear herself out
    B) moved and sp0ken slowly and softly while keeping body language relaxed
    C) assertively commanded the client to stop, breathe, and relax
    D) matched the client in tone, volume, and posture

11. Which aspect of DBT would be most helpful for this client?
    A) emotional regulation
    B) cognitive reprocessing
    C) contingency management
    D) family therapy

12. What purpose can role-play serve as a therapeutic intervention with this client?
    A) It can allow the client to vent her frustrations.
    B) It can help the client process trauma.
    C) It can give the client a safe place to practice communication and relationship skills.
    D) It can reprimand the client for fighting with others.

13. What might be an appropriate long-term goal for this client?
    A) to learn job skills
    B) to attend group therapy with other inmates
    C) to make reparations to the people she hurt
    D) to create a medication regimen

Case Study 4

Intake Session

Age: 15

Sex assigned at birth: male

Gender: masculine

Sexuality: heterosexual

Ethnicity: Hispanic or Latino

Relationship status: single

Counseling setting: adolescent drug court

Type(s) of counseling: individual

Presenting problem: drug use

Diagnosis: F12.10 cannabis use disorder, mild, in early remission

Presenting Problem

The client is mandated to individual therapy as a component of the adolescent drug court program and is diagnosed with cannabis use disorder in the referral paperwork. The program includes goals the client has to meet, and if he complies with all goals, he can avoid jail time. Program goals include meeting with a probation officer; attending school; participating in individual, family, and group counseling sessions, attending a life skills group; and performing community service. During the intake, the client is resistant to talking to the counselor, stating, "You don't know me" throughout and saying that he is only attending the sessions because the program makes him do so.

Mental Status

The client sits with his arms crossed, staring at the counselor; his affect is congruent with an angry mood. He is well-groomed and is oriented to person, place, and time. Although he refuses to offer information to the counselor, he shares that he has not had auditory or visual hallucinations or suicidal or homicidal ideation. He demonstrates fair judgment and limited insight by complying with the program requirements at a minimal level.

Family History

The client states that he does not want to talk about his family and that his "brothers" are his real family. According to the referral paperwork, the client, his mother, and his sister live with his paternal grandparents. His father is currently serving a prison sentence for assault and battery. The report also notes that the client is a member of a local gang that engages in criminal activity and drug sales.

Counseling Session 1

In this session, the counselor brings out a deck of cards and proposes a game of "war" to the client, but with different rules. Whoever wins the "battle" gets to ask the other person a question. The client agrees. During the course of the game, the counselor points out that the questions the client asks are insightful and demonstrate that he is a deep thinker. The counselor learns that the client loves to do work with his hands and that his community service is at an auto body shop, which he really likes. The owner is someone he respects, and he is fascinated with metalworking.

Counseling Session 2

When the client arrives, he asks if they can play the card game again. He appears more relaxed, smiles more, and asks more insightful questions. The counselor asks the client questions, such as what are his strengths, what would he like to be doing in five years, what does he value, and what are some of his favorite things. The counselor reflects on the client's answers, highlights his strengths, and provides positive reinforcement of his questions.

1. What is a potent challenge when working with a client who is mandated to treatment?
    A) treatment compliance
    B) establishing a trusting relationship
    C) early dropout
    D) aggression and violence in session

2. What was the client nonverbally communicating during the intake?
    A) fatigue
    B) interest
    C) defiance
    D) submission

3. Why would it NOT be appropriate to conduct assessments during the intake?
   A) The client does not trust the counselor and therefore will likely not be truthful.
   B) There is already a diagnosis; further assessment is not needed.
   C) The counselor has all the information needed to begin treatment with this client.
   D) The counselor already has assessment results in the referral paperwork.

4. If the client does not articulate goals, what should the counselor do?
   A) write goals for the client in compliance with the judicial program
   B) write that the first goal is to establish rapport with the client
   C) save writing goals for later
   D) give the client an ultimatum that he must set goals

5. What is a reasonable, client-focused short-term goal that could be written after session 1?
   A) The client will read more books about therapy in the next two weeks.
   B) The client will process his feelings about his father.
   C) Career counseling assessments will be conducted within thirty days.
   D) The client will explore mentorship or apprenticeship programs in metalworking.

6. Which type of counseling intervention is the counselor using by complimenting the client's questions?
   A) EMDR
   B) exposure therapy
   C) strengths-based
   D) motivational interviewing

7. When providing the client with a summary of the session, what might the counselor emphasize to get him to think about changing his lifestyle?
   A) how much time he has left in the program
   B) his strengths, values, and goals and how his current choices will likely not help him reach them
   C) the penalties for not complying with the program
   D) the remaining expectations of drug court and how well the client has done so far

8. What would be the next step in the counseling intervention?
   A) continuing to play the card game and getting the client to process his emotions
   B) discussing the client's familial relationships and how they impact his choices
   C) discussing the resources that could help the client achieve his goals and use his strengths
   D) finding ways to improve the client's grades in school

9. What strategy could the counselor have used to address the client's resistance to therapy during the intake?
   A) treated the client with respect and refrained from over-questioning
   B) ignored the resistance and continued with treatment
   C) reported the resistance to the drug court to force the client's participation
   D) pointed out that if the client does not participate, he will not pass

10. What purpose did the card game serve?
    A) It was a distraction from the real reason the client is in therapy.
    B) It took up time, so the session went by faster.
    C) It got the client thinking about his childhood.
    D) It equalized power between the client and counselor.

11. How can the counselor counter the client's initial defiance?
    A) tell the client he is required to participate
    B) equalize power by differentiating the counselor from authority figures
    C) act like the client's friend by mimicking his language and behavior
    D) ignore the client's defiance and proceed as usual

12. What stage of change is the client in regarding cannabis use?
    A) maintenance
    B) action
    C) contemplation
    D) precontemplation

13. What strategy is appropriate for the counselor to use with the client, given the stage of change he is in?
    A) approach the client with curiosity and nonjudgment
    B) give the client psychoeducation with a list of reasons to quit using cannabis
    C) require the client to attend Narcotics Anonymous meetings in addition to individual therapy
    D) set up a contingency management plan for abstinence

Case Study 5

Intake Session

Age: 35

Sex assigned at birth: female

Gender: feminine

Sexuality: heterosexual

Ethnicity: West African (Nigerian)

Relationship status: married

Counseling setting: outpatient

Type(s) of counseling: individual

Presenting problem: in domestic violence relationship, depressed, anxiety

Diagnosis: F43.10 post-traumatic stress disorder; T76.21XA spouse or partner violence, sexual, suspected, initial encounter

Presenting Problem

A thirty-five-year-old married woman from Nigeria immigrated to the United States three years ago when she married a man from this country. They had met when he visited Nigeria on business. He courted her and requested permission to marry her in accordance with Muslim customs, which she appreciated. A condition of their marriage was that she would move to the US with him but would return to Nigeria every year for three weeks to visit her family. The early part of the marriage was good. They enjoyed cooking and reading together, and he took her sightseeing all around the US. He is five years older than her, works in banking, and is very well off financially, so he told her she could work if she wanted to but did not have to. She works in a child care center and wants to go to school to become a teacher. The problems started because she was not getting pregnant. At first, he would get mad and call her names. Then he told her she could not work and must stay at home because he thought she was having an affair and using birth control against his wishes. In the past six months, he has taken to forcing her into sexual relations and threatening her. She fears for her life, but if she leaves, she will be forced to return to Nigeria, and that would disgrace her entire family. She reports feeling scared and helpless, having a loss of appetite, being unable to sleep, and crying all the time.

Mental Status

The client presents as well-groomed, with a traditional Muslim hair covering and a long-sleeve, floor-length dress in bright colors. During the intake session, she sat on the edge of her seat, fidgeted her hands, and changed position often. Her speech and facial expressions are congruent with her stated fear and anxious mood. She demonstrates no perceptual disturbances and is oriented to person, time, and place. She denies auditory or visual hallucinations as well as suicidal or homicidal thoughts. The client has no history of previous mental health problems and appears in good health. She reports decreased appetite and sleeping disturbances and has difficulty with concentration, memory, and focus.

Family History

The client is the youngest of five children in a traditional Muslim family, with both her parents still living and together. Both sets of her grandparents also live in their family's home. She reports having a "normal childhood" and that her family was considered wealthy due to her father's business acumen. Because of this, she and her siblings went to an international school where most of her classes were in English. She also speaks French. Before meeting her husband, she had earned an accounting certificate and worked in her father's business assisting with bookkeeping tasks. She says her relationships with her parents are based on respect and love and that she is fairly close with her siblings; however, if she were to return home divorced, the family would suffer socially due to the stigma involved.

Counseling Session 1

The client reports that her husband has not forced sex on her in over a week, and this brings her great relief. She also says that he is planning a business trip to another state and will be gone for three days. The counselor and the client discuss safety planning and a referral to an immigration attorney. The counselor also guides the client through processing how she will tell her family if she decides to leave her husband. They also discuss whether the client's husband would be open to couples counseling.

Counseling Session 2

Three weeks later, the client returns and reports feeling much better. When her husband returned from his trip, he brought her a gift and was kind to her. She says it was like when they were first married. She is sleeping better and eating regularly again. Her husband's behavior gives her hope that they will not have to get divorced. She did not bring up the idea of couples counseling to him and does not think she will because she does not want to make him angry.

1. As a mandated reporter, what is the counselor's professional obligation toward the client regarding the abuse she reports?
   A) The counselor must report the husband's abuse to law enforcement.
   B) The counselor should work with the client to establish a safety plan.
   C) The counselor may only call law enforcement if the client requests it.
   D) The counselor has no professional obligation.

2. What other assessment might be appropriate for this client?
   A) CAPS-5
   B) intelligence test
   C) DAST-10
   D) marital communication assessment

3. Which part of the client's report suggests that a PTSD diagnosis may be appropriate?
   A) growing up in a wealthy family
   B) learning English in school
   C) forced sexual relations
   D) not being able to return to Nigeria

4. What should be a short-term goal for this client?
   A) returning to Nigeria
   B) getting a job
   C) leaving her husband immediately
   D) creating a safety plan

5. What could be an appropriate long-term goal for this client?
   A) reduce anxiety symptoms by learning one mindfulness activity per week
   B) learn a new trade or skill for gainful employment
   C) attend education courses concerning people suspected of domestic violence
   D) persuade her parents to allow a divorce

6. What can the counselor say to the client to show empathy for her family situation?
   A) "How would your family feel if something happened to you?"
   B) "Your consideration for your family demonstrates your love and respect for them."
   C) "Does your family give you the same consideration you give them?"
   D) "You really should not worry about your family; they are an ocean away."

7. Why would the counselor NOT object to the client's decision to stay with her husband?
   A) It is up to the client if, when, and how she wants to leave.
   B) The counselor should convince the client to leave her husband.
   C) The counselor knows it is not possible to persuade the client.
   D) The client should obey her husband according to their cultural values.

8. What counseling intervention can the counselor use to help the client prepare for change if it becomes necessary?
   A) provide psychoeducation about the effects of domestic violence
   B) recommend she start saving money
   C) help the client strengthen self-efficacy
   D) guide the client in processing childhood memories

9. What can the counselor say to demonstrate cultural awareness early in the relationship?
   A) "Help me understand how your marriage influences your family's social standing in Islam."
   B) "Why do you stay in the relationship if you are afraid?"
   C) "Is it true that all Islamic marriages are arranged?"
   D) "Is your family forcing you to stay married because of a religious belief?"

10. What skill is the counselor using by saying to the client, "Your hands tremble when you describe how your husband treats you."
    A) sharing an observation to invite the client to talk about her feelings
    B) asking an open-ended question to invite a detailed answer
    C) conducting an assessment to make a correct diagnosis
    D) practicing self-awareness to build rapport

11. Which of the following goals could increase the number of protective factors for the client?
    A) secure a teaching job
    B) save money separately from her husband
    C) visit a medical provider
    D) increase social support

12. What can the counselor do to improve cultural competence?
    A) take a college course on working with women
    B) pursue knowledge about Islam and Nigerian culture
    C) share information with the client about the counselor's culture
    D) ask the client to teach the counselor about Islam

13. Which of the following is a strengths-based question about the client's relationship with her husband?
    A) "What do you love about your husband?"
    B) "What does a good day with your husband look like when your relationship is going well?"
    C) "What do you want from your husband?"
    D) "What can you do to improve your relationship with your husband?"

Case Study 6

Intake Session

Age: 11

Sex assigned at birth: male

Gender: masculine

Sexuality: unknown/not applicable

Ethnicity: White

Relationship status: unknown/not applicable

Counseling setting: outpatient

Type(s) of counseling: individual

Presenting problem: recently released from a psychiatric hospital

Diagnosis: F90.1 ADHD, predominantly hyperactive/impulsive type, moderate; F31.81 bipolar 2 disorder

Presenting Problem

The client is brought to therapy by his father, who says he was just released from the psychiatric hospital. The client had a breakdown at home, during which he was yelling, crying, and breaking things in the house. He also threw objects at his father's live-in girlfriend and threatened to hurt her son, who is the same age. The father brought his son's records from the psychiatric hospital, which diagnosed him with bipolar 2 disorder and ADHD and put him on medication. Since the client started the medication, the father reports that he has been lethargic, sleeping a lot, not wanting to do much, and barely eating—"kind of like a little zombie." The father says this is unlike him, but he is afraid to take him off the medication because of his tantrums.

Mental Status

The client presents well-groomed in shorts and a T-shirt. He sits very close to his father and looks at the floor while his father provides the information about him. The client does not fidget but appears lethargic and tired. When responding to questions, his eye contact is brief, and he answers with short answers or a shrug. The client denies hearing voices or seeing things that no one else could see, and he says he does not want to hurt himself or anyone else.

Family History

The client lives with his father, his father's girlfriend, and her son in a small home in a rural area. The client's father divorced his mother five years ago due to her drug use and infidelity. The client sees his mother every other weekend. The father works in construction. The father's girlfriend moved into his home six months ago with her eleven-year-old son, who shares a room with the client. They get along most of the time unless the client gets mad.

Counseling Session 1

One week later, the father and client return, and the father initially comes into the therapy room. The counselor, however, asks the client and his father if it is okay if she meets with only the client. Once the father leaves, the counselor asks the client if he would like to just hang out and color some pictures of cars. The client smiles and nods in response. The counselor brings out coloring pages for him to choose from, and he tells her which model car each one is. The counselor asks how he knows so much, and he says that his dad gets *MotorTrend* magazine and the client reads them all. As he colors in the cars, he explains why he colors them that way by referencing car models in real life. Throughout the session, the client is talkative, responsive, and animated. When asked if his dad understands how much he knows about cars, the client responds, "No, he doesn't ask . . . nobody asks."

Counseling Session 2

The next session occurs two weeks later, and the client asks if he can color cars again because he has something in mind. While he is coloring, the counselor asks him about how he landed in the hospital. The client says it was after he went to visit his mom. He says he hates visiting her because she drinks too much beer and does not do anything with him, so he does not see the point of going there. When he got back, his dad was in the field with his girlfriend's son teaching him how to use a bow and arrow; then they kept talking about what they did while the client was at his mother's house, and he got mad. "He doesn't want me for a son, he wants Caleb. I just wish they'd both leave."

1. Based on the information from sessions 1 and 2, what additional services are appropriate for this client?
   A) disability testing
   B) family therapy for father and son
   C) referral to child protective services
   D) tutoring for school

2. What suggests that the client's diagnosis may not be bipolar disorder?
   A) evidence of family dysfunction
   B) evidence of manic episode
   C) evidence of depressive episode
   D) suggestion of conduct disorder

3. What type of further assessment would benefit the client?
   A) cognitive assessment for children
   B) DAST-A
   C) CAPS-CA-5
   D) Beck Anxiety Inventory

4. What would be an appropriate short-term goal for this client?
   A) start engaging in healthy lifestyle activities
   B) behave more appropriately in school
   C) apologize to the family
   D) learn and practice one anger management technique

5. What would be an appropriate long-term goal for this client?
   A) comply with his father's rules and directions
   B) learn healthy coping skills for managing anger
   C) meet with a pediatrician regarding health issues
   D) process early childhood experiences

6. What does the client's statement, "nobody asks," at the end of session 1 indicate?
   A) The client is self-deprecating.
   B) The family does not give the client attention.
   C) The client misinterprets family actions.
   D) The client has no friends.

7. What could the counselor have said at the end of session 2 to explore the client's feelings?
   A) "What would it be like if Caleb and his mom left?"
   B) "That is up to your dad to decide, and he has the right to have a girlfriend."
   C) "What does your mom think about Caleb's mom living with you?"
   D) "It can be dangerous to talk like that, they may put you back in the hospital."

8. What could be an explanation for the client's lack of symptom presentation in the counseling sessions?
   A) Clients tend not to display symptoms in therapy.
   B) The counselor is giving the client attention and encouragement.
   C) The environment is professional, which promotes good behavior.
   D) The father may have lied about the client's issues.

9. What did the coloring activity do for the therapeutic relationship?
   A) It distracted the client from his problems.
   B) It made the counselor look more fun.
   C) It gave the client a constructive activity to do.
   D) It took the focus off the client's problems, making him feel more comfortable.

10. What reflection could the counselor use with this client?
    A) "What kinds of things do you do when you're at your mom's house?"
    B) "Thank you for sharing more about your life."
    C) "It sounds like going to your mom's is a difficult experience and makes you feel left out."
    D) "Your coloring skills are excellent."

11. When a child presents with a diagnosis of ADHD, what should the counselor rule out for a thorough differential diagnosis?
    A) post-traumatic stress disorder
    B) schizophrenia
    C) personality disorder
    D) developmental disorder

12. What about the client's history suggests an attachment problem?
    A) his premature birth
    B) the fact that his father's girlfriend's son shares his name
    C) his many friends at school
    D) neglect from both biological parents

13. How might the counselor educate the client's father on the client's issues?
    A) provide psychoeducation about attachment and explain the difference in the client's behavior during the session
    B) explain the side effects of the medications the client is on and how they can harm him in the future
    C) give the father a detailed explanation about the proposed diagnosis
    D) explain the method of therapy that will be used

Case Study 7

Intake Session

Age: 18

Sex assigned at birth: female

Gender: feminine

Sexuality: lesbian

Ethnicity: Black/African American

Relationship status: single

Counseling setting: college counseling office

Type(s) of counseling: individual

Presenting problem: failing grades

Diagnosis: F43.22 adjustment disorder with anxiety, rule out cannabis use disorder

Presenting Problem

The client is attending therapy because she is in danger of being expelled from college in her first semester. The client says that school is not what she expected, and she feels lost and out of place. It makes her feel jittery and nervous, and she worries that she will never be good enough to finish school. She says she knows she is failing, but she cannot motivate herself to do the "crazy" amount of reading necessary because the material is boring and not relevant to anything. This causes her stress and worry, and she often skips classes to avoid the shame she feels. She lives in a dorm and gets along fine with her roommate but spends most of the time at her girlfriend's off-campus apartment. Her family cannot know about her girlfriend because "they would flip out." The girlfriend is a junior, and they met at a campus orientation event, where she was recruiting for an organization. They started talking and "just clicked." The girlfriend smokes a lot of marijuana, and the client recently started because she wanted to know what the fuss was about. She enjoys it and says it relaxes her. She currently smokes approximately four times per week and does not experience cravings, tolerance, or withdrawal. The client says that maybe counseling will "help me get my head on straight."

Mental Status

The client is well-groomed and oriented to person, place, and time. Her facial expressions and speech are appropriate, and her attitude toward the counselor is genuine and open. The client's mood is agreeable and congruent with her stated feelings of frustration and lack of direction. She denies hallucinations, delusions, suicidal ideation, or self-harm. She demonstrates fair judgment and insight conducive to her age and maturity.

Family History

The client is the middle child of three children and grew up with both of her married parents living together. She describes the family as suburban, churchgoing, and "normal." Her older brother is at another university on an athletic scholarship, and her younger brother is an athlete in high school and will probably get a scholarship too. She went to college because she felt like her parents expected her to but does not know what she wants to do with her life.

Counseling Session 1

In this session, a week later, the client announces that she thinks she will just quit school and deal with her parents being disappointed. The counselor guides the client through a decisional balance about that choice. During the session, the client says multiple times, "Why did I even come here?" When asked to clarify, the client says she does not know why she decided to go to college. The counselor helps the client explore her motivations for doing so, which leads to a discussion of family expectations. The client agrees to do some journaling as homework to brainstorm ideas about what she wants to do without factoring in familial expectations.

Counseling Session 2

Two weeks later, the client returns and again announces that college is not for her; however, instead of being angry about it, she presents her various reasons, stating that the journaling exercise was a good one for her. She states that the problem is going to be with her parents, and she does not know how to tell them. The counselor invites the client to participate in a role-playing exercise where she practices telling her parents.

1. The counseling office only allows clients six sessions. How should the counselor address this?
   A) The counselor should cover it in the informed consent information and offer a referral if needed.
   B) The counselor should pack as much therapy as possible into the time allotted.

C) It is not necessary to pay attention to the number of sessions.
D) The counselor should let the client know that counseling is for six sessions and after that, she is on her own.

2. Which of the following assessments would be appropriate based on what the client said during the intake?
    A) a learning disability assessment
    B) a substance use assessment
    C) a gender dysphoria assessment
    D) a sexual assault assessment

3. What symptoms support the diagnosis of adjustment disorder?
    A) Although the client lives in a dorm, she spends a lot of time off-campus.
    B) The client reported marijuana use.
    C) The client has a relationship with another student off-campus.
    D) Symptom onset coincides with college attendance.

4. What can the counselor ask the client in order to identify the priority of values and develop a treatment plan goal?
    A) "What are your long-term life goals?"
    B) "How can I help you accomplish your goals?"
    C) "How will you know when the problem is solved?"
    D) "What brings you to therapy?"

5. Is it appropriate to address the client's feelings of inferiority?
    A) Yes, the client needs to process this to move on.
    B) No, this is not an issue the client wants to discuss.
    C) Yes, because if she does not, she may continue failing in college.
    D) No, there is not enough time to process it effectively in only six sessions.

6. Which intervention is most likely to help the client achieve her goals within the short time span?
    A) learning DBT skills
    B) practicing ACT
    C) using EMDR
    D) building on the client's strengths

7. What might the counselor have said in session 1 to prevent the client from making an impulsive decision?
    A) "I wonder if you would feel better about your decision if we talked through the pros and cons a little bit."
    B) "If you're going to act that way, maybe college is not for you."
    C) "What would your parents say if you quit so soon?"
    D) "I'm not sure if that's a good idea, you already paid for the whole semester, so you might want to finish."

8. What purpose did the role-playing exercise serve in session 2?
    A) It helped the counselor understand the client's perspective.
    B) The counselor was able to give the client instructions on what to say.
    C) The client needed to make sure she got it right the first time.
    D) It gave the client a safe place to practice and process communicating with her parents.

9. What could the counselor have said to the client to demonstrate empathic attunement in session 1?
   A) "Your brothers sound wonderful, but I imagine you feel lost amid all the attention they receive."
   B) "How did you make your presence known in your family?"
   C) "How did that make you feel?"
   D) "Tell me more about how you feel about your family."

10. The counselor did not bring up the client's sexual orientation for what reason?
    A) It is forbidden in this counseling session.
    B) The client did not bring it up as an issue.
    C) It is not noted on the client's intake paperwork.
    D) The client's parents would not approve.

11. In which stage of change was the client during session 1?
    A) contemplation
    B) action
    C) preparation
    D) maintenance

12. Is the counselor, as a mandated reporter, required to report the client's drug use?
    A) Yes, especially if smoking marijuana is a criminal offense.
    B) Yes, it is beneficial for the client's health.
    C) No, the client is not in danger of harming herself or others.
    D) No, it is none of the counselor's business.

13. Which of the following is a strengths-based question that could help the client figure out what to do with her life?
    A) "What career ideas have you tried in the past?"
    B) "What have been your favorite classes so far?"
    C) "Have you had any jobs in your life that you enjoyed?"
    D) "What is your earliest memory of having an idea of what you wanted to be when you grew up?"

Case Study 8

Intake Session

Age: 56

Sex assigned at birth: female

Gender: feminine

Sexuality: heterosexual

Ethnicity: White

Relationship status: married

Counseling setting: outpatient

Type(s) of counseling: individual

Presenting problem: depression

Diagnosis: F32.0 major depressive disorder, mild, single episode with melancholic features

Presenting Problem
The client comes to therapy stating that she is depressed and thinks she wants to end her marriage. Her children are grown, and she is bored, so maybe she will just divorce her husband and find someone else. The client works as an accountant. She says that she and her husband are well off, so they can afford to get divorced. They have been married for twenty years; their children live out of state. She describes her symptoms as apathy, lethargy, boredom, emotional detachment, social isolation, having no appetite, and being unable to sleep. At night she feels like there is a motor inside her that will not shut off, and she has no interest in doing things she used to enjoy. If she has a half bottle of wine, that helps. She does not drink wine every night, but sometimes she thinks she should. She goes to work only because it keeps her from getting bored. There is a consultant who comes to the office that she finds good-looking and appealing, so she might flirt with him. She is hoping counseling might help her make up her mind or maybe get her a referral to a psychiatrist for some medication.

Mental Status
The client is well-dressed in a business pantsuit with expensive-looking jewelry. Her facial expression and mood are congruent with her stated apathy. Her thought processes follow a flight of ideas and a preoccupation with herself and how others view her. She has little to say about her emotional status and avoids questions about love, suggesting poor social and emotional intelligence. She denies suicidal ideation but casually comments that her family would pay more attention to her if she did express thoughts about suicide.

Family History
The client describes her family of origin as poor and abusive. She was an only child of her parents, who remain married to this day; however, when she was growing up, they both drank excessively and would have explosive "knock-down-drag-out fights." She describes being annoyed by their behavior—not afraid—saying, "I couldn't get any sleep with all that racket, and they expected me to get good grades?" She did well in school and earned an accounting degree. She and her husband met through friends, and she married him because "I liked him well enough, and he was fun at times." They have two daughters; both are married and living in other states. She says she is not close with either of her daughters.

Counseling Session 1
Before the client's next session, her husband sends the counselor an email expressing concern that his wife has a history of going to therapy and playing "the victim." He says they have had problems for years because she has affairs with men at work. They go for couples counseling, things work out for a time, and then it starts again. He says they have been through this four times so far, but this is the first time it has happened since their daughters moved out. He concludes by stating that he understands the rules of confidentiality and does not expect the counselor to respond, but he is filing for divorce, so this time she might actually need therapy.

Counseling Session 2

The client arrives for the session late, saying she is overwhelmed at work. She says she almost did not make it to the session but knew that she needed this time for self-care. In stream-of-consciousness fashion, she starts talking about the consultant at work that she finds attractive, but the counselor interrupts to say that there is something they need to discuss. The counselor gives the client a printout of the email sent by her husband. As the client reads the email to herself, her facial expression changes to anger. When she finishes, she balls up the paper, throws it across the room, and starts cursing her husband. The counselor validates the client's feelings and invites her to share her point of view on the email.

1. Which professional ethics principle was the counselor upholding by sharing the information sent by the client's husband?
    A) transparency and clarification of roles
    B) avoiding dual relationships
    C) appropriate transfer of services
    D) professional competency

2. What do the client's focus on herself, evidence of emotional detachment, and a story different from her husband's suggest about the diagnosis?
    A) The client obviously lied and does not care.
    B) The diagnosis could be a personality disorder.
    C) Perhaps the client is faking her symptoms.
    D) The client's husband might be abusive to her.

3. How does the information from the husband influence the assessment?
    A) The counselor cannot use the information for the assessment.
    B) The counselor should believe the husband's report.
    C) It does not influence the assessment.
    D) It suggests a concerning pattern of behavior that may change the diagnosis.

4. What is required for this client before creating a treatment plan?
    A) an accurate diagnosis
    B) the client admitting she has a problem
    C) payment up front for all sessions
    D) the client's records from previous counselors

5. What barrier will affect the client treatment plan?
    A) not enough time with the client
    B) agency services not appropriate for this client
    C) the likelihood that the client is not truthful
    D) the husband's interference

6. What must the counselor do to determine which interventions to use with this client?
    A) force the client to comply with therapy
    B) establish a therapeutic alliance
    C) refer the client to a psychiatrist
    D) wait for the client to articulate goals

7. Which therapeutic technique could the counselor have used when the client arrived late for the session?
   A) confrontation
   B) summarizing
   C) active listening
   D) treatment planning

8. The client says in her intake that she might need a referral for a psychiatrist. How could the counselor respond to get more information?
   A) "A referral is not indicated at this time."
   B) "Help me understand what you hope a psychiatrist will find."
   C) "I'll give you a psychiatrist referral if you tell me what is really going on."
   D) "I don't think medication will help you."

9. What could the counselor have said to the client to demonstrate nonjudgment about the husband's information?
   A) "Your husband is attacking you; I wonder why?"
   B) "What do you have to say for yourself? Because it seems like you lied to me."
   C) "Is your husband's account right, or is yours? I'm not sure what to believe."
   D) "I imagine you are feeling angry and hurt that your husband sent this information."

10. What could the counselor have said to the client to address her emotional state after revealing the husband's email?
    A) "This is the first time I have seen you angry."
    B) "How is this different from any other day?"
    C) "How do you feel about this information?"
    D) "Does this information contribute to feeling depressed?"

11. Which assessment might reveal more data for a diagnosis?
    A) Wechsler Adult Intelligence Scale (WAIS)
    B) Minnesota Multiphasic Personality Inventory (MMPI)
    C) Beck Depression Inventory (BDI)
    D) Addiction Severity Index (ASI)

12. What could the counselor have said to the client to get more information about the husband's email without damaging the relationship with the client?
    A) "Why would your husband say such things if they are not true?"
    B) "Is what your husband says true?"
    C) "If you were in counseling before, I would like to get copies of those records."
    D) "Your husband made some allegations about previous problems and said you went to counseling before. Do you agree with what he said?"

13. What personality disorder do the client's symptoms suggest?
    A) paranoid personality disorder
    B) borderline personality disorder
    C) narcissistic personality disorder
    D) dependent personality disorder

Case Study 9

Intake Session

Age: 24

Sex assigned at birth: female

Gender: feminine

Sexuality: heterosexual

Ethnicity: White

Relationship status: single

Counseling setting: substance use outpatient

Type(s) of counseling: individual

Presenting problem: opioid and benzodiazepine addiction

Diagnosis: F11.20 opioid use disorder, moderate, on maintenance therapy; F13.10 sedative use disorder, mild, early remission

Presenting Problem

The client is attending outpatient treatment following discharge from a residential detox facility. She is mandated to attend treatment through child protective services, which has removed her three-year-old daughter from her care while she is in treatment. She is currently on medication-assisted treatment for opioids, as she has co-occurring physical ailments that cause her significant pain. The client states that she has been in treatment before, but this time she means it because she wants her daughter back. She has a high school education and no job skills; she engaged in prostitution to pay for her drug habit. She says a neighbor called child protective services because she passed out and her baby was crying for a long time. She almost overdosed that night, she says. She has significant health issues after breaking her pelvis and lower vertebrae when she was pushed off a second-story balcony at a party. She says she does not remember it very well because she was high at the time. The client reports mood problems and feeling worthless, lonely, and sad most of the time. Her only family is her father, who is currently caring for her daughter. All of her friends use drugs, and she is trying to stay away from them. She also needs to figure out how to support herself, and she starts to cry when explaining that she does not know what to do.

Mental Status

The client is adequately groomed yet appears malnourished. She walks slightly bent over, which she says is due to her back and hip pain. Her vocabulary is commensurate with her stated education level, her thought processes are tangential at times, and she is very open and not afraid to talk about anything. Her speech slows down when she talks about negative events and speeds up when she talks about pleasant events. The client reports understanding why she is in treatment, but she also struggles with long-term memory loss due to extensive drug use. The client demonstrates some acceptance of her circumstances, yet with limited insight.

Family History

The client reports growing up with her father because her mother left when she was young. She has no siblings. When she was fourteen, her father had a gambling problem and would often have strangers over at the house to play cards all night. They were poor, so when he could not pay his debts, he "pimped her out" to pay them. He got her started on drugs so she could get through those traumatic events. He has since been in treatment and recovery. For the past seven years, he has been sober, working a good job, and trying to get her straight. She states that she loves and hates her father at the same time.

Counseling Session 1

A week after intake, the client reports that she has an evaluation coming up with child protective services to see if she can increase her contact with her daughter. She is tearful and anxious, stating that "everything rides on this" and keeps repeating, "I can't lose my daughter." She reports feeling worthless and that maybe her daughter would be better off without her. The counselor guides the client through emotional regulation exercises and then helps her create a plan for getting through the evaluation.

Counseling Session 2

A week later, the client returns for a session looking happy and reports that she passed the evaluation with child protective services. She is now allowed to have unsupervised visits with her daughter, and as long as she remains sober and on her recovery plan, the visits will continue. She says she needs help to stay on track because most days she feels like she is on an emotional roller coaster, constantly worried that she is doing something wrong.

1. How should the counselor explain to the client what will be disclosed to child protective services about her attendance?
    A) emphasize the minimal disclosure principle
    B) explain the need for collaboration with child protective services
    C) promise not to disclose any information the client does not want revealed
    D) review confidentiality policies with the client

2. What is the strongest indication that co-occurring disorders may be present?
    A) The client had her daughter taken away from her.
    B) The client reports history of early sexual trauma and mood disturbances.
    C) The client is in medication-assisted treatment.
    D) The client has made multiple attempts at recovery.

3. Given the client's disclosure of early childhood sexual abuse, which additional assessment should be conducted?
    A) intelligence testing
    B) substance misuse assessment
    C) career counseling assessment
    D) trauma assessment

4. What should be the focus of treatment for this client?
   A) substance use recovery
   B) management of trauma symptoms
   C) both substance use and trauma at the same time
   D) parenting skills

5. What is the first goal of trauma therapy?
   A) establish safety
   B) provide social support
   C) process the trauma
   D) develop resilience

6. What kind of psychoeducation would help frame the client's co-occurring disorders?
   A) describing how therapy works and the importance of treatment plans
   B) demonstrating the connection between trauma and substance use
   C) explaining what co-occurring disorders are
   D) clarifying how the client can get her child back

7. Which symptom cluster of PTSD is likely associated with the client's substance use and can be a target of intervention?
   A) avoidance
   B) reexperiencing
   C) intrusive memories
   D) trouble sleeping

8. Which feature of DBT would be an appropriate intervention for this client?
   A) cognitive reprocessing
   B) interpersonal skills
   C) parenting skills
   D) distress tolerance

9. What can the counselor say to the client to demonstrate unconditional positive regard and empathy?
   A) "I am on your side."
   B) "I am sorry for everything you have been through, and I admire your tenacity."
   C) "I don't know how you survived all of that."
   D) "I don't understand why you even want a relationship with your father after what he did to you."

10. How can the counselor acknowledge the client's conflicting feelings about her father?
    A) let her know it is okay to love and hate her father at the same time
    B) suggest that maybe she and her father should do family counseling
    C) share a personal story to make the client feel validated
    D) tell her to get her daughter back quickly, so she can get away from him

11. Which of the following referrals would be MOST appropriate to help this client improve recovery capital?
    A) visit a medical provider for a checkup
    B) join a peer support group for women in recovery
    C) engage in restorative justice
    D) pursue vocational training

12. Given the client's traumatic relationship with her father, which of the following might she struggle with?
    A) communication
    B) finding a job
    C) boundaries
    D) parenting skills

13. What is a good short-term goal for this client?
    A) learn healthy coping skills
    B) start an exercise regimen
    C) address and reframe maladaptive thoughts
    D) reestablish a relationship with her father

Case Study 10

Intake Session

Age: 42

Sex assigned at birth: female

Gender: feminine

Sexuality: heterosexual

Ethnicity: Black/African American

Relationship status: divorced

Counseling setting: outpatient

Type(s) of counseling: individual

Presenting problem: grief, trauma

Diagnosis: persistent complex bereavement disorder, traumatic bereavement; rule out PTSD

Presenting Problem

The client is attending therapy to deal with the one-year anniversary of her oldest son's suicide. She says that her three children are her life, and when her oldest son killed himself, her "world imploded." She has a daughter, and her youngest child is a son. The client reports that she does not believe her son killed himself. They were very close, and she knows he would not do that to her. She does not trust that the authorities told her the truth or that they will. Her other children are becoming upset with her because she cannot get over what happened to her oldest. She says her daughter accused her of not loving them as much and ignoring them. The client cries throughout the session, and the counselor stops periodically to allow her time to compose herself. The client has been divorced for five years, and her ex-husband is remarried. Her two children spend more time with him now because they are mad at her, so she has more time alone to think and cry. She reports feeling depressed and sad, often crying at any reminder of her son. She used to go to church, but she stopped. Sometimes friends from church come to her house to visit her. She is unemployed and lives on the alimony and child support from her ex-husband. She used to enjoy crafting and volunteer work but lost interest in those activities too. Sometimes she feels intense pain and loss, and other times she feels completely numb and cut off from life. She recognizes that she needs help coping with this, or she will lose her other two children.

Mental Status

The client is well-groomed and overweight. She is oriented to person, place, and time. Her affect is congruent with her stated depressed mood and with intermittent crying. She denies auditory and visual hallucinations as well as suicidal ideation or self-harm. Her thought processes are clear, with indications of paranoid thinking regarding her son's death. The client was emotionally labile throughout the session.

Family History

The client grew up in a small town in a two-parent home, the youngest of four children. She describes her family as "normal," with her mother at home caring for the children and her father working for the railroads. She reports good relationships with her family, even though they live out of state. They have been supportive of her since her divorce, and her siblings help her with finances when they can.

Counseling Session 1

In this session a week after the intake, the client talks more about what she thinks happened to her son. She explains his brief experience with drugs but says that she knows he quit. She believes he was murdered by drug dealers who wanted him to work for them and that the police are covering it up. She further expands on her beliefs that she needs to protect her other two children. The counselor uses cognitive techniques to probe her beliefs, thoughts, and emotions.

Counseling Session 2

Six months into therapy, the client comes to a session with her daughter; they are both crying and disheveled. The client reveals that her youngest son was shot and killed in a drive-by shooting four days prior. The client says that there was no reason for her youngest son to be shot, as he was at a friend's house playing video games. She says the police are calling it a random event, not targeted. The counselor offers condolences and space for the client to express her grief.

1. What should the counselor say to the client about confidentiality when her daughter accompanies her to a session?
   A) "I'm not sure it's a good idea to bring your daughter into the session because of confidentiality."
   B) "I need you to sign a HIPAA release form that allows us to talk with your daughter in the session."
   C) "I am okay with your daughter in the session if you are."
   D) "No one else is allowed in your session unless advanced notice has been given."

2. Should the counselor consider a diagnosis of depression for this client?
   A) No, because the client's symptoms are the result of her son's death a year ago.
   B) No, because the client can only have one diagnosis at a time.
   C) Yes, because the symptoms exhibited by the client indicate depression.
   D) Yes, because depression can co-occur with bereavement.

3. What is an appropriate long-term goal for this client following session 1?
   A) decrease symptoms of depression
   B) process her childhood memories
   C) accept her son's death
   D) attend a mutual aid group

4. How would the client's treatment plan change after session 2?
   A) It should focus on establishing safety amid a new trauma.
   B) The treatment plan would not change.
   C) It depends on the client's stated goals.
   D) The entire treatment plan needs to start over.

5. Which type of resources should the counselor recommend for this client?
   A) economic resources
   B) social support
   C) psychiatric referral
   D) family therapy

6. What can the counselor say to the client to move her from focusing on her son's death story to remembering their relationship?
   A) "At some point, you're going to have to move on."
   B) "You have one other child; perhaps you should focus on her instead."
   C) "Tell me about your son."
   D) "Let the police do their job."

7. What counseling skills should the counselor have focused on in session 2?
   A) working on cognitive behavioral skills
   B) allowing the client a safe space to grieve
   C) identifying unhealthy beliefs
   D) teaching the client healthy coping skills

8. What could the counselor have said to the client in session 1 to show empathetic understanding?
   A) "I sense you feel a real fear for the safety of your remaining children."
   B) "I don't understand why you're not over this yet."
   C) "It sounds like your son might have been involved with some nasty characters."
   D) "No one is after you; I'm sure your children are safe."

9. Why might the counselor have pointed out the client's strengths in session 1?
   A) to move the client toward treatment plan goals
   B) to introduce the idea that maybe she is not depressed
   C) to challenge her beliefs about herself
   D) to remind the client that she has the resources to cope with her grief

10. Which of the following in the client's case indicates a cultural issue that the counselor should be sensitive to?
    A) divorce from her husband
    B) distrust of police officers
    C) unemployment
    D) history of depression

11. What kind of assessment should have been at least informally explored in session 2?
    A) substance use
    B) depression assessment
    C) relationship assessment
    D) suicide assessment

12. What is an appropriate diagnosis for this client?
    A) adjustment disorder
    B) persistent complex/traumatic bereavement
    C) seasonal affective disorder
    D) generalized anxiety disorder

Case Study 11

Intake Session

Age: 32

Sex assigned at birth: male

Gender: masculine

Sexuality: heterosexual

Ethnicity: Indian/South Asian

Relationship status: single

Counseling setting: outpatient

Type(s) of counseling: individual

Presenting problem: anxiety, depression

Diagnosis: F43.10 post-traumatic stress disorder

Presenting Problem

The client is from India and has lived in the United States for five years. He is undocumented. He grew up in India, and his family was involved in a farming organization that was expected to pay bribes to local officials. When he was a teenager, his father fled the country because the officials threatened his life. At that time, the client took over the family farm and the organization. Not long after he took over, the officials threatened his life as well. He and his family moved to another part of India, but they could not find work. His mother and sisters joined his father in Australia, and he came to the US because a friend lived there and could give him a job. When he arrived, he worked in a gas station for twelve hours each day, seven days per week, and lived in a small apartment nearby. Approximately six months ago, while he was working, he was robbed at gunpoint by three men. After the men left, he called the police and the owner. The police took his statement, and the owner told him he would take the stolen money out of his paychecks. The client does not know if this is allowed, but he is afraid to fight it because of his immigration status. It has been six months since the incident, and the police have not found the men responsible. He states that he lives in fear that they will find him and kill him. He says he does not trust anyone. He startles easily, wakes up at any noise in his apartment, only goes to work, and comes straight home. When at work, he has vivid memories of the gunmen coming into the store and has to remind himself that they are not there. He has no appetite and feels jumpy all the time. He is afraid to press the police because he does not know if they will come after him as well. He is still working at the gas station, but he is terrified every night he works. He is afraid to look for other work because he believes no one else will hire him.

Mental Status

The client presents in casual dress, is well-groomed, and appears depressed with constricted range of affect. He shows no positive emotional response, even when talking about pleasant experiences. He speaks slowly and softly, making little eye contact with the counselor. When discussing the robbery, he stares into space and stops talking, suggesting dissociation. He is oriented to person, time, place, and situation, and presents no signs of psychosis or delusional thinking. He denies suicidal ideation. His thought processes are goal-directed. His judgment is good, and his insight is fair.

Family History

The client grew up the oldest of six siblings in a two-parent home in India. They lived in an agricultural community and were considered very poor. When the client was an adolescent, his father was the head of the farming organization and was harassed and threatened by government officials. He reports good relationships with his family and has a responsibility to help them financially, but it has been hard to do that with his current job.

Counseling Session 1

In the first counseling session, the client announces that he wants to quit his job but does not know how he will make a living without it. He does not know many people in town, and he is afraid. The counselor guides the client in identifying his thoughts regarding fear, and he shares that he is ashamed of himself. He says he thinks he should have fought back when he was robbed, stating, "Maybe I am not much of a man." The counselor explores these thoughts and beliefs using cognitive techniques and invites the client to talk about how the trauma of the robbery influences how he thinks about himself. The counselor also provides the client with a referral for an immigration attorney.

Counseling Session 2

The client reports that he met with the immigration attorney and now has hope that he will be able to stay in the country because he cooperated with the police. The attorney contacted the police and found out that the robbery suspects fled to another state. The client says this makes him feel a little safer, but he still feels at fault. The counselor helps the client go through the trauma again, considering alternatives to his actions and examining which aspects of the event were outside of his control.

1. Why does the referral to an immigration attorney have therapeutic value?
    A) It gets the client into the system.
    B) Fear of deportation and not knowing the law prevents the client from making life changes.
    C) A referral relieves the counselor of some of the work.
    D) The counselor cannot provide services to undocumented immigrants.

2. Which type of assessment can be used to evaluate client progress as well as a diagnosis?
    A) mood chart
    B) trauma symptom checklist
    C) habit checker
    D) mental status evaluation

3. Since the client has not been in the United States very long, what other assessment can help the counselor understand his experience in a cultural context?
    A) diversity evaluation
    B) biopsychosocial assessment
    C) mood disorders scale
    D) cultural formulation interview

4. What is a short-term goal the counselor can help this client work toward?
    A) learning coping skills to reduce hyperarousal symptoms
    B) helping the client find a new job
    C) beginning volunteer work in the community to promote acclimation
    D) assessing for co-occurring disorders

5. Which type of referral would help the client build resources that contribute to resilience?
    A) psychiatry
    B) social support group
    C) career counseling
    D) social welfare programs

6. Why might psychoeducation about trauma be appropriate for this client?
    A) His English is very poor, and he may not understand the counselor.
    B) It will help him understand the American legal system.
    C) Psychoeducation will reduce the client's fear of the symptoms getting worse.
    D) It will help the client understand that his reaction to a traumatic event is normal.

7. Which emotions and beliefs seem most important to the client and should therefore be addressed in counseling?
    A) self-efficacy
    B) low self-esteem
    C) fear and shame
    D) family neglect

8. Which type of intervention was the counselor using in session 1?
    A) cognitive therapy
    B) EMDR
    C) exposure therapy
    D) ACT

9. What is an appropriate statement the counselor could have made after the intake?
    A) "Don't all people from India do yoga? That will help with your symptoms."
    B) "You feel afraid because of the robbery and because it interferes with your ability to provide for your family."
    C) "How might you make changes in your life to address the fear?"
    D) "You don't seem to understand the legal process in this country; it is very different from the system back home."

10. How can the counselor bring culture into the discussion?
    A) tell the client everything she knows about India
    B) ask the client how PTSD is addressed in India
    C) tell the client she loves Indian food
    D) ask how a Hindu would deal with PTSD

11. What stage of change is the client in regarding his job?
    A) precontemplation
    B) contemplation
    C) preparation
    D) action

12. What can the counselor do to help the client move to the preparation stage?
    A) explore the pros and cons of making a change or staying with the same job
    B) make a list of small steps the client can take now
    C) provide psychoeducation about the need for change
    D) set long-term goals for overcoming PTSD

13. What type of referral could help the client move beyond his trauma?
    A) referral to a job center that can help him find a new job
    B) family therapy referral to help him address issues with his family
    C) a psychiatrist who can prescribe medication to help him with trauma symptoms
    D) referral to a housing specialist to find him a new place to live

Answer Key

Case Study 1

1. **B)** While the counselor must report the incident, doing so could cause the family significantly more distress. Therefore, inviting the client and the parents into the reporting process can be a proactive way to minimize that distress. It also shows the client that the counselor will support and advocate on her behalf.

2. **A)** Significant behavior changes tend to indicate a traumatic event or another noteworthy incident that caused distress.

3. **C)** Significant changes in behavior are a risk factor associated with suicide.

4. **A)** The mother spoke for the whole intake session, so establishing a therapeutic alliance with the client is essential before implementing an intervention. The therapeutic alliance will also provide the counselor with more assessment data about what the client is experiencing.

5. **B)** The first step in trauma therapy is to facilitate the reestablishment of physical and psychological safety for the client. While the other options might be appropriate interventions at some point, the priority is safety.

6. **D)** With this statement, the counselor acknowledges that the client disagrees with what the mother reported and validates what the client says.

7. **B)** The sexual assault is likely the triggering event, which means that the client's aggressive behaviors are better explained as symptoms of post-traumatic stress disorder (PTSD).

8. **A)** This statement does not discount what the mother says; rather, it conveys to the client that the counselor knows the behavior is there, does not judge the client for it, and suspects that there may be a reason for it other than what the mother reports. This statement is also nonconfrontational.

9. **C)** This statement reflects what the client has already stated, but it uses different words and sends the message that the counselor understands.

10. **A)** The client mentioned art and music as interests. The counselor can use these pastimes to help the client express emotion and process trauma.

11. **B)** The family could benefit from help dealing with the significant change to the family dynamic, especially since the client described her brother as being considered the favorite.

12. **C)** The client has expressed an interest in music and poetry; therefore, art therapy may be a good fit.

Case Study 2

1. **B)** Professional ethics require the counselor to refer the client and his wife to a couples counselor, as it would be considered a dual relationship if the counselor provides both types of therapy to the client.

2. **B)** Suicide risk factors include major life changes and feelings of hopelessness.

3. **D)** Unresolved trauma is a risk factor for substance use and can interfere with successful recovery if not addressed.

4. **B)** Because the client does not have recovery support in his life right now, connecting him with those resources is a crucial component of his ability to maintain abstinence from the substance in between counseling sessions.

5. **A)** People who experience childhood trauma can develop symptoms that substance use can mitigate; therefore, addressing the childhood trauma would likely reduce the need for the substance.

6. **D)** The client is in contemplation stage during session 1 because he says he wants to change but has not yet taken action. The counselor's use of the decisional balance intervention is meant to solidify the client's reasons for change and use those to move toward action.

7. **B)** Normalizing the relapse contributes to minimizing the shame involved and turns the client's focus to what can be learned from the experience.

8. **C)** A significant percentage of people with substance use problems also have a history of childhood abuse; substance use can be a form of self-medicating.

9. **D)** It is important to separate the behavior from who the client is as a person; doing so gives the client hope for making positive change.

10. **A)** Some people raised in Hispanic or Latino culture subscribe to the concept of machismo, or strict gender roles regarding masculinity. From this perspective, discussing the abuse with someone else would be admitting weakness.

11. **C)** Trauma-focused cognitive behavioral therapy (CBT) will help the client address the consequences of the thoughts and beliefs related to his childhood trauma that led to his substance use.

12. **A)** Since the client talks about being afraid to tell others, drawing attention to what it feels like to tell the counselor will help the client build self-awareness about his feelings.

13. **D)** The correlation between insecure attachment styles and substance use is very high because people who are insecurely attached have trouble with emotional regulation, and substances often act as self-medication for strong emotions.

Case Study 3

1. **B)** Counselors are bound by professional ethics to report the minimal amount of information that complies with requirements, thus abiding by requests while maintaining client confidentiality.

2. **A)** Attachments with caregivers provide children with models of relationships and examples of how to handle emotions. The client did not get these from her mother.

3. **D)** While the other assessments could all be helpful, an anger management scale can be used every thirty days to measure the client's progress in implementing coping strategies.

4. **A)** The client's most immediate challenge and presenting problem is her inability to control her anger and anger-related behavior, which gets her into trouble in the prison.

5. **D)** Dialectical behavior therapy (DBT) includes treatment modules that address distress tolerance and teach emotional regulation skills.

6. **A)** This shows nonjudgment and understanding that fighting serves a real purpose for the client.

7. **B)** The client seeks calm, but she has no way to achieve it except through this maladaptive behavior cycle.

8. **D)** The client's mother did not provide a secure attachment for her, so the client did not learn the skills she needed, which explains why the client has developed her behaviors.

9. **C)** The client was defensive during the intake and said that she felt like the system was against her. By allying with the client against the system, the counselor separates himself from the system.

10. **B)** By modeling calm, relaxed behavior, the counselor lets the client know he is not a threat and that the client is safe.

11. **A)** Dialectical behavior therapy (DBT) teaches emotional regulation skills that can help clients manage the strong emotions that lead to impulsive behaviors.

12. **C)** The client needs to learn new ways of expressing herself, so the therapeutic relationship can be a place to practice and receive constructive feedback.

13. **A)** Learning job skills will give the client purpose and a skill that she can use upon her release.

Case Study 4

1. **B)** While the other options may also be a challenge, the most important one is that the client resists establishing a relationship with the counselor because the counselor is seen as part of the system mandating the client to treatment.

2. **C)** The crossed arms, direct eye contact, and refusal to participate in the intake suggest defiance of authority.

3. **A)** The client exhibits defiance and is therefore not likely to be honest in the assessments. The counselor should work on establishing rapport first.

4. **B)** The client is already suspicious and defiant toward authority, so the first goal should be to build a relationship with him before establishing treatment goals. Client buy-in for treatment goals is essential to success.

5. **D)** While the other options might be appropriate, the client specifically mentions an interest in metalworking, which the counselor can use as an opening to work out a treatment goal with him.

6. **C)** The counselor is using strengths-based intervention by pointing out strengths seen in the client to help him begin to look for strengths in himself.

7. **B)** By emphasizing the client's strengths and contrasting his values and goals with his current choices, the counselor shows the client the discrepancies between his actions and what he hopes to achieve.

8. **C)** The client may or may not realize what resources are available to him, but by identifying the potential resources, the client can decide to use them and work toward his goals.

9. **A)** Resistance is usually a result of feeling powerless, and questioning the client too much will make him feel like he is being confronted, which is another display of power.

10. **D)** The rules of the game were fair, and allowing the client to ask questions equalized the power position between him and the counselor.

11. **B)** The client is defiant and suspicious of authority. To build trust and establish a rapport, the counselor needs to show the client that she is not part of the authority establishment.

12. **D)** The client is in the precontemplation stage because he does not talk about changing his cannabis use at all nor does he consider it a problem.

Case Study 5

1. **B)** The client is not of an age that falls under mandated reporting laws (e.g., under eighteen or over sixty-five). However, the client's safety is a priority, so a plan should be created that helps her and does not put her in more danger.

2. **A)** A trauma symptom checklist, such as the Clinician-Administered PTSD Scale for DSM-5 (CAPS-5), will help determine if the client's experiences with her husband have resulted in post-traumatic stress disorder.

3. **C)** Forced sexual relations are a traumatic experience in and outside of marriage.

4. **D)** In domestic violence situations, leaving—or the threat of leaving—can escalate the violence. Therefore, establishing a safety plan in advance can help the client make the right decision about when to leave, if she decides to do so.

5. **A)** The client does not want a divorce at this time, but she could learn to manage her anxiety symptoms, which will improve her ability to make decisions.

6. **B)** Mentioning the client's consideration for her family does not convey judgment; rather, it shows appreciation for the client's values.

7. **A)** All counseling should be client-led, but in domestic violence situations where the abuser

13. **A)** The client is in the precontemplation stage. The goal of the intervention is to get him thinking about and noticing the problems caused by cannabis use, with the hope that he will consider that cannabis is not helpful to him.

has all the power, it is especially important to safeguard the client's autonomy.

8. **C)** Strengthening the client's self-efficacy will help her make a decision she can feel confident about and help her take action with more confidence.

9. **A)** This statement acknowledges the cultural differences between the counselor and the client and communicates the counselor's interest in understanding Islamic culture according to the client's experience.

10. **A)** The counselor describes what he sees in the client's body language to show empathy and positive regard, thus inviting her to trust the counselor with emotional sharing.

11. **D)** The client does not seem to have social support in this country outside of her husband. Increasing her social support will give the client other people to turn to if she needs help.

12. **B)** Learning more about Islam and Nigerian culture can help the counselor understand the client better and improve cultural competence.

13. **B)** This question inspires the client to think concretely about times when the relationship was good. She may realize that she has resources to repair the relationship or move on in another way if she desires to do so.

Case Study 6

1. **B)** The client describes feeling neglected by his father, so the two of them could benefit from family counseling.

2. **A)** Family disruption and dysfunction can cause behavioral reactions in children that mimic

other disorders. Further, there is no evidence of manic/depressive cycling in the client's history.

3. **C)** The Clinician-Administered PTSD Scale for DSM-5—Child/Adolescent Version (CAPS-CA-5) evaluates the client for symptoms of post-

traumatic stress disorder (PTSD), which are often similar to attention deficit hyperactivity disorder (ADHD) symptoms.

4. **D)** Learning an anger management technique, like counting to ten or deep breathing, will help the client begin to understand how to manage strong emotions.

5. **B)** While some of the other options might be appropriate, the presenting issue is the client's impulsivity and anger. The treatment priority is learning how to cope with strong feelings. Managing strong emotions will help the client navigate family relationships and function better in school.

6. **B)** Children need attention and affection from their parents. The client's statement suggests that from his perspective, his father does not take an interest in him.

7. **A)** Asking the client to imagine what his life would be like if Caleb and his mom left is a miracle question—it will get the client to think and talk about what he needs from his father.

8. **B)** The counselor shows interest in the client, which gives him time to be himself and encourages him to share his interests.

9. **D)** By being taken to see the counselor, the client may have felt he was in trouble, which would make him less likely to feel comfortable in the therapeutic setting. The coloring activity offered the client an opportunity to take the focus off of his concerns and, therefore, feel more comfortable.

10. **C)** This statement acknowledges a feeling the client has already implied and addresses a deeper feeling.

11. **A)** Hypervigilance and overreactive startle can be confused with hyperactivity and impulsivity.

12. **D)** The client's parents divorced when he was young, and neither parent pays enough attention to him.

13. **A)** The client feels like his father does not care about him and that his father prefers the girlfriend's son. Additionally, the neglect the client feels as a consequence of the divorce damages his ability to manage his emotions and create relationships.

Case Study 7

1. **A)** The counselor has an ethical obligation to be transparent with the client and provide for continuation of care.

2. **B)** The client reported marijuana use. An accurate assessment of use habits will provide insight into the influence the use has on the client.

3. **D)** Adjustment disorder symptoms relate directly to a stressful event, and in this client's case, the stressful event is starting college.

4. **C)** This is modeled after the miracle question, which is based on a strengths-based approach that causes the client to focus on the issue that will change her life the most, thus identifying her values as well as a goal.

5. **D)** Although it may help the client to process these feelings, it is not appropriate to start something that may take more time than what is available.

6. **D)** Although all of these options could be adapted as brief interventions, strengths-based interventions have strong evidence-based support for this application.

7. **A)** By questioning whether the client would feel better about her decision after discussing its pros and cons, the counselor validates the client's feelings while inviting her to process the decision so that she will feel confident in what she decides later.

8. **D)** By practicing and processing her feelings in advance, she can more effectively communicate with her parents and anticipate their reactions.

9. **A)** The client describes her brothers as having a plan for their lives, yet she chose to attend college because she felt it was expected of her, so it is likely that she feels left out.

10. **B)** In client-centered therapy, counselors address issues of importance to the client.

11. **A)** Contemplation is the stage wherein a person is aware that change is needed, is motivated to change, but is unsure how to change.

12. **C)** Mandated reporting is required in cases of abuse or if clients are in danger of harming themselves or someone else.

13. **D)** By asking about the earliest memory, the counselor prompts the client to think about what her wishes were before she felt influenced by her family.

Case Study 8

1. **A)** Sharing this information established the counselor's relationship with the client. By asking for the client's version of the story, the counselor communicated nonjudgment and invited the client into a more honest therapeutic relationship. In couples counseling, a counselor does not take sides, but in individual counseling, the counselor advocates for and supports the client.

2. **B)** While the other options are possible, they are unlikely and not supported by information from the client; however, several things do signal a personality disorder: no emotional reaction to her parents' alcohol-fueled fighting, emotional detachment from her daughters, and considering an affair with no emotional reaction when her marriage is in danger.

3. **D)** The counselor cannot do anything about having received the information, but it suggests that the client may not have been truthful about her symptoms or her situation.

4. **A)** An accurate diagnosis informs the goals for the treatment plan, and while the client presents with textbook depression symptoms, the information shared by the husband suggests that a diagnosis of depression may not be accurate.

5. **C)** There are multiple barriers to effective treatment planning; dishonesty from clients is a significant one.

6. **B)** Interventions will remain ineffective without a therapeutic alliance.

7. **A)** Confrontation can be used to draw attention to disrespectful behavior that suggests the client is not taking therapy seriously.

8. **B)** This response conveys nonjudgment and invites the client to explain her issues more.

9. **D)** This statement calls attention to the client's feelings—not the husband's actions—and demonstrates empathy and nonjudgment.

10. **A)** The counselor recognizes the client's emotional presentation and calls attention to noticing the client's other emotional states.

11. **B)** The Minnesota Multiphasic Personality Inventory (MMPI) is a validated measure used to help with diagnosis and has multiple methods of detecting discrepancies and false reporting.

12. **D)** This lets the client know that the counselor heard what the husband said but is asking for the client's perspective on it, showing that the counselor's alliance is with the client.

13. **C)** While the client does not meet all of the criteria for narcissistic personality disorder, she does demonstrate some its symptoms: lacking empathy, requiring attention from others and to be the center of attention, and exploiting relationships for personal gain.

Case Study 9

1. **A)** The minimal disclosure principle suggests that the counselor share only the minimum amount of information necessary to comply with the request of another agency.

2. **B)** While the other options may also indicate co-occurring disorders, the childhood sexual trauma is the strongest indication.

3. **D)** A trauma assessment will reveal if the client meets diagnostic criteria for a trauma disorder, which would guide the treatment plan.

4. **C)** Treatment of the co-occurring disorders will increase the likelihood of recovery.

5. **A)** The first goal of trauma therapy is to establish physical and psychological safety to allow the client to engage in recovery.

6. **B)** Evidence suggests that many who experience trauma use substances as a coping strategy.

7. **A)** The client reports first using drugs to "get through" the sexual assaults, which means she learned to avoid harm by using drugs.

8. **D)** Drugs helped the client avoid distressing situations, thoughts, and feelings; the client needs to learn new ways to manage distress and strong emotions without using substances.

9. **B)** The counselor admits feeling hurt with the client while pointing out a quality that is a strength.

10. **A)** People who experience trauma often have conflicting feelings about the person who inflicted trauma on them. Letting the client know that it is okay to both love and hate her father normalizes and validates the client's conflicting feelings.

11. **B)** The client currently does not have friends or other social support, so a recovery-focused social support group could provide her with those resources.

12. **C)** Her father violated the parent-child boundaries by not keeping her safe, so it is likely that she does not know how to establish and maintain boundaries.

13. **A)** After establishing safety with clients who have experienced trauma, the next step is to help them learn healthy coping skills to replace the unhealthy ones they have used in the past.

Case Study 10

1. **B)** Health Insurance Portability and Accountability Act (HIPAA) rules must be adhered to, and the client needs to provide consent for her daughter to participate.

2. **A)** Depression cannot be diagnosed if there is a significant event that can better explain the client's symptoms; in this case, the death of the client's son is a cause of her symptoms.

3. **C)** Moving the client through the stages of grief includes helping the client accept her son's death.

4. **A)** The death of the client's second son four days prior is a new trauma that exacerbates the existing trauma of her older son's death and thus requires a return to the basics of safety.

5. **B)** Family tends to be a strong form of support during grief, but the client's family is not readily available. Connecting her with other social support is an important component of grief therapy.

6. **C)** Moving the client from the death story to remembering the relationship can help her move through the grieving process.

7. **B)** This new grief is fresh, and the counselor should allow the client to express it.

8. **A)** This statement validates the client's feelings without judgment and acknowledges the reality of her fear.

9. **D)** Clients can forget what life was like before their grief and that they have the tools to move through it.

10. **B)** Many Americans of African descent distrust authority figures and police officers, due in part to historical systemic oppression in the United States.

11. **D)** Extremely stressful life events and tragedy are both strong suicide risk factors.

12. **B)** The deaths of two children a year apart, and the trauma of losing two sons unexpectedly and violently, suggests persistent complex bereavement.

Case Study 11

1. **B)** The client's fear is a barrier to change, and eliminating that barrier will improve his sense of autonomy.

2. **B)** The trauma symptom checklist can measure symptom presentation over time and show client progress.

3. **D)** The cultural formulation interview in the Diagnostic and Statistical Manual of Mental Disorders, Fifth Edition (DSM-5) provides an assessment of the impact of culture on the client's symptom presentation.

4. **A)** The client's hyperarousal symptoms are the most distressing since they are the major contributors to functional impairment.

5. **B)** The client currently does not have any social support in the United States; therefore, a support group may help him develop some friendships.

6. **D)** Normalizing and validating the client's experience can reduce shame, which is a barrier to effective therapy.

7. **C)** Since the client states that he is afraid for his life and ashamed that he did not fight back during the traumatic event, fear and shame should be addressed in counseling.

8. **A)** The counselor was exploring the client's thoughts and beliefs with cognitive therapy techniques.

9. **B)** The counselor acknowledges both the surface-level and deeper fears that the client feels.

10. **B)** This question invites the client to share his perspective of how people in his country of origin would look at what he is experiencing. This gives the counselor cultural insight and helps the client explore the way in which he thinks about post-traumatic stress disorder (PTSD), which could affect treatment.

11. **B)** During contemplation, a person wants to change and is motivated to change but does not know how and/or does not have a plan.

12. **A)** This exercise helps the client make a stronger commitment to change, which makes him ready for preparation.

13. **A)** The client believes that his job and his responsibility to provide are very important; a new job would get him away from the scene of the trauma.

www.ingramcontent.com/pod-product-compliance
Lightning Source LLC
Chambersburg PA
CBHW081151290426
44108CB00018B/2511